CHANGING LOC
GOVERNANCE, C
CITIZENS

Edited by Catherine Durose, Stephen Greasley and
Liz Richardson

This edition published in Great Britain in 2009 by

The Policy Press
University of Bristol
Fourth Floor
Beacon House
Queen's Road
Bristol BS8 1QU
UK

t +44 (0)117 331 4054
f +44 (0)117 331 4093
e tpp-info@bristol.ac.uk
www.policypress.co.uk

North American office:
The Policy Press
c/o International Specialized Books Services
920 NE 58th Avenue, Suite 300
Portland, OR 97213-3786, USA
Tel +1 503 287 3093
Fax +1 503 280 8832
info@isbs.com

British Library Cataloguing in Publication Data
A catalogue record for this book is available from the British Library.

Library of Congress Cataloging-in-Publication Data
A catalog record for this book has been requested.

ISBN 978 1 84742 217 0 paperback
ISBN 978 1 84742 218 7 hardcover

The right of Catherine Durose, Stephen Greasley and Liz Richardson to be
identified as editors of this work has been asserted by them in accordance with the
1988 Copyright, Designs and Patents Act.

The statements and opinions contained within this publication are solely those of
the editors and contributors and not of the University of Bristol or The Policy
Press. The University of Bristol and The Policy Press disclaim responsibility for
any injury to persons or property resulting from any material published in this
publication.

The Policy Press works to counter discrimination on grounds of gender, race,
disability, age and sexuality.

Cover design by Qube Design Associates, Bristol
Front cover: image kindly supplied by www.alamy.com
Printed and bound in Great Britain by MPG Books Group

Thanks to all of our parents and families

Contents

List of boxes and tables

Boxes

Tables

Acronyms

A2	Accession two
A8	Accession eight
BBC	British Broadcasting Corporation
BCU	borough command unit
BME	black and minority ethnic
BNP	British National Party
CEE	Central and Eastern Europe
CIC	Commission for Integration and Cohesion
CLG	Communities and Local Government
CPP	children's participation partnership
CUF	Church Urban Fund
CULF	Commission on Urban Life and Faith
CYPP	Children and Young People Plan
CYPU	Children and Young People's Unit
DCLG	Department for Communities and Local Government
Derby CSP	Derby Community Safety Partnership
DfES	Department for Education and Skills
DIUS	Department for Innovation, Universities and Skills
DRR	Drug Rehabilitation Requirement
EMDA	East Midlands Development Agency
ESOL	English for speakers of other languages
ESRC	Economic and Social Research Council
EU	European Union
FCCBF	Faith Communities Capacity Building Fund
GP	general practitioner
GRP	governance, representation and policy
HA	housing association
HMR	housing market renewal
IDeA	Improvement and Development Agency for local government
IPEG	Institute for Political and Economic Governance
IPPR	Institute for Public Policy Research
JRF	Joseph Rowntree Foundation
LA	local authority
LAAs	local area agreements
LGA	Local Government Association
LGRU	Local Governance Research Unit
LSBs	local safeguarding boards
LSPs	local strategic partnerships

MCC	Manchester City Council
MNI	Mediation Northern Ireland
MSP	Manchester Salford Housing Market Renewal Pathfinder
NDC	New Deal for Communities
NEM	New East Manchester
NGO	non-governmental organisation
NHF	National Housing Federation
NRU	Neighbourhood Renewal Unit
NSNR	National Strategy for Neighbourhood Renewal
NWIN	North West Improvement Network
ODPM	Office for Deputy Prime Minister
PCPS	Policy Commission on Public Services
PCTs	primary care trusts
PVE	preventing violent extremism
RCUK	Research Councils UK
RUN	Regenerating Urban Neighbourhoods
SEU	Social Exclusion Unit
TARAs	tenants' and residents' associations
UNCRC	UN Convention on the Rights of the Child
URC	urban regeneration company
VCS	voluntary and community sector
YC	Youth Council

Notes on contributors

Rebecca Askew is due to start a PhD in criminology at the University of Manchester in September 2009. She was a researcher in the Institute for Political and Economic Governance at the University of Manchester from 2006-09. During this time she worked on two projects using design experiment methodology, one aimed to prevent anti-social behaviour in young people and the other a holistic treatment programme for problematic substance abusers. She also led an evaluation for Lifeline in Salford and won a project with the children of substance-misusing parents. Her research interests include risk, resilience and social exclusion, drug use identity and the law, and drug treatment and strategy in the UK.

Rachael Chapman is a senior research fellow at the Local Government Centre, University of Warwick. She was previously employed at the Local Governance Research Unit, De Montfort University, where she conducted the research on which her contribution to this book is based. Her expertise and research interests focus around governance, particularly in relation to faith and third sector engagement, partnership working, democracy and regeneration. Recent publications include 'Faith and the voluntary sector in urban governance: distinctive yet similar?' in A. Dinham, R. Furbey and V. Lowndes (eds) *Faith in the public realm: Controversies, policies and practices*(The Policy Press, 2009); and 'Democracy through multi-level governance? The implementation of the structural funds in South Yorkshire', *Governance*, vol 21, no 3, pp 397-418 (2008).

Harriet Churchill is Lecturer in Social Work at the Department of Sociological Studies, University of Sheffield. Harriet's research interests include children and young people's citizenship, sociological changes in family life and social welfare reform. She has recently published articles and book chapters on lone mothers' experiences of welfare to work policies, New Labour's reform of children's services in England and community engagement. Harriet is also co-author of *Getting your PhD* (with T. Sanders; Sage Publications, 2007).

Sarah Cotterill is a research associate at the Institute for Political and Economic Governance at the University of Manchester. Sarah is currently working on a project funded by the Economic and Social Research Council and Communities and Local Government:

Rediscovering the Civic and Achieving Better Outcomes in Public Policy, using experimental methods to evaluate interventions to stimulate civic. Her research interests are public sector partnerships, citizen participation and civic engagement. Sarah was previously a programme manager for a Health Action Zone and a New Deal for Communities partnership

Catherine Durose is RCUK Research Fellow at the Local Governance Research Unit at De Montfort University. Catherine has recently coordinated a systematic review of evidence on community empowerment for the Department for Communities and Local Government. Her research interests include neighbourhood working, public service delivery, community development and social entrepreneurship. Recent publications can be found in *Public Administration* and *Critical Policy Analysis.*

Matthew J. Goodwin is ESRC Research Fellow at the Institute for Political and Economic Governance, University of Manchester. Matthew's main areas of interest include political behaviour, the politics of race and immigration and organised extremism. His research has appeared in *The Political Quarterly, Politics,* the *Journal of Contemporary European Studies* and *Representation.* Matthew is currently completing a book that examines extreme right party members and activists.

Stephen Greasley is a lecturer in comparative public policy/politics of regulation in the School of Political, Social and International Studies, University of East Anglia. He was previously a research associate at the Institute for Political and Economic Governance, University of Manchester. His research interests include bureaucracies, local government systems and political leadership.

Bethan Harries worked as a researcher at the Institute for Political and Economic Governance, University of Manchester, from 2007 to 2008. Her principal research interests are in ethnicity and representation of minority identities. She is currently studying for her doctorate in the Department of Sociology at the University of Manchester.

Peter John is the Hallsworth Chair of Governance in the School of Social Sciences at the University of Manchester, where he is a co-director of the Institute for Political and Economic Governance. He is known for his work on local governance, public policy and citizen involvement, and is currently directing a project funded by the

Economic and Social Research Council and Communities and Local Government called 'Rediscovering the civic: achieving better outcomes in public policy', which is using the experimental method to evaluate interventions to stimulate citizen engagement.

Rabia Karakaya Polat is Assistant Professor of Political Science at Işık University in Istanbul. She received her PhD degree in political science in 2004 from De Montfort University and worked at the university's Local Governance Research Unit as a visiting fellow until 2005. Her research interests include political participation, electronic democracy, local democracy, democratisation in Turkey and securitisation theory. She worked as part of research projects funded by the Office of the Deputy Prime Minister (UK), Turkish National Science Foundation, Işık University Research Fund and Turkish Informatics Foundation. She has published articles in *European Journal of Communication*, *Parliamentary Affairs*, *International Journal of e-Government Research*, *Security Dialogue*, *Australian Journal of International Affairs* and *Insight Turkey*.

Lawrence Pratchett is Professor of Local Democracy and Head of the Department of Public Policy at De Montfort University. His research interests focus on all aspects of local democracy but especially political participation, both offline and online. He has published several edited books and numerous articles on the topic. He was academic adviser to the UK government's Local e-Democracy National Project, as well as sitting on the Council of Europe's advisory group for its Green Paper on the *Future of democracy in Europe*. He is also expert adviser to the Council of Europe's ad hoc committee on e-democracy.

James Rees is a research associate at the Institute for Political and Economic Governance, University of Manchester. His research interests centre on: critical approaches to the urban housing market and social change; regional and city-regional governance and economic development; and neighbourhood regeneration. In 2007 he completed his PhD, which examined contemporary debates on state-led gentrification in the context of Housing Market Renewal in Manchester.

Liz Richardson is a senior researcher in the Institute for Political and Economic Governance (IPEG) at the University of Manchester. Prior to joining IPEG in August 2006, she was co-ordinator of LSE Housing, based in the Centre for Analysis of Social Exclusion at the London School of Economics and Political Science. Her research interests are: community engagement in decision making and user involvement in public services; civic renewal and civil society; public service delivery; and neighbourhood governance structures. Her research has had a strong policy and applied focus. Liz is author of *DIY community action: Neighbourhood problems and community self-help* (The Policy Press, 2008).

Leila Thorp is a research fellow in the Local Governance Research Unit at De Montfort University, working on community cohesion. She is currently working on a project exploring citizenship for Polish new migrants in the UK. Her other research interests include changes to political interest representation, group recognition and identification within the context of globalising trends. Her PhD assessed the changes to Polish civil society within this context, and in other work she has conducted an action research project on the UK policy of preventing violent extremism.

Acknowledgements

The editors and contributors would like to acknowledge and thank the organisations and participants who have provided great insights into their everyday work and lives, without which this publication could not have been produced.

The editors would also like to thank the Local Governance Research Unit (LGRU) at De Montfort University together with the Institute for Political and Economic Governance (IPEG) and Governance, Representation and Policy (GRP) research group at the University of Manchester for their support in developing this book.

Further, the editors would like to acknowledge the support of colleagues at both the De Montfort University and the University of Manchester for their contributions to developing both the overall theme of the book and specific chapters. In particular, Tessa Brannan, Martin Burch, Francesca Gains, Rachel Gibson, Alan Harding, Paul Hepburn, Tomila Lankina, Steve Leach, Vivien Lowndes and Melvin Wingfield. In addition, Gerry Stoker has provided great support, useful comments and a welcome foreword to this edition.

The editors would also like to thank Charlotte Jackson at IPEG and Suzanne Walker at LGRU for their assistance in proofreading, copy-editing and formatting the text of this book. Also, thanks to Emily Watt and Leila Ebrahimi at The Policy Press for their support throughout the process of producing this book.

The editors would finally like to acknowledge the support of the North West Improvement Network, which provided some financial support for this publication. The GRP research group at the University of Manchester provided funds for the first of two writing colloquia; the second was supported by the LGRU at De Montfort University.

Foreword

Unlike most UK citizens, I do spend many hours reflecting on the details of our governance structures and processes. What drives me to these issues, and gives them great importance for me, is a concern about how enfeebled citizens feel about their engagement with our political system and more broadly their lives in neighbourhoods and communities. Over the last decade and more I have worked with colleagues from Local Governance Research Unit, De Montfort University and the Institute for Political and Economic Governance, University of Manchester on issues of citizen engagement. I know the depth of understanding and insight they bring to the table so it's a pleasure to be able to support this book.

In a globalised and interdependent world it is increasingly challenging to offer citizens a direct sense of empowerment, which makes the importance of affording opportunities at the local level even more vital. This book is valuable above all because it recognises that if citizenship is going to be a living practice rather than a spectator sport for most citizens we need to create a far wider set of opportunities for real decisions to be made at the local level that people care about.

The 2008 White Paper *Communities in control* notes:

> In the period from April to December 2007, only two fifths
> (38%) of respondents to the Citizenship Survey felt they
> could influence decisions in their local area and one fifth
> (20%) of people felt they could influence decisions affecting
> Great Britain. (p 10)

These figures suggest a gap between the local and the national sense of subjective empowerment. We are building on a stronger base at the local level but there is still a long way to go. This book offers us much valuable evidence about some the hurdles to be faced and how they might be overcome.

The Labour government since 1997 has been slow to recognise the importance of the issues of active citizenship. Its agenda for local government has been more managerial and focused on service delivery. And to an extent the agenda has delivered; local government is better managed, more strategic and more joined up than ever before. It delivers many services with efficiency and many of its practitioners have delivered real and imaginative community leadership. The trouble is that citizens have been largely left behind in this managerial revolution.

But there are several reasons to believe that a more robust and effective system of local democracy and engagement would benefit our attempts to reinvigorate our practice of citizenship. The local is an arena where a less partisan, more free-flowing politics that addresses issues that people care about could flower. Doing what is right for your area or community is a positive basis for a more consensus-building politics. Moreover because it is local it can offer an engagement that is accessible to all. That is not to say that all is well with local politics but the potential of local politics can be seen not only through abstract argument but also on a regular basis in practice. This book is valuable because it shows what can be achieved and what remains to be achieved.

Local government practitioners and residents who have promoted citizen engagement have to an extent been swimming against a tide of managerial and centrally driven directives. Although the government in *Communities in control* rather belatedly recognises what has been achieved and calls for more, it does so without a suitably radical approach and without a full evidence base.

Above all we need to be more radical in devolving power if citizen engagement at the local level is going to get beyond the promising signs of practice identified in this book. To make space for a more vibrant local citizenship we need to take steps to change attitudes and practices in the Westminster and Whitehall village. We need to challenge the unthinking centralism that pervades the way national decision makers respond to policy problems. What are required are not ever more elaborate strategic partnerships where centrally funded agencies and local authorities sign off on agreed plans and targets – rather, something that breaks the mould. We need a fundamental shift of responsibility to local government and this will require a wider set of constitutional changes. Some movement on local government finance is essential. A democratic system where all but a small proportion of revenues are raised and allocated centrally through Whitehall is odd in comparative democratic terms and unsustainable. Given the highly politically charged nature of local tax changes, as the poll tax fiasco demonstrated in the late 1980s and early 1990s, the only long-term way forward if substantial changes are going to be implemented is to have a cross-party group charged with coming up with a consensus set of proposals for a better system of local government revenue raising. Above all we need to break a culture that assumes that Westminster is the focal point for accountability. The key question is: if something goes wrong, who will be on the media to explain why? We need local politicians and citizens much more involved in that process.

We also need to return to the agenda of how to reconstruct local politics so that it works better in its representative, direct and participative aspects. Here the agenda for change is vast and the range of institutional devices that could be brought into play developing on from our own and others' practices is vast. The options stretch from more elected mayors or electoral reform, through citizen initiatives or referenda to participatory budgeting or internet-focused deliberation.

This book gives considerable food for thought in tackling a challenging agenda of change. We need both better ideas and better evidence about what works if a genuine strengthening of local citizenship is to occur. This book delivers both and deserves to be read not only by academics but also by practitioners operating at all levels of our governance systems.

Gerry Stoker
Centre for Citizenship and Democracy
University of Southampton
www.soton.ac.uk/ccd

Preface

This edited collection came about as a result of a series of discussions in internal team meetings, over drinks and around the edges of conferences. We are a collection of academic colleagues who enjoy being engaged in hands-on primary research with citizens, with local government, in neighbourhoods; our active research focus is one of the things that unite us. We are also proud of our links to practitioner and citizen audiences, and the fact that our work tried to bridge the gap between academia and practitioner perspectives. Active as we were, the downside was that some of our work was through small or medium size commissions for a range of clients on myriad topics. These types of pieces of work tended to involve an intense period of fieldwork, then writing up, before moving on to the next piece of paid work. We wanted to have the space to sit back a little from our activity and think through what it amounted to, if anything. Our individual projects appeared incredibly disparate at first glance. But gradually it became clear that some of the same questions, issues and debates came up time and time again in relation to these very disparate pieces of work. We realised we were wrestling with some common questions: was this more of the same or was something new happening in the way that neighbourhoods and areas were being governed? Did citizens really welcome the extra demands being made of them? Had governance activity produced outcomes for citizens, society, or local agencies? What did this mean for how we think about what it means to be a citizen in the UK? The idea for *Changing local governance, changing citizens* finally crystallised when we searched for other literature on this topic. We found many great books theorising governance and governance changes, but very little that looked at the issue from both governance and citizen perspectives. Much of the theoretical discussion was somewhat abstracted from the day-to-day experiences and engagement of the citizen. Much of the literature on local government focuses on technical and internal changes in decision making and service delivery, neglecting the wider relevance of such discussions to the lives of local people.

So, we proposed a volume on that would take a citizen-centred empirical approach to some of the key questions facing local governance. We set out with the aim of providing a pertinent and robustly empirical contribution to current debates among policy makers, academics, practitioners and local communities about how to respond to a changing policy framework that encourages greater citizen participation. We hope that this volume helps to redress the balance in the literature on governance towards the 'missing citizen'.

Liz Richardson, 17 July, 2009

ONE

Changing local governance, changing citizens: introduction

Catherine Durose, Stephen Greasley and Liz Richardson

Introduction

Renegotiating the roles of citizens and their relationships to public governance have been policy preoccupations of New Labour during its period in office. As Clarke (2005: 447) observes: 'at different points, citizens have been activated, empowered, and made the subjects of responsibilities as well as rights'. This is not just a New Labour fixation; Cameron's Conservatives have also been interested in the limits of state action and the scope of personal responsibility. *Changing local governance, changing citizens* brings together recent empirical analyses of this renegotiation in a variety of contexts.

The recent efforts to remodel the citizen–governance relation are part of a long running and evolving agenda (John, this volume). Some of the trends that are contributing to change are long-term – an increasingly diverse and demanding public, the continuing globalisation of the economy and a fracturing of the institutional landscape. Yet, despite the continuities, we would argue that over the last decade policy efforts appear to have intensified and developed a particular character. Across the ideological spectrum, what citizens expect of governance and what governance can expect of citizens are up for grabs.

The chapters in this book all focus empirically on aspects of the attempted renegotiation between public governance and citizens. Inevitably, given the variety of contexts considered, a single consistent picture of changing citizenship fails to appear. Nonetheless, strong connections exist between the various areas discussed, similar questions can be posed and similar pressures are at play. The purposes of this introductory chapter are to briefly situate the subsequent contributions in relation to some key concepts and describe the gap that we believe the book fills.

Changing language, changing practice?

If the language used to talk about public services, governance and citizens is anything to go by there has already been a revolution in the way the state engages with citizens. Communities and citizens are to be empowered as co-producers of public value. Communities must be cohesive, while children and new migrants are understood as almost, but not quite, full citizens. However, the practice sometimes lags behind the language and sometimes our language and concepts do not keep up with changing practice. The language of politics is used to both describe and shape the application of public authority. It can be difficult, and arguably futile, to try to completely separate these two linguistic functions. However, it is possible to contrast 'merely' rhetorical change with changes that have influenced the behaviour of relevant actors. The much discussed turn from 'government' to 'governance' attempts to describe changes in the structures and processes of public institutions but has also been used to influence the way reform develops. The meaning of citizenship and how it relates to the 'public as client' or 'public as consumer' and to concepts such as 'civicness' and 'co-production' has also garnered attention, partly trying to reflect changes, partly trying to influence the way that 'the public' acts. An aspect of the new language of citizenship and governance is that people are understood from a collectivist perspective – as members of neighbourhoods, communities and groups – while simultaneously being understood from a highly individualised perspective as differentiated users of responsive and tailored services. Depending on the underlying normative commitments, the new language is either trying to describe a form of collectivist social organisation that respects and responds to individual and group differentiation, or trying to find a form of individualism that does not erode all social obligation and civic responsibility.

Is this merely linguistic churn or is something more substantial going on? The contributors to this volume shed light on that question by moving beyond the highly abstract debates surrounding citizenship and governance to examine the citizenship relation in situ.

The practice of citizenship

The chapters of this book focus on changing demands made by and of citizens. It is difficult to engage in a discussion of the changing conceptions of the relationship between the citizen and the state without delving into the more theoretical debates around conceptions of citizenship. Recent work has introduced some important shifts in theorising citizenship (see Lewis, 2004; *Citizenship Studies*, 2007; Kivisto and Faist, 2007; Clarke and Newman, 2008).

Some of our contributors do dip a toe into these deep waters. Churchill (Chapter Ten) for example discusses the liberal and communitarian thinking that underpins New Labour's notion of children's citizenship. In her chapter Thorp (Chapter Seven) discusses the impact of globalised identities and explores the concept of cosmopolitan citizenship. Polat and Pratchett (Chapter Eleven) discuss the expansion of citizenship at both the global and local level and the differing dimensions of citizenship, as status, rights and responsibilities and identity. All three chapters probe the boundaries of citizenship, exploring whether children and new migrants can be understood as citizens; and the impact of new technologies on citizenship.

However, by and large the chapters steer clear of extensive theoretical debates. The contribution of this book is centrally empirical and so, while acknowledging citizenship as 'the relationship between the individual and state, in which the two are bound together by reciprocal rights and duties' (Heywood, 2000: 119), the book focuses on the *practice* rather than the *status* of citizenship, borrowing from Prior et al's (1995) distinction between citizenship as a *status* which people possess and as a *practice* which people engage in. The former identifies citizens as those who are members of a particular political community, through which they have certain rights and obligations. For Prior et al (1995: 6) a political community is a 'collectivity whose members share a common system of governance, which includes both the institutions of government and the process of collective decision-making ... individual members of the community who are entitled to participate in these political arrangements have the status of citizens'. Citizenship as practice, on the other hand, refers to the activities of citizenship linked to citizen rights and responsibilities. Such activities include but are not limited to participation in public affairs. This book focuses on the *practice* of citizenship. We focus on practice in the belief that the implicit understandings of the nature and limits of citizenship are exposed in the actual interactions between governance and citizens.

Changing local governance

The new language of citizenship presents public institutions with a distinct set of challenges. Of course, the traditional politics of 'who gets what, when?' has not disappeared. However, that formulation of politics paints a picture of the citizen as the passive recipient of public benefits and it portrays public action as competitive and zero-sum in nature. The language of empowerment and co-production on the other hand both implies a more active understanding of citizens and seeks to emphasise common solutions to problems rather than conflict over resources. Simply adding 'em' to 'power' cannot achieve this redrawing of the character of politics; the institutions designed to answer the 'who gets what, when?' question also need to re-examine their organisation and practices.

Governance structures and processes, and the skill and attributes of staff, are designed to deal with particular problems in particular ways and with particular groups. In much of the government arena such unreflective action is exactly what is required. The bureaucratisation and standardisation of action aids the efficient, reliable and transparent delivery of public services. In other instances, however, such governance biases have less benign effects: they can divide people based on constraining and out of date social categories; they can generate dependent relationships where public sector interventions first help then disempower people; they can lead to the provision of inappropriate and ineffective services.

The much discussed 'turn' from government to governance can be partly understood as an attempt to adjust the biases of structures designed largely to deliver standardised goods and services to a grateful and unquestioning public. A historical narrative exists, describing a shift away from the Westminster model of British government as a unitary state (Gamble, 1990) towards governance by and through networks (Bevir and Richards, 2009). This is characterised as a series of shifts from the hierarchies or bureaucracies of the post-war welfare state; through the marketisation reforms of the Conservative governments of the 1980s and 1990s; to the emphasis now given by New Labour to networks (Etzioni, 1961; Lindblom, 1977; Clarence and Painter, 1998). This move partly reflected a growing perception that the classical hierarchical model of government and public administration 'does not work' (Hendriks and Topps, 2005: 476). As a result, the process of governing is now carried out by numerous and varied stakeholders operating in new governance sites (Hirst, 2000; Rhodes, 2000) and government is reduced to 'only one of many actors' (Rhodes, 2000: 63). Networks of organisations from public and private sector are drawn into the policy process as reflected by the observation that 'partnership is the new language of public governance' (Sullivan and Skelcher, 2002: 1). These changes are partly designed to shift the nature and approach of public bodies from paternalistic styles of mono-government to possibly more facilitative styles of governance.

However, this narrative of governance is 'one-sided' (Bevir and Rhodes, 2003) and neglects complexities and contradictions (Newman, 2001; Stoker, 2002). Greater flexibility, if achieved, generates problems of political and bureaucratic accountability and hence New Labour's rhetoric of governance through networks, of a more inclusive policy process and of the decentralisation of control to local government has gone hand in hand with a tendency towards centralisation, performance management and targeting (6 and Peck, 2004; Hood, 2006). The relationship between the 'new public management' and citizenship is discussed by Peter John (this volume). He argues that it is too simplistic to present managerialism as antithetical to citizen influence. However when central control becomes too tight we see 'a growing tendency to sacrifice civic engagement on the altar of centrally determined efficiency' (Marquand, quoted in Stone, 2009: 265). By the mid-2000s, some commentators were despairing of what seemed to be the backwards progress of New Labour's policy on local government, arguing that the situation was dangerously close to the position of mid-1980s: 'when it seemed that local government in this country might gently expire, starved of financial and democratic oxygen by the Thatcher regime' (Davies, 2004).

An alternative method for ensuring accountability that is currently being given more emphasis is to establish new ways of drawing citizens into public decision making. The turn to a local governance of networks and partnerships has therefore been seen as an opportunity to innovate around the concept of 'citizenship'.

The missing citizen

The changes that are characterised as a 'turn to governance' have largely been analysed in terms of their impact on the shape of public sector organisations, as well as on local government's relations with other organisations – the first two of Goss's (2001) elements of governance. Until recently, less attention has been given to the third of Goss's elements – the role of citizens or dialogue between state and citizens (Goss, 2001; for exceptions see HM Treasury et al, 2001; Audit Commission and IDeA, 2005; DCLG, 2008; Stone, 2009). One link as mentioned above is that the institutional complexity and fragmentation associated with governance is a challenge to the traditional chains of accountability associated with representative democracy. This is an important issue, but it should not obscure the potential for alternative mechanisms for representation and accountability and for innovations in the meaning of citizenship to be developed.

5

The chapters in this book report on the practice of citizenship in specific places and in relation to specific issues. Within those basic parameters, authors were asked to keep in mind three themes. Not all the chapters address each theme directly or comprehensively and authors were not asked to explicitly consider them in their writing. The themes relate to how citizens and groups are understood; what is at stake in the relation between governance and citizen; and the sustainability of new demands being made of governance and citizens.

Policy makers and researchers have agonised about the issues around the involvement of representatives of the voluntary and community sectors in partnerships but have paid less attention to citizens outside that milieu. That is to say that when citizens have been engaged in governance it has often been in the traditional manner of group politics and representation. The basis of this representation and in particular its inclusiveness may have changed though. While functional representation of unions and business still exists, a wider array of groups defined by religion, culture, sexuality and ethnicity are being engaged in governance. Sections of the public who are ineligible to vote – because they are too young, or because they are economic migrants, asylum seekers or refugees – are in some instances becoming involved in governance.

The first theme that authors were asked to think about was the different ways that citizens and groups of citizens are defined, self-defined and grouped together in particular contexts. In addition, how does governance deal with people and groups who do not enjoy the traditional rights of citizenship? This is not only an issue of identity politics it is also an issue of how the needs and interests of citizens are understood. For example, an influential report on public service transformation argued that public services need to increasingly focus on 'the totality of the relationship with the citizen' (Varney, 2006: 1). Rather than the citizen adapting in order to engage with public services, the relationship needs to be shifted so that public services adapt to deal with citizens 'in the round'.

A second set of questions we asked authors to reflect on was what is at stake? What are the motives and goals of the various institutions of public governance and of the citizens and groups of citizens as they engage in defining and redefining citizenship at a local level? In part, the government's citizenship agenda is driven by long-term trends and changes in the political and civic culture of the country, but there are more immediate goals being pursued. One motive for central government in trying to strengthen citizenship has been to maximise the chances that centrally channelled resources will translate locally into better outcomes for citizens and service users (HM Treasury and Cabinet Office, 2004). Some doubt that citizen engagement on its own is a sufficient mechanism to initiate thoroughgoing or large-scale organisational changes (Entwistle et al, 2003) but government policy is clearly becoming more sympathetic to community or service user involvement (Richardson, 2005). With changes to the performance management system in English local government that at least in theory will loosen the grip of the centre, the hope is that local citizens will keep up the pressure on the quality of local service provision – not just through the ballot box but also via election engagement at neighbourhood level, as user groups and as individual citizens.

In addition to the managerialist motive of strengthened accountability a debate has been developing nationally and locally about the need to involve citizens directly in service provision. The idea is to match the shift from paternalism to facilitation with a shift from citizens as passive recipients to active partners. As one politician has expressed it: 'the biggest untapped resource in education provision is not teachers but pupils ... in health [it] is not doctors ... but patients ... in social care [it] is not social workers but citizens' (Miliband, 2005). This strain of thought has a long tradition, but its most recent academic expression is found in work on social capital (Putnam, 1995; Lowndes, 2004) and is also found in recent policy debates around co-production and personal responsibility.

A third issue at stake relates to citizens as policy makers (see John, this volume), selecting and prioritising policy goals. Participatory budgeting (DCLG, 2008) is a step in this direction and the continued move towards neighbourhood working also provides a site for citizens to influence priorities (Durose and Richardson, this volume). Citizen influence at the more strategic level can also be identified in particular policy areas – such as community cohesion.

The final set of questions we asked our authors to consider was what demands were being made on governance and citizens? How could the emerging relationships be best characterised? Can changes be sustained? The changes under discussion make demands of both the system of public administration and the public. We have argued above that greater reliance on networks might facilitate and will require the more active involvement of citizens in governance. However, it is not inevitable that professionals in networks will take a more facilitative stance, will treat citizens equally or will submit to popular control. Public servants do not always serve the public. On the other side of the table, do the goals identified make demands of citizens that are unlikely to be met? Reforms that require a sudden flowering of civic activism are unlikely to be successful.

Renegotiating citizenship?

As noted, changes in the organisation and operation of the state would seem to require a renegotiation of the relationship between state and citizens. The word 'negotiation' carries with it connotations of parties bargaining to find mutual benefit and has the advantage that it privileges neither state-centred nor society-centred explanations. Instead it suggests that outcomes will develop from public institutions and citizens playing the game and adjusting their strategies in response to each other. The themes and questions we have suggested to our authors reflect the idea that the changes in citizenship relationships will reflect such interaction. The approach taken in this book is to try to address these questions empirically.

The structure and key arguments of this book

The chapters in *Changing local governance, changing citizens* look at the different ways in which citizens are conceptualised in local governance; the new demands citizens are facing from local governance; and how citizens themselves perceive and respond to these changes and demands. The chapters discuss a range of issues relevant to local governance but they do not cover the entire terrain. However, they reflect contemporary concerns of both citizens and local government. Moreover, the chapters reflect the research and expertise of the Local Governance Research Unit (LGRU) at De Montfort University and the Institute for Political and Economic Governance (IPEG) at the University of Manchester.

The book opens with an overview chapter by Peter John (Chapter Two). This chapter illuminates the UK debate about different forms of representation as the country moved from being an established mature democracy based on long-embedded political institutions to a more fragmented political system that is less clear about the role of the citizen. The chapter discusses changing citizen attitudes and behaviours since the 1960s and the participation reforms of the 1970s; it then considers the debate about consumers and citizens during the new public management reforms of the 1980s and 1990s. It moves on to plot the various citizen-centred initiatives that have emerged during the last three decades, concentrating on those the Labour Party introduced since entering government in 1997. The final section assesses the significance and impact of these changes, in particular whether citizen engagement introduced by the state can create an effective and autonomous civic input into decision making.

The main part of the book reports empirical and applied citizen-centred research in local governance on a range of topical issues including multiculturalism, economic migration, community cohesion, housing markets, neighbourhoods, faith organisations, behaviour change and children's services in order to establish a differentiated, contemporary view of the ways that citizens are constituted at the local level today. The empirical work can be broadly divided into three sections: a focus on place, on ethnicity and on public services. The chapters are organised to reflect this. The structure of the book is as follows. Focusing on issues of place, Catherine Durose and Liz Richardson (Chapter Three) consider the potential and inherent difficulties of the 'neighbourhood' as a potential site for citizen empowerment. James Rees (Chapter Four) examines citizens' experience of Housing Market Renewal and the differential conceptions of citizens within Housing Market Renewal. Bethan Harries and Liz Richardson (Chapter Five) explore the housing aspirations of minority citizens, specifically second-generation South Asian women and how well these are reflected in local authority housing strategies.

Focusing on the politics of ethnic, national and religious identity, first, Matthew Goodwin considers group contact as a possible tool for facilitating community cohesion (Chapter Six). Then, Leila Thorp considers the different conceptions of citizenship affecting new economic migrants and the barriers to them achieving 'full' citizenship (Chapter Seven). And finally, Rachael Chapman examines the role of citizens and organisations of faith in governance (Chapter Eight).

Focusing on services, Rebecca Askew, Sarah Cotterill and Stephen Greasley (Chapter Nine) look at the concept of behaviour change and its impact on citizens in a variety of policy settings. Harriet Churchill considers how children and young people are consulted and engaged around service provision and the meaning this has for our understanding of their roles as citizens (Chapter Ten). Rabia Karakaya Polat and Lawrence Pratchett (Chapter Eleven) look at local e-government provision and the prospects for its contribution to local citizenship.

The chapters provide insights on citizen governance relations from a disparate range of policy areas and contexts. Drawing these insights together into a single coherent picture is impossible. Indeed, it is part of the argument of the book that the practice of citizenship varies with place and purpose. The conclusion then surveys how citizens have been variously empowered, activated, ignored, neglected and misunderstood by local governance. It returns to the three themes we asked authors to consider, and in particular discusses in more general terms the limits and potential of reforms.

References

6, P. and Peck, E. (2004) '"Modernisation": the 10 commitments of New Labour's approach to public management', *International Public Management Journal*, vol 7, no 1, pp 1-18.

Audit Commission and IDeA (Improvement and Development Agency) Performance Management Measurement and Information (PMMI) Project (2005) *Interim findings from research into performance management in well-performing local authorities,* London: IDeA.

Bevir, M. and Rhodes, R.A.W. (2003) *Interpreting British governance,* London: Routledge.

Bevir, M. and Richards, D. (2009) 'Decentring policy networks: a theoretical agenda', *Public Administration*, vol 87, no 1, pp 3-14.

Citizenship Studies (2007) Special issue 'Citizenship beyond the state', vol 11, no 2, pp 117-228.

Clarence, E. and Painter, C. (1998) 'Public services under New Labour: collaborative discourses and local networking', *Public Policy and Administration*, vol 13, no 3, pp 8-22.

Clarke, J. (2005) 'New Labour's citizens: activated, empowered, responsibilized, abandoned?', *Critical Social Policy*, vol 25, no 4, pp 447-63.

Clarke, J. and Newman, J. (2008) *Publics, politics and power: Remaking the public in public services*, London: Sage.

Davies, H. (2004) 'Can local government survive a third term of New Labour?', Speech to LSE/LGA conference, London School of Economics and Political Science, 7 September.

DCLG (Department of Communities and Local Government) (2008) *Communities in control: Real power, real people,* London: HMSO.

Entwistle, T., Dowson, L. and Law, J. (2003) *Changing to improve: Ten case studies from the evaluation of the best value regime*, London: ODPM.

Etzioni, A. (1961) *A comparative analysis of complex organisations*, New York: The Free Press.

Gamble, A. (1990) 'Theories of British politics', *Political Studies*, vol 38, no 3, pp 404-20.

Goss, S. (2001) *Making local governance work: Networks, relationships and the management of change*, Basingstoke: Palgrave Macmillan.

Hendriks, F. and Topps, P. (2005) 'Everyday fixers as local heroes: a case study of vital interaction in urban governance', *Local Government Studies*, vol 31, no 4, pp 475-90.

Heywood, A. (2000) *Key concepts in politics*, Basingstoke: Palgrave.

Hirst, P. (2000) 'Democracy and governance', in J. Pierre (ed) *Debating governance: Authority, steering and democracy*, New York: Oxford University Press, pp 13-35.

HM Treasury et al (2001) *Choosing the right FABRIC: A framework for performance information*, London: HM Treasury.

HM Treasury and Cabinet Office (2004) *Devolving decision making: Delivering better public services – refining targets and performance measurement*, London: HMSO.

Hood, C. (2006) 'Gaming in target world: the targets approach to managing British public services', *Public Administration Review*, July/August, pp 515-22.

Kivisto, P. and Faist, T. (2007) *Citizenship: Discourse, theory and transnational prospects*, Oxford: Blackwell.

Lewis, G. (2004) *Citizenship: Personal lives and social policy*, Bristol: The Policy Press.

Lindblom, C.E. (1977) *Politics and markets: The world's political-economic systems*, New York: Basic Books.

Lowndes, V. (2004) 'Getting on or getting by? Women, social capital and political participation', *British Journal of Politics and International Relations*, vol 6, no 1, pp 45-65.

Miliband, D. (2005) Speech to *Guardian* Public Services Summit, 2 February.

Newman, J. (2001) *Modernising governance: New Labour, policy and society*, London: Sage.

Prior, D., Stewart, J. and Walsh, K. (1995) *Citizenship: Rights, community and participation*, London: Pitman.

Putnam, R. (1995) 'Bowling alone: America's declining social capital', *Journal of Democracy*, vol 6, no 1, pp 65-78.

Rhodes, R.A.W. (2000) 'Governance and public administration', in J. Pierre (ed) *Debating governance: Authority, steering and democracy*, New York, Oxford University Press, pp 54-90.

Richardson, E. (2005) 'Social and political participation and inclusion', in J. Hills and S. Stewart (eds) *A more equal society? New Labour, poverty, inequality and exclusion*, Bristol: The Policy Press, pp 93-116.

Stoker, G. (2002) 'Life is a lottery: New Labour's strategy for the reform of devolved governance', *Public Administration*, vol 80, no 3, pp 417-34.

Stone, C. (2009) 'Who is governed? Local citizens and the political order of cities', in J.S. Davies and D.L. Imbroscio (eds) *Theories of urban politics* (2nd edn), London: Sage, pp 257-73.

Sullivan, H. and Skelcher, C. (2002) *Working across boundaries: Collaboration in public services*, Basingstoke: Palgrave MacMillan.

Varney, D. (2006) *Service transformation: A better service for citizens and businesses, a better deal for taxpayers*, London: HM Treasury.

TWO

Citizen governance: where it came from, where it's going

Peter John

Introduction

Democratic theory presents different conceptions of the role of the citizens as policy makers.[1] At one extreme is the classical ideal of active citizens, who directly participate in public decisions in a face-to-face context alongside their peers; at the other end of the spectrum is the Schumpeterian elitist conception, whereby relatively passive individuals choose between different elites that compete for the vote, leaving experts in charge of day-to-day affairs between elections. It is probably the case that the practice of a democracy never reaches either extreme; all political systems have some direct forms of participation built into them as well as summative occasions whereby citizens elect leaders who are then left to be able to do their job. There is no pure form of democracy, but only combinations of institutions and practices that persist over time.

The differences between these forms of democratic connection are a matter for endless debate and affect the frequent projects for institutional reform. The elites of political systems tend to want to move between one and the other type of mechanism. By necessity, the busyness of modern life; the relative lack of interest in politics on the part of the average citizen; the longevity of existing representative political institutions; and the exigencies of a large country needing methods of preference aggregation almost inevitably ensure the continuing importance of representation and the passivity of the individual. More direct forms of engagement may not be viable in the modern context. On the other hand, a sense of loss for a more vibrant democratic age inspires policy makers to introduce institutions to engage people more directly in public policy decisions. Politicians are apprehensive about the decline in conventional forms of participation, such as voting and membership of political parties, and seek to revive it in other contexts. Citizens themselves have embraced more active styles of participation, questioning the decisions of bureaucracies and becoming more assertive in getting their views across. These factors point in the opposite direction, towards a rediscovery of the civic and to placing citizens at the heart of public administration. Whether what may be called citizen governance can be effective without reconstructing other aspects of the political system, in particular the current forms of bureaucratic organisations, is a question that this chapter seeks to answer. But what it does mean is there is a dialogue between citizen behaviours and aspirations on the one hand, and policy makers' responses on the other.

What this chapter seeks to understand is how the debate about different forms of representation took place in England. Over the last 40 years it has moved from being an established mature democracy based on long-embedded political institutions to a more fragmented and less legitimate political system, which is less clear about the role of the citizen. To this end, the chapter discusses changing citizen attitudes and behaviours since the 1960s and the participation reforms of the 1970s; it then considers the debate about consumers and citizens during the new public management reforms of the 1980s and 1990s. It moves on to plot the various citizen-centred initiatives that have emerged during the last three decades, concentrating on those the Labour party has introduced since entering government in 1997. The final section assesses the significance and impact of these changes, in particular whether citizen engagement introduced by the state can create an effective and autonomous civic input into decision making.

The origins of the reform agenda

It is probably the case that the radical political movements of the 1960s changed the way in which experts and citizens viewed public institutions in the Anglo-American democracies. Before that time, there was a high level of satisfaction with democracy and a positive relationship between citizen orientations/behaviour and the outputs of government. The classic Almond and Verba (1963) surveys into the civic culture carried out in the late 1950s reported a balance between what they called participatory and subject roles, indicating the high degree of deference to established authority in Britain, albeit not inconsistent with some activism.

In the 1960s, the world changed. Almost at once, public authorities seemed to have become out of touch with a younger cohort of citizens. There was a public debate about the lack of responsiveness of existing elites. Popular movements sought to challenge existing policies, such as the war in Vietnam, through demonstrations and – at first – peaceful protests. The decade saw the rise of more assertive and confrontational forms of participation – both collective in the form of protests and community organisation and individual through more contacting of officials and politicians. Citizens increasingly preferred to challenge the dominant values rather than bargain within the existing framework of distributive politics. Habits of deference declined (Barnes and Kaase, 1979). The vocabulary of participation expanded to include a larger range of contents, such as boycotting products on the basis of a political campaign. Formerly neglected groups, such as minority ethnic groups and women, advocated different kinds of preferences to those of conventional left–right politics.

Some believed that values had shifted towards what Inglehart (1977) called post-materialism. Critics have questioned Inglehart's conceptualisation and the extent to which citizens have gone beyond materialistic concerns (for example, Clarke and Dutt, 1991), but it is clear that there were value changes in European democracies during that period (Klingemann and Fuchs, 1995) that are still playing out today in the different forms of political participation and the promotion of a wider set of political objectives than those of the post-war period of consensus politics. These changes should not be exaggerated, of course. The study of public opinion indicates that public attitudes and beliefs change very slowly. Surveys show only very gradual changes in habits and styles of political participation.

The political system was not passive in the face of these changes in political values and behaviour. Policy makers sought to accommodate citizens, giving them opportunities to participate. For example, the Skeffington Committee (1969) proposed extending the citizen's right to contribute to public planning decisions, particularly before the final decision had been made. There followed a series of reforms of the planning process, which incorporated citizen involvement on a statutory basis. The government experimented with community forms of participation by setting up community development projects in 1969, which promoted a participatory approach to neighbourhood development (Loney, 1983).

These initiatives waned in the 1970s, though formal participation in planning has remained part of the statutory framework. Community development lost its impetus and was wound up in 1977. This was before the Conservative government came into power in 1979, which shows it was not right-wing hostility to community empowerment that was the factor that caused its demise. Rather the decay of these initiatives resulted from considerable implementation difficulties, the loss of interest by central government and an environment of financial retrenchment as the economic crisis hit home in the 1970s.

The rise and decline of community participation in the 1960s and 1970s provide some useful lessons for contemporary reformers. They show that the current interest in empowerment as a supplement to the institutions of representative democracy is not a new idea, but is rediscovered periodically, usually with a different nomenclature. Governments seek to respond to the reoccurring frustrations with British democratic institutions and aim to co-opt more assertive citizen participants. But the experiments do not last. The cycle of official interest starts with initial enthusiasm, proceeds to the institutional experiments, and then moves to decline as the costs and implementation problems kick in. Crucially, the 1970s' experience reveals the importance of civil servants in sustaining these innovations and how their indifference can kill a project over the long term (Loney, 1983). Of course, the current interest in community participation does not have the radical underpinnings of those heady years, which may have made those projects more risky than the current wave and less likely to get embedded in mainstream policy making. But the comparison may also show that community participation is not an essential activity for both the public and the state. There is a danger it is subject to ministerial interest and the vicissitudes of fashion. *absolutely.*

Citizen participation since the 1970s

The trends in civic participation that began in the 1960s carried on into the following decades. The decline of conventional and habitual forms of political behaviour continued with the emergence of a more individualistic and choosing citizen (Norris, 1999; Clarke et al, 2004). For example, party identification, the attachment of voters to a political party, weakened. In 1964, 44% of people described themselves as party identifiers; by 2001 only 14% placed themselves in this category (figures from Whiteley, 2003: 611). The more striking example was the decline in voter turnout in national elections, which fell from over 70% in the 1950s to 59% in 2001. There have also been significant declines in measures of political trust (Catterberg and Moreno, 2005), confidence in institutions and perceptions of the trustworthiness of politicians. Indicators of the health of political parties are in great decline, such as party membership (Webb et al, 2002).

Some of these declines caused commentators to pronounce a general crisis of political participation. The idea that there is a problem with the social bases of democracy is a powerful message for both media pundits and policy makers. But research on democracy in Britain resists the idea that there is a crisis of participation and an erosion of the social bases to political life (Hall, 1999; Pattie et al, 2004). Some of the key measures of social capital, such as social trust, have stayed at a constant level over several decades. The turnout dive was partially due to the extent to which elections were closely fought. The fall in turnout in the general election of 2001 was partially due to the lead that Labour had in the polls rather than a general turning off of the electorate from politics, and it duly increased in 2005 when the race was much closer. *See also Power Inquiry*

The decline in conventional measures of participation and attitudes is matched by continuing interest in politics and rise in participation in non-conventional forms of activity, such as protest, boycotts and various kinds of community-based action (Pattie et al, 2004). But these new kinds of civic activity create problems for the political elites. Citizens have become more critical of existing institutions and there are fewer opportunities for party leaders to converse with people outside their narrow networks because of the decline of the mass membership of political parties. *Hence, 'listening events'*

Even if political participation is not in crisis, the perception of it has generated much official interest in the topic. From the 1980s, several investigations examined the strength of civic engagement. Prominent among them was the Speaker's Commission on Citizenship (1990), which drew interest from across the political parties. Then there was the Crick Report on citizenship education in English and Welsh schools (Qualifications and Curriculum Authority, 1998), which led to the introduction of citizenship education in secondary schools. Recently there was Lord Goldsmith's Citizenship Review (DCA, 2008) and the wider debate about constitutional reform launched by the Brown government, which stressed the importance of direct citizen participation (DCA, 2007). More generally, there have been research initiatives based on the perceptions of a problem with the state of participation in Britain, such as the ESRC's Democracy and Participation programme[2] the Democratic Audit reports,[3] and the successive audits of engagement carried out by the Hansard Society and the Electoral Commission (2004, 2005, 2006, 2007, 2008).

The perception of crisis may have encouraged the government and parliament to consider measures to involve the citizen more in public decision making. As a result there was a whole series of changes to public management, which have sought to include and to encourage citizen voice. There is now extensive contact between the citizen and the state, perhaps far more than in conventional political activities. From a set of gradual reforms, particularly from the entrepreneurial initiatives of some ministers, a series of public spaces for discussion have emerged within bureaucracies and away from conventional party and representative politics. One key question is whether this is a significant move away from conventional politics, towards a rediscovery of a form of direct democracy, or whether these initiatives are cynical exercises by politicians and bureaucrats keen to maintain their legitimacy in an anti-civic age.

New public management and citizen voice

Before this chapter moves to discuss the key period of the reforms in the 2000s, it is important to clear away one claim that can easily get in the way of a proper analysis of the role of the citizen in the contemporary English state. This is the idea that the new public management is necessarily inimical to citizen voice. The proposition is that the reforms of the public sector since the early 1980s removed the citizen from direct control over public services in favour of strong management by objectives. Systems of hierarchical management may have been replaced by mechanisms designed to improve efficiency and to yield savings in government. Procedures of accountability, review and redress may have weakened as a result. In part, this argument rests on a wider critique of the public choice inspired reforms of the public sector, with the idea that it aimed to remove or limit the voices of employees, especially in trades unions, and of established interest groups, to allow the bureaucracy to be managed effectively. More broadly, these reforms are thought to be based on a narrow conception of citizenship, reducing the citizen role to that of a chooser and consumer of services (Walsh, 1995).

In this way, many critics believed the reforming Thatcher governments limited the rights of citizens and reduced the public space. The main example was the removal of functions from control by locally elected government and their transfer to unelected agencies controlled by boards appointed by central government (Payne and Skelcher, 1997). The government removed statutory forms of consultation with the trades unions. Instead of rights and formal methods for having dialogue, it put in place mechanisms for consumer choice and transferred activities outside the public realm to the private sector. Examples are the contracting of local government services, which seemed to imply they would be beyond public scrutiny. In some cases these agencies relied on quasi-markets to generate choices from citizens to stimulate or curtail production from the agencies themselves, such as parents choosing places in school or patients selecting hospitals. Many of the new organisations had direct methods of including the public in their decisions. But, to the critics, these mechanisms seem to be forcing citizens into a narrower form of participation, encouraging them to be self-interested rather than to take on a broader set of actions based on the values and norms of citizenship.

It is, of course, easy to find examples of where competitive forms of new public management shut out the citizen. But the reforms of the Conservative years in government, 1979-97 may also be seen as part of a more general movement in the direction of greater citizen orientation in public services – even if the Conservatives emphasised more the market and competitive parts of this agenda – for it is important to recall how these reforms emerged. They reflected the growing awareness of the public of the actions of public bureaucracies and rising expectations of fair treatment; they also were the influence of the dissemination of good practice among public authorities that has gradually become the norm. Gyford (1991) identified sets of changes that placed citizens more in the driving seat in bureaucracies. This had its roots in the development of citizen expectations. Citizens were no longer so deferential to established professionals, such as social workers and planners, but sought to put their legitimate point of view to the bureaucrats and the experts. Increasingly, it seemed that citizens were becoming dissatisfied with public services in a general way (Lowndes et al, 2001; PIU, 2001), which reflected not only past failures but also an increasing willingness to question the kind of procedures that had been acceptable during the period of the classic bureaucratised version of the welfare state in post-war years. The idea that professionals and bureaucrats are left free to make allocation decisions is not consistent with today's more diverse social structures and higher expectations of citizens. Deference and acceptance may have been the norm for the older generations, but changing attitudes to authority created what some refer to as the critical citizen (see Norris, 1999 for discussion of that term). Rising living standards may be part of this change, as may be the experience of consumers in the private sector. Parts of the private sector have moved away from serving mass markets where long-term sales are generated by advertising and peer pressure to identifying and managing niche markets, which need to respond to the consumer's unique needs with a differentiated product. Companies learn to respond more effectively to complaints and seek to anticipate them by changing aspects of their product before the complaint emerges. Consumers have become used to making more sophisticated choices, such as over holidays. In the past, the average consumer would have chosen a package holiday from a brochure showing pictures of near identical hotels and swimming pools on each page. The focus now is on choosing, perhaps using the internet, different elements to a holiday, such as the hotel, the cities to visit, with specialist activities along the way, all purchased from different suppliers. With these experiences as increasingly the norm in private consumption, it is not surprising there should be a read across to the public sector. Public sector consumers expect the same degree of choice they experience in the private sector (Dowding and John, 2009).

While a lot of these activities involve market research to respond to the more discerning consumer, they also prompt public organisations to involve the public more broadly in their decisions to help provide services more appropriately to avoid failures. This new thinking sees the citizen behaving as an individual, such as a complainer, or acting collectively in a representative function. If some citizens are happy to sit back and make passive choices, others are prepared to come forward to represent concerns about standards or the responsiveness of these services to their client group. This happened right from the early days in public management reform, with the greater participation of school governors in schools, for example. In regeneration, there is the requirement to consult and to form partnerships in bids for funding, such as in the Single Regeneration Budget programme, which ran from 1994. More generally, more effective kinds of regulation mean that agencies are opened up to the public gaze and consultation, whether they are directly controlled by elected politicians, or whether they are in the public or private sector. And it has always been the case that public law guidelines, requiring fairness and consultation, apply not just to public sector agencies but also to all bodies carrying out public tasks. The expansion of regulation is an extension of this principle.

 It is important to realise that community participation emerged from within local public agencies as well as being imposed from above by central government. Thus the neighbourhood decentralisation movement of the 1980s (Lowndes and Stoker, 1992a, 1992b) was a radical initiative from within local government, which depended on giving services to decentralised units where services were guided by consultation forums. This had support from the left of the political spectrum. Significantly, these initiatives did not survive and fell by the wayside, rather like the community development experiments of a decade earlier. Is this the fate of community empowerment generally, at least in England? But communities have become more vocal in their representation, whether it is over planning decisions or when community champions challenge elected local councillors (Barnes et al, 2004).

The UK experiments did not happen in isolation. Community empowerment is a cross-national phenomenon that sits alongside more general public management reforms. Though these measures have appeared in many countries, they have been more pronounced in the Anglo-American democracies. Fung (2006), for example, examines the participation experiments of many cities in the US, whereby citizens have sought to use new forums to control the political agenda and to achieve social objectives, such as the reduction of crime. Gaventa and Goetz (2001) and Gaventa (2004a) have charted the cross-national experience of these activities, especially in the less developed countries. They articulate a critical point of view, suggesting these forums compete with locally elected organisations. Other public management writers discuss a change in the character of the bureaucracy in response to these changes, what Bryer (2007) calls a deliberative form characterised by negotiated or collaborative management. Collaborative public management involves initiatives to include stakeholders to try to improve policy making.

Labour in power since 1997

The previous section stressed the continuity of approaches to citizen involvement since the early 1980s and how they are part of an international movement promoting citizen engagement. In contrast, this section explores the distinctive contribution the Labour governments have made in the years since 1997, when the party entered office after a long period of opposition. The Labour party was keen to start anew in government and wanted to broaden its connection to the citizens, rather than just rely on traditional supporters, such as trades unions and party members, which seemed to represent the past from which the party's leadership was so desperate to try to escape. It wanted to encourage new forms of governance to maintain the party's legitimacy and standing with non-core Labour voters. It was also the time when the perceived crisis of British democracy hit home, which made it seem that the conventional representative foundations of democracy, in terms of citizen support for elected politicians, were in need of attention. Hence there were reforms for local government, for example in the proposals for directly elected mayors, which were designed to stimulate local democracy and the citizens' interest in council affairs. The devolution experiment was a way of reinvigorating democracy, as were other constitutional projects, such as the 1998 Human Rights Act and the attempted reform of the House of Lords.

The other factor behind the move to strengthen citizen voice was the initiative of some key Labour politicians. Tony Blair is one example, with his initial seizing of what was called the Third Way political agenda. Another is David Blunkett, who became a champion for citizen direct involvement with public services, what he called civil renewal. At the time of the first Labour government, Blunkett was a serious and respected politician, who had been introduced to theories of democracy by his former university teacher, the late Bernard Crick. Blunkett had a long interest in the subject, being a key figure on the Speaker's Commission on Citizenship referred to above. With his working-class origins, Blunkett could get away with intellectual pronouncements that in other politicians' voices would sound pompous and overblown. But Blunkett's speeches and writings made ample use of ideas from political theory. He wished to re-engage with the classical ideal of democracy, with its strong focus on citizen duty (for example, Blunkett, 2003). As Education Secretary, he promoted the reform of the curriculum to introduce citizenship education. Then, as Home Secretary, he pushed consultation further by opening up crime partnerships to public consultation. Finally, Labour wanted to follow the reform of the public sector according to new public management techniques with even more vigour than the Conservatives. It was no surprise that this wish to reform should be accompanied by attempts to involve the public in decision-making forums. There would be both more choice and more voice.

The best term for describing these diverse arenas for engagement is citizen governance, where the state creates institutions that involve the citizen in a degree of influence of decision making. There are several published descriptions of these initiatives (see Brannan et al, 2006), so only a brief summary is needed here. Examples are forums for council house tenants in tenant participation compacts and housing cooperatives. Another policy field is health where there is statutory consultation by primary care trusts (PCTs) and health panels to encourage long-term involvement and representation of communities in policy making. In addition, foundation hospitals are accountable to local communities and include members of the public on their governing bodies. Crime is another area, especially the public participation on crime and disorder partnerships created in 2004. The 2006 Local Government White Paper (CLG, 2006), and subsequent legislation, applied these participatory ideas directly to local government. It introduced community calls for action; powers so councils may create parish councils; and recommendations that councils should deal with petitions and delegate budgets. It also expanded the power of the ombudsman; empowered people to manage their own neighbourhoods; increased opportunities for communities to take on the management and ownership of local assets and facilities such as underused community centres or empty schools; simplified and extended the scope of tenant management of housing; encouraged local charters between communities and service providers; provided a new power of well-being for the best parish councils to improve the development and coordination of support for citizens, communities groups and local authorities; and changed the best value duty to ensure that authorities inform, consult, involve and devolve to all citizens and communities.   *Duty to Involve*

The contribution of citizen governance to democracy

There is no doubt that citizen governance is a permanent feature of the political landscape, which has survived the transfer from Conservative to Labour and from Tony Blair to Gordon Brown as premier. The Conservatives under David Cameron are sympathetic to these ideas as *doesn't mean much!* the party retreats from advocating pure market solutions and stresses the organic and decentralised character of politics (Norman and Ganesh, 2006). The Liberal Democrats, with their community activist roots, have always championed citizen rights though they pay more attention to the constitutional framework governing participation. The wide adoption of citizen governance as a desirable feature of public administration across political parties and different ideological standpoints suggests that these reforms are compatible with a range of views of citizenship, linking them to debates about alternatives to representative democracy. But there remains a broader question of the extent to which they deepen democracy or whether they are more like an appendage, even if a useful one, to existing representative institutions.

On the positive side, citizen governance involves a wider group of citizens in its deliberations, about 8.3% of the population (John, 2009, forthcoming), with about 3.5% doing this as their only form of citizen activity outside voting. There is also evidence that citizen governance reaches to citizens who have been excluded from decision making, such as minority ethnic communities and young people. From these figures it is not possible to dismiss citizen governance quite so much as a minority sport as some do (Walker, 2006), though it still does not involve 90% of the population.

But what is the experience of these activities? One view is that they are simply consultation devices, perhaps of similar ilk to the supposedly democratic Soviets who used to legitimate oppressive socialist governments before the fall of the USSR. Judge (2006), for example, regards them as a diversion from the effective business of representative government, an example of the failure of New Labour's vision for democracy in spite of good intentions to restore trust in government. Some case studies seem to bear out the symbolic character of these participation experiments. Cole's (2004) study of Exeter, for example, suggests that the exercise aimed to manufacture consent rather than genuinely influence policy. The case studies reported in Barnes et al (2007) focus on the limitations of participation exercises and the failure to transfer power to them. Newman et al's (2004) examination of participation in two cities found dissatisfied participants who reported unacceptable delays in responses to participation.

But it would be wrong to see these forums as merely legitimation exercises. Some studies show citizens make policy (see Brannan et al, 2006). The conclusion of many accounts of citizen governance is one where there are good experiences and practices, but there is more to be learnt (Skidmore et al, 2006). And then there are the often unnoticed but extensive community self-help activities that complement the wider participation initiatives (Richardson, 2008).

But it would be fair to say that English participation activities tend to lack formal grounding and rely too much on bureaucratic discretion rather than handing over significant institutional power to citizens. Gaventa (2004b: 24) comments, 'though there have been a number of white papers, guidelines and committee reports promoting community participation in the UK, unlike in other countries the legal and statutory frameworks supporting participation have been relatively weak'. It appears that participators tend to lack formal rights of redress or for information, which may reflect the weak conception of the role of the citizen in the process and the sense in which it is not possible to have formal alternatives to representative democracy. This tension is felt very much in local affairs where elected councillors see themselves as the representatives and tend to resist community representatives (Barnes et al, 2004). The Ministry of Justice (2008) consultation paper *A national framework for greater citizen engagement* proposed extending participation of citizen forums, summits/deliberation, participatory budgeting and e-petitions, but recommended that consultation should occur only on topics the core decision-makers wanted to be debated, such as greater consultation can occur 'on policy options on which government has an open mind' (Ministry of Justice, 2008: 11), which implies there are many other proposals where the government has a closed mind and the public should not be involved!

Conclusion

There is no doubt that England continues to be a largely legitimate and effective representative democracy. Its long-lasting democratic political institutions are sustained by expectations from the citizen about the appropriate role of government. In spite of worries about declining participation and the reduced efficiency of the system, it functions reasonably well by delivering responsive but decisive governments, with periodic changes in power to renew public policy. Overall, the citizens regard these arrangements as legitimate – they are happy to elect governments into power, to let them get on with the job of governing and – in due course – to punish or reward them accordingly at the polls. And most of the basic indicators of the health of democracy, such as voting and forms of citizen involvement, are not in freefall decline. Citizens increasingly find new arenas in which to participate, whether it is holding demonstrations or posting e-petitions. The alternatives that this chapter discusses, which envisage a direct role for the citizen in deciding and co-producing public services, are an addition not a replacement for representative mechanisms.

One view would be that citizen governance forums are at best a distraction to the effective running of parliamentary government. They dilute traditional representative mechanisms, but they do not get enough power to make a difference. They are symbolic rather than actual democratic exercises. But the innovations that have occurred cannot be dismissed as the paraphernalia of new public management, or the favourite ploy of populist or right-wing governments keen to tear down corporatist and consensual decision-making structures. The structures that have emerged to involve the citizen in decision making, in contrast to earlier experiments in community development in the 1970s and the decentralisations of the 1980s, appear to be permanent fixtures to the delivery of policy that offers benefits to citizen and policy maker alike through a full and professionally administered dialogue. It is likely that these mechanisms of direct democracy will develop in time, as policy makers increasingly have to justify their actions. Such changes can challenge or redefine the roles of existing representatives, like members of parliament and locally elected councillors.

But, if the progress has been positive, these forms of governance could be enhanced. They could take advantage of good examples from elsewhere in the globe where citizens develop formal rights of redress in the decision-making process. With such tools in the hands of citizens, there could be a revival of community-based decision-making, which would overcome some of the cumbersome features of local government with its vast jurisdictions and overprofessionalised administration. But it would need much more of a rethink about the constitutional language and the practice of government. England lacks a well-developed vocabulary of constitutional argument and public involvement with decision making. The ideas that could push in this direction, in the rule of law and delegated forms of public accountability, have been buried and constrained within elite-centred discourse concerned to protect executive autonomy and to concentrate the rights of criticism in an official opposition. A wider set of constitutional understandings, with more articulated formal rights for the citizen, could both make the existing experiments work better and lead to a more mature debate about politics and participation.

Notes

[1] There are many summaries of the tension in democratic theory, but there is a useful review in Parry et al (1992: 3-5).

ПL 320. 0942 PAR

[2] www.esrcsocietytoday.ac.uk/ESRCInfoCentre/research/ research_programmes/democracy.aspx?ComponentId=9262&SourcePageId=9102.

[3] www.democraticaudit.com/

References

Almond, G. and Verba, S. (1963) *The civic culture: Political attitudes and democracy in five nations*, Boston, MA: Little, Brown & Co.

Barnes, S. and Kaase, M. (1979) *Political action: Mass participation in five western democracies*, Beverly Hills, CA: Sage.

Barnes, M., Newman, J. and Sullivan, H. (2007) *Power, participation and political renewal: Case studies in public participation*, Bristol: The Policy Press.

Barnes, M., Sullivan, H., Knops, A. and Newman, J. (2004) 'Power, participation and political renewal: issues from a study of public participation in two English cities', *IDS Bulletin*, vol 35, no 2, pp 58-66.

Blunkett, D. (2003) 'Active citizens, strong communities: progressing civil renewal', Scarman Lecture, Citizens' Convention, 11 December (www.communities.gov.uk/publications/communities/activecitizensstrong)

Brannan, T., John, P. and Stoker, G. (2006) *Re-energising citizenship*, Basingstoke: Macmillan.

Bryer, T. (2007) 'Towards a relevant agenda for responsive public administration', *Journal of Public Administration Research and Theory*, vol 17, no 3, pp 479-500.

Catterberg, G, and Moreno, A. (2005) 'The individual bases of political trust: trends in the new and established democracies', *International Journal of Public Opinion Research*, vol 18, no 1, pp 31-48.

Clarke, H. and Dutt, N. (1991) 'Measuring value change in western industrialized societies: the impact of unemployment', *American Political Science Review*, vol 85, no 3, pp 905-20.

Clarke, H., Sanders, D., Stewart, M. and Whiteley, P. (2004) *Political choice in Britain*, Oxford: Oxford University Press.

CLG (Communities and Local Government) (2006) *Strong and prosperous communities: The local government white paper* (www.communities.gov. uk/localgovernment/strategies/strongprosperous/)

Cole, M. (2004) 'Consultation in local government: a case study of practice at Devon County Council', *Local Government Studies*, vol 30, pp 196-213.

DCA (Department of Constitutional Affairs) (2007) *The governance of Britain*, London: HMSO.

DCA (2008) *Citizenship: Our common bond*, London: DCA.

Dowding, K. and John, P. (2009, forthcoming) 'The value of choice in public policy', *Public Administration*, vol 87, no 2, pp 219-33.

Fung, A. (2006) *Empowered participation: Reinventing urban democracy*, Princeton, NJ: Princeton University Press.

Gaventa, J. (2004a) 'Towards participatory local governance: assessing the transformative possibilities', in S. Hickey and G. Mohan (eds) *From tyranny to transformation? Exploring new approaches to participation*, London: Zed Books, pp 25-41.

Gaventa, J. (2004b) 'Representation, community leadership and participation: citizen involvement in neighbourhood renewal and local governance', paper prepared for the Neighbourhood Renewal Unit, Office of Deputy Prime Minister.

Gaventa, J. and Goetz, A.M (2001) *Bringing citizen voice and client focus into service delivery*, Brighton: IDS, University of Sussex.

Gyford, J. (1991) *Citizens, consumers, and councils: Local government and the public*, London: Macmillan.

Hall, P. (1999) 'Social capital in Britain', *British Journal of Political Science*, vol 29, no 3, pp 417-61.

Hansard Society and the Electoral Commission (2004, 2005, 2006, 2007, 2008), *Audit of political engagement*, London: Hansard Society.

Inglehart, R. (1977) *The silent revolution: Changing values and political styles among western publics*, Princeton, NJ: Princeton University Press.

John, P. (2009, forthcoming) 'Making representative democracy more representative: can new forms of citizen governance in the UK open up democracy?', *Public Administration Review*, vol 69, no 3, pp 494-503.

Judge, D. (2006) 'This is what democracy looks like: New Labour's blind spot and peripheral vision', *British Politics*, vol 1, no 3, pp 367-96.

Klingemann, H.-D. and Fuchs, D. (1995), *Citizens and the state: Beliefs in government, volume one*, Oxford: Oxford University Press.

Loney, M. (1983) *Community against government: The British community development project, 1968-1978: A study of government impotence*, London: Heineman.

Lowndes, V., and Stoker, G (1992a) 'An evaluation of neighbourhood decentralisation – part 1: customer and citizen perspectives', *Policy and Politics*, vol 20, no 1, pp 47-61.

Lowndes, V. and, Stoker, G. (1992b) 'An evaluation of neighbourhood decentralisation – part 2: staff and councillor perspectives', *Policy and Politics*, vol 20, no 2, pp 143-52.

Lowndes, V., Pratchett, L. and Stoker, G. (2001) 'Trends in public participation: part 2 – citizens' perspectives', *Public Administration*, vol 79, no 2, pp 445-55.

Ministry of Justice (2008) *A national framework for greater citizen engagement*, London: Ministry of Justice.

Newman J., Barnes M., Sullivan, H. and Knops, A. (2004) 'Public participation and collaborative governance', *Journal of Social Policy*, vol 33, no 2, pp 203-23.

Norman, J. and Ganesh, J. (2006) *Compassionate conservatism: What it is, why we need it*. London: Policy Exchange (www.policyexchange.org.uk/assets/Compassionate_Conservatism.pdf).

Norris, P. (ed) (1999) *Critical citizens: Global support for democratic government*, Oxford: Oxford University Press.

Parry, G., Moyser, M. and Day, N. (1992) *Political participation and democracy in Britain*, Cambridge: Cambridge University Press.

Pattie, C.J., Seyd, P. and Whiteley, P. (2004) *Citizenship in Britain: Values, participation and democracy*, Cambridge: Cambridge University Press.

Payne, T. and Skelcher, C. (1997) 'Explaining less accountability: the growth of local quangos', *Public Administration*, vol 75, no 2, pp 207-25.

PIU (Performance and Innovation Unit) (2001) *Satisfaction with public services*, London: PIU (www.cabinetoffice.gov.uk/media/cabinetoffice/strategy/assets/satisfaction.pdf).

Qualifications and Curriculum Authority (1998) *Education for citizenship and the teaching of democracy in schools (Crick Report)*, London: QCA.

Richardson, L. (2008) *DIY community action*, Bristol: The Policy Press.

Skeffington Committee, (1969) *Report of the Committee on Public Participation in Planning*, London: HMSO.

Skidmore, P., Bound, K. and Lownsbrough, H. (2006) *Community participation: Who benefits?* York: Joseph Rowntree Foundation.

Speaker's Commission on Citizenship (1990) *Encouraging citizenship*, London: HMSO.

Walker, D. (2006) 'Perils of empowering the people', *The Guardian*, 22 November.

Walsh, K. (1995) *Public services and market competition, contracting and the new public management*, London: Macmillan.

Webb, P., Farrell D. and Holliday, I. (2002) *Political parties in advanced industrial democracies*, Oxford: Oxford University Press.

Whiteley, P. (2003) 'The state of participation in Britain', *Parliamentary Affairs*, vol 56, no 4, pp 610-15.

THREE

'Neighbourhood': a site for policy action, governance ... and empowerment?

Catherine Durose and Liz Richardson

Introduction

'Neighbourhood' is a longstanding concept in public policy, with numerous initiatives and policy directives focusing on 'neighbourhood' being part of the policy agenda from the 1960s onwards. The 'neighbourhood' has re-emerged under New Labour as an organisational anchor for the promotion of planned change, a site for local governance and latterly as a site for encouraging more active citizenship. The concept of 'neighbourhood' has achieved significant normative appeal and resonance in public policy. The new governance and policy spaces created at the neighbourhood level, particularly under the reforms introduced by New Labour, offer unprecedented opportunities to reshape democracy, decision making and the delivery of services. This chapter examines to what extent those opportunities have been used, and used effectively.

Neighbourhoods are often the sites where the issues that matter most to people's lives are in sharpest relief. Neighbourhoods are areas where citizens identify with and feel a sense of belonging (CLG, 2007). However, there is no single generalisable definition of neighbourhood and 'top-down' administrative definitions often fail to capture the scale and nuance of citizens' own understandings of their neighbourhoods.

This chapter uses Lowndes and Sullivan's (2008) typology of neighbourhood-based working under New Labour as a framework for exploring the different understandings of why neighbourhood working is happening, and how far this matches citizens' needs and preferences. We find that there are several clear gaps between citizens and local government in how the neighbourhood agenda is being operated.

The chapter draws on extensive primary and applied research conducted by the authors over the last five years (Richardson, 2004, 2006; White et al, 2006; Durose, 2007; Durose and Lowndes, 2008; Richardson forthcoming).

What is neighbourhood-based working?

The rhetoric and policy drivers around neighbourhoods produced by central government are diverse and fluid and have led to an almost overwhelming array of neighbourhood-based initiatives. As Lowndes and Sullivan (2008: 6) comment: 'neighbourhood based working is out there'. We use the term 'neighbourhood-based working' in this chapter as a generic term for a variety of forms of neighbourhood structures and processes. Two definitions of neighbourhood-based working are set out in Box 3.1.

Box 3.1: Definitions of neighbourhood-based working

A 'neighbourhood approach' is understood as a set of arrangements for collective decision making and/or public service delivery at the sub-local level. This implies the transfer of political and/or managerial authority from 'higher' to 'lower' level actors, though who gains power and over what depends on the purpose and design of devolution. 'Neighbourhood' is not an objective category; consequently, the idea of the 'sub-local' is a relative concept, referring to an area smaller than the local authority boundary, though such areas may contain 1,000 residents or 10,000.

Source: Lowndes and Sullivan (2008: 62).

'Neighbourhood governance' is the practices and arrangements at a neighbourhood level that:
- provide leadership;
- develop shared values and a shared vision for an area;
- exert influence over decisions that affect an area;
- take decisions about an area;
- monitor both the execution and the impact of decisions;
- recognise the development of local institutions and processes that are responsible for making decisions and allocating resources locally.

The definition of a neighbourhood is relatively broad, will vary according to locality and should be locally defined to offer a viable neighbourhood in terms of ensuring sustainable governance arrangements.

Source: White et al (2006).

As Box 3.1 shows, definitions of a neighbourhood are hard to pin down. We look at different definitions of neighbourhood later in this chapter, as these differences are at the heart of key debates over what neighbourhood working is trying to achieve, and for whom.

Neighbourhood-based working allows for a variety of structures or systems to operate in each sub-local area. Neighbourhood structures have very different institutional designs, ranging from community forums with no decision-making powers; to neighbourhood committee systems with delegated decision making and devolved budgets where a wide range of decisions are taken by a group of councillors (influenced by and answerable to a wide group of residents); to neighbourhood management structures with a dedicated manager and team of staff responsible for extensive community consultation, and providing and adapting services in the area in line with community needs.

In this chapter we are less concerned with a descriptive catalogue of the forms that neighbourhood working takes locally and more concerned to look at the underlying aims of neighbourhood working and what this implies for citizens. We now turn to a typology of the different aims of neighbourhood-based working. We then use this typology in the rest of the chapter to explore how the neighbourhoods' agenda has evolved, and how well the needs of citizens and local government are being met by current neighbourhood working practices.

Typologising 'neighbourhood' under New Labour

As noted, the re-emergence of neighbourhood under New Labour was driven by multiple agendas with differentiated aims. Lowndes and Sullivan (2008) have provided a useful typology of the emergence of neighbourhood under New Labour, highlighting underlying rationales about the benefits of neighbourhood working and 'ideal' institutional forms and citizen roles, shown in Table 3.1.

Shifting rationales for neighbourhood policy under New Labour

A neighbourhood approach re-emerged at the start of the 1997 New Labour administration and was a key part of the branding of the new government, beginning with the setting up of the Social Exclusion Unit (SEU). Much of the work of the SEU was based on the understanding that social exclusion and deprivation had a spatial element, as reflected in the National Strategy for Neighbourhood Renewal (NSNR; SEU, 2001), targeting the most deprived neighbourhoods, with the aim of

Table 3.1: A typology of the turn to neighbourhoods under New Labour

Rationale	Civic	Economic	Political	Social
	Opportunities for direct citizen participation and community involvement	Focus on efficiency and effectiveness gains in local service delivery; tax/spend bargain	Improvements in the accessibility, accountability and responsiveness of decision making	Holistic and citizen-centred approach to delivering services; designing services around the citizen
Form of democracy	Participatory democracy	Market democracy	Representative democracy	Stakeholder democracy
Institutional design	Neighbourhood empowerment	Neighbourhood management	Neighbourhood governance	Neighbourhood partnerships
Citizen role	Citizen: voice, co-production	Consumer: choice	Elector: vote	Partner: loyalty, problem solving

Source: adapted from Lowndes and Sullivan (2008).

narrowing the gap between deprived neighbourhoods and the rest of the country. A key element of the strategy was around the 'social' rationale of providing better outcomes in the most deprived areas. There were a number of neighbourhood-based working programmes, including Neighbourhood Management Pathfinder Programme and the flagship programme the New Deal for Communities (NDC). The policy was underpinned by a 'civic' rationale of the need for citizen engagement and ownership.

The neighbourhood was used initially by New Labour in government as a site for policy action to tackle inequality and social exclusion. Over time, neighbourhood became a prominent theme in many parallel agendas focusing on developing a more participative, decentralised form of local governance in a much wider range of neighbourhood types, not just the most deprived (Lowndes and Sullivan, 2008). Running alongside policy on social inclusion and neighbourhoods has been the 'civil renewal' agenda or 'civic' rationale. This agenda emerged more explicitly slightly later in the New Labour second term and was initially coordinated by the Home Office and importantly led and championed by David Blunkett. It was partly in response to widespread concern about the state of democracy and the performance of public services (Blunkett, 2003). The three core elements of the agenda were: 'active citizenship', where citizens are able to define and address their own key problems; 'strengthened communities', where communities can develop their own community-based organisations to respond to key concerns; and 'partnership' in meeting local needs, including more involvement of citizens in the decisions of local agencies. All these elements emphasise the 'interdependence and mutuality' of all stakeholders in society (Blunkett, 2003). Following Blunkett's political demise this agenda has been restated in several policy documents, most recently in the more prosaic Hazel Blears' 2008 White Paper on community empowerment (CLG, 2008a).

Local government modernisation has been an ongoing policy agenda under New Labour. The objectives of this agenda are: to improve the efficiency and effectiveness of service delivery (an 'economic' rationale); including 'joining up' services so as to be more citizen-centred (a 'social' rationale); but also to increase accessibility to decision making and empower citizens to get involved in these processes and in their own communities (a 'political' rationale). The most recent forms that this agenda has taken are in 'new localism' (Corry and Stoker, 2002) and 'double devolution' (Miliband, 2006). The 'new localism' agenda under New Labour has had a strong focus on a political rationale, looking at the role for 'modern councillors' and new roles for ward members as 'community champions', as can be seen in the recent White Papers (ODPM/Home Office, 2005; CLG, 2006a).

Many of the initiatives coordinated by the Neighbourhood Renewal Unit (NRU) were implemented initially directly in neighbourhoods. Local authorities were involved in bidding for central funds, but were largely bypassed in the initiation and development of neighbourhood projects. However, local government and its partners have since taken up the neighbourhood agenda and developed varying forms of neighbourhood-based working. Rather than focusing on neighbourhood renewal and aiming to narrow the gap in social and economic outcomes between deprived areas and the rest, local government has taken up the neighbourhood agenda in the form of providing leadership and vision, and influencing or taking decisions across all neighbourhoods. Local authorities now often use a model of a 'sliding scale' of governance structures, including those in better-off areas that do not require 'neighbourhood management'. As a result the neighbourhood agenda as seen in local authority areas is being more closely aligned with 'civic' and 'political' agendas and is being decoupled from such a close association with the resource-intensive area-based initiatives seen under central government policy. One executive councillor in a large metropolitan authority objected to the idea of a 'minimum standard', but expressed the distinction thus: 'McDonald's say: there's deluxe then super deluxe. Well, regeneration areas get super deluxe and everywhere else gets deluxe' (Durose and Lowndes, 2008, p 17).

Despite this continued political interest in neighbourhoods in relation to building civic attitudes, behaviour and community empowerment, the neighbourhood agenda has been subject to shifting interest and commitment from government. The early 2000s saw significant amounts of government money go into neighbourhood renewal. Investment from central government into citizen engagement in neighbourhoods has now tailed off, with the hope that statutory bodies at a local level will commit to their own policy innovations as and where necessary.

Does neighbourhood working empower citizens?

Our use of a typology of rationales for neighbourhood working, which has been established by and operates within local authorities is not meant to imply that neighbourhoods are all the property of institutional designers and local government modernisers; they are also spaces for bottom-up involvement, which may or may not be incorporated into neighbourhood-based working. In assessing neighbourhood working against the rationales as expressed by local governance actors themselves, we argue in the rest of this chapter that:

- the 'civic' rationale is limited in its uptake and success;
- local authorities tend to focus predominantly on the 'economic' rationale for neighbourhood-based working;
- there has been a focus on the 'social' rationale within moves towards efficiency and effectiveness, although to a lesser extent than the economic rationale
- neighbourhood working around the 'political' rationale is beginning to deliver benefits for both citizens and local politicians. *not sure*

The chapter will now explore the variations in the take-up of different rationales for neighbourhood working.

Neglect of the 'civic' within neighbourhood working

Talking to local authorities about their own articulations of the rationales behind neighbourhood-based working indicates that they have clear underlying 'economic' and 'political' rationales, and within this a less powerful but still present emphasis on the 'social' rationale. Authorities themselves acknowledge the difficulties in simultaneously achieving all four agendas and the potential tensions that exist between the four rationales. Local governance structures were making choices where focusing on and achieving 'economic', 'political' and 'social' aims was often at the expense of 'civic' objectives. The case study evidence in Box 3.2 illustrates this point forcefully.

Box 3.2: Examples of the economic, political and social rationales in practice

'Economic' rationale for neighbourhood working
In one large metropolitan council, the stated aims of the neighbourhood management system that was developed were to address the key challenges of New Labour's policy agenda and all four of the rationales for the move towards neighbourhoods. However, beyond the rhetoric, it did not seem possible or desirable for neighbourhood-based working to fulfil all of these rationales and be, as one senior officer commented, "the panacea for all the problems of a city". Although it is important "to make sure that neighbourhood management has an input into all of these work strands", it is also important "that it isn't seen as the answer to all the ills ... and isn't left alone to tackle it". While rhetorically

agreeing with different objectives for neighbourhood-based work, clear priority was given in the city to using neighbourhoods as a means of improving service delivery – an economic rationale. The alignment of neighbourhood working with service improvement is clear from this demarcation of 'neighbourhoods' as large areas, previously labelled 'service delivery areas'. Other indications are the emphasis on citywide implementation of the scheme, rather than solely in areas of marked deprivation; and the emphasis given to coterminous and complementary organisation with other service deliverers (Durose, 2007).

The focus on service improvement was seen by employees of the same authority to undermine 'civic' work by neighbourhood actors and there were tensions between the two aims (Durose, 2007). As one community development worker commented:

> '... community development work and neighbourhood management are not the same thing and there's some tension between them. Neighbourhood management is all about the effectiveness and the efficiency of services ... a sort of top-down sort of structure; whereas community development work is the complete opposite, we're working with local needs ... I'm there to support local needs ... but not to be the face of [X] Council.'

'Political' rationale for neighbourhood working

For example, in one county council, officers and members said that neighbourhood working aimed in theory to combine rationales, but work to engage and empower citizens around 'civic' goals was taking place. As one officer commented, "we are doing participatory work elsewhere, there is not a gap" (Richardson, forthcoming). The 'political' rationale was central (Richardson, forthcoming):

> Very few officers see members because they don't go to Cabinet and they don't see them locally ... Directorates saw local committees as encouraging poor performance, and they see [current neighbourhood structures] as bad – idiot councillors making stupid decisions ... It is not easy to deliver on the model, but there is significant member support for devolving. Members understand place because it's place that elects them ... Democracy is all about members. We are focusing on representative democracy to give [members] the ability to put community leadership into practice.

'Social' rationale for neighbourhood working

In another authority, the inclusion of two social housing estates in a neighbourhood management pilot area were based on the level of social and economic problems and the fact that those neighbourhoods were 'difficult to manage' for service providers (as opposed to 'difficult to live in' for residents). A previous iteration of neighbourhood working had attempted to deliver on a 'social' rationale. New multidisciplinary environmental services teams were created. Part of the idea was to encourage pride among staff about their areas and to encourage residents to approach staff with issues: 'It was a genuine attempt to involve local people in shaping services or at least responding to message from local people.' However, links to a civic agenda were patchy – for example, the initiative did not fully engage citizens as it was promoted via the area forums, which had limited citizen participation, and through 'standard leaflets that no one reads'. Where it had engaged residents, this successful civic response was not matched by successful social response, where services are designed around the citizen. The multidisciplinary teams were a commitment to be responsive to local people, 'which is not always easy to do' (Richardson, forthcoming).

Defining the 'neighbourhood'

The particular rationales for neighbourhood working being assumed or followed clearly relate to the definitions of the neighbourhood. The emphasis on the 'economic' rationale is reflected in the dominance of 'top-down' definitions of neighbourhood over more socially constructed boundaries. As Kearns and Parkinson (2001: 2103) note: 'there is no single generalisable interpretation of the neighbourhood', but this is not simply an abstract argument over definitions. The selection and definition of target neighbourhoods is a highly political and negotiable process (Chaskin, 1998: 11). The question of who defines neighbourhood is the first crucial stage of starting to deliver neighbourhood working. This question is currently not being resolved in favour of citizens. Many governance structures do not use residents' own definitions or definitions that make sense to citizens. The implications of this mismatch are that there needs to be a major descaling of the size of area at which local government works for neighbourhoods to be meaningful for citizens. This is not taking place in the majority of local authorities; indeed, in some places, authorities are not just staying at their current scale of working, but scaling up.

The substantial intervention activity and multiple initiatives being developed for and at the neighbourhood level are underpinned by the belief that neighbourhoods are 'viable, recognisable units of identity and action, and are therefore the appropriate locus for the planning and delivering of a range of services and activities' (Chaskin, 1998: 11). Chaskin's concept of neighbourhoods helps us to ask the question:

what sorts of neighbourhoods are viable and recognisable, and for whom? Looking at different stakeholders' perspectives, what becomes clear is there is a disparity between what constitutes an appropriate locus for action for residents versus that for local government. The fact that there are conflicting definitions of neighbourhood illustrates the point that local government is focused on 'economic' and 'political' rationales in direct contradiction to a 'civic' rationale and what makes sense to citizens.

The 'neighbourhood' is both an enduring concept in public policy and a space that citizens identify with. Neighbourhood is a salient idea for people – for example, a national survey in 2007 found that 77% felt that they 'strongly belonged' to their neighbourhood, up from 71% in 2003 (CLG, 2007). What people mean by neighbourhood is different for different groups of citizens, who have different relationships to neighbourhoods. How individuals define and use neighbourhoods depends in part on their status in and relationship to the larger society, as influenced by their position in the life course (Chaskin, 1998). For example, those most integrated into the larger society – people who are married or middle aged, people with higher incomes and education – tend to have larger, more dispersed, more casual neighbourhood networks (Barrett et al, 1991: 13; Barrett and Campbell, 1992, 1993). It is acknowledged that neighbourhoods are complex, dynamic, and multifaceted.

But, while 'different residents and organisations will not always agree on the actual boundaries' (Power, 2004: 2), broadly citizens understand neighbourhood to have a physical and social element. Even citizen definitions of neighbourhood as a physical space are partly related to their own use of the space. As Lowndes and Sullivan (2008: 5) note, 'the debate about the constitution of neighbourhoods is now largely based upon an acceptance that neighbourhoods are socially constructed'. For residents, perceptions of what constitutes the 'neighbourhood' will usually be based on 'the location of family and social networks, amenities such as shops and schools and physical boundaries such as roads and railways' (Taylor and Wilson, 2006: 5; see also Kotecha et al, 2008: 27). There is a strong social component to neighbourhoods, 'people connect with neighbourhoods in many, often unspoken ways'(Power, 2004: 2).

Therefore, because neighbourhoods for citizens are about social relationships and their day-to-day lives, it means that the scale at which people understand neighbourhood is relatively contained. It is the scale at which they can easily walk to the local shops (a 15-20 minute walk), and a scale at which they feel comfortable greeting neighbours at the shops (CLG, 2008b). Residents' definitions of neighbourhood are of what have been called 'home' or 'natural' neighbourhoods – that is, areas of between 500 and 2,000 homes (Young Foundation, 2005). In other research by the authors, residents' definitions of neighbourhood were focused on small neighbourhoods of under 2,000 homes, mostly fewer than 1,000 homes (Richardson, 2008a; see also Power, 2004).

Citizens have incentives to engage in the neighbourhood, because it is at this level that they consume many of the most important public services and experience the issues most likely to mobilise them (Lowndes and Sullivan, 2008). The neighbourhoods' agenda is therefore based on the premise that people are most likely to engage with services and policy making at a very local level. This is particularly resonant in the most disadvantaged neighbourhoods, where people's choices are more likely to be dictated by their immediate surroundings (Taylor and Wilson, 2006: 5). This suggests that, in order to fulfil civic aims, 'neighbourhoods' need to be relatively small areas that citizens relate to, structured around things that matter to them.

However, Taylor and Wilson (2006: 5) note that: 'there is often a discrepancy between top down "administrative" definitions that rely on ward boundaries or other boundaries used for the collection of statistical information and those that residents themselves apply'. Other primary research has found similar discrepancies where people's definitions of neighbourhood 'are not likely to share boundaries with any "formal" division of areas', such as parishes or wards (Kotecha et al, 2008: 27). Much of what is being termed 'neighbourhood working' still operates on a ward, district or wider area level. Local government has confused area-based working with neighbourhood-based working. Although the former is potentially an important step towards the latter, the two should not be conflated (Power, 2004).

Local authorities trying to achieve 'economic' and 'political' goals are using what have been called 'public' or 'strategic' neighbourhoods of 4,000 to 15,000 residents upwards (up to roughly 8,000 households) 'where more structured governance starts to make sense' (Young Foundation, 2005, p 7). White et al (2006) looked at 17 case studies of neighbourhood governance with populations that ranged from nearly 8,500 to 30,000 and around 3,400 to 8,000 households.

These discrepancies between definitions of neighbourhood are not easily resolved. One reason for this is that, where there is political will to descale, it is still a major undertaking. A senior manager described the process in one large metropolitan council:

'You need to organise yourself in a way to encourage community involvement.... You need to identify your neighbourhoods first ... we have 52 different neighbourhood plans! I [the senior manager] wanted 25 neighbourhoods not 52, but the communities drew lines on an actual map, so I didn't argue.' (Quoted in Richardson, 2004)

Neighbourhood action planning is gathering momentum in many authorities where plans are created jointly with residents and professionals for small areas. Despite this, neighbourhood decision making and working structures remain at a larger scale in many places, and there is not the political will to try to alter the scale. The expectation is that citizens will learn to fit into local government's perspective, rather than the other way round. One officer in a large metropolitan authority commented, "People don't learn about how the city works, they don't learn about what [the council] can and can't do ... you need to build people's knowledge of how the system works" (Durose, 2007).

Existing administrative boundaries are also convenient for data gathering and do not require major upheaval in ways of working. More significantly, it is not in the interests of local government to resolve discrepancies between top-down definitions and residents own definitions if 'economic' and 'political' rationales are being followed.

For those with an underlying 'political' rationale, existing administrative and ward boundaries are also 'recognisable' to local politicians, and therefore more viable in terms of representative democracy. Where neighbourhoods, as defined by citizens, cross ward boundaries, this has sometimes resulted in political problems of power sharing between local elected representatives for those wards; broadly, this has not been well received by councillors in the local authorities studied.

For local authorities interested in efficiency and effectiveness gains (the 'economic' rationale), a viable and recognisable neighbourhood for management purposes is based on a collection of around two to five wards, containing up to 15,000 to 20,000 residents (or up to roughly 12,000 households). Based on the annual management and administrative costs of one specific New Labour initiative, there were increased costs from about £10 per head of resident population for neighbourhoods with populations of 15,000 plus, to £40 per head for smaller neighbourhoods of about 5,000 people (White et al, 2006). Authorities have also made a strong case for scaling up to achieve economies of scale or 'more bang for your buck'.

Defining the neighbourhood is one of the most initial stages of neighbourhood working and a critical one. Decisions are being made even before governance structures have been created. Here we see real tensions between citizens' perspectives and those of local authorities, based on the competing rationales being used. This presents clear risks to the 'civic' and 'social' rationales for neighbourhood working. If residents do not share in the construction of what a neighbourhood is, then there is less likelihood of people relating to and engaging with neighbourhoods that do not make sense to them.

As Jacobs (1990: 7) notes, '[neighbourhoods] have no real significance as collections of physical entities until they are imbued with value by citizens'. It is more appropriate to understand neighbourhoods not as simple spatial or geographical units, but as 'socially constructed realities that are built through a dialogue between individual actors and structural forces that contain spatial, social and experiential dimensions' (Chaskin, 1998: 14). However, without a primary focus on a social or civic rationale, the value of people's own constructions is not recognised. The dominance of 'economic' and 'political' rationales means that neighbourhoods are defined and implemented at too large a scale, and based on political control rather than people's day-to-day experiences.

Does the lack of a 'civic' rationale matter?

It is perhaps not surprising that working with the 'economic' rationale comes easiest to local authorities as it most closely reflects their traditional role and practice; but does the lack of success of neighbourhood working to deliver on the 'civic' rationale actually matter to citizens? There is a strong argument that citizens just want local government to get on with the jobs of managing and delivering low council tax – that is, deliver on 'political' and 'economic' rationales. Although the vast majority of citizens feel a sense of belonging to their neighbourhood, this does not translate to people playing the active role expected of them, despite levels of interest and support for neighbourhood governance as an idea. Actual levels of engagement in neighbourhood-based initiatives are limited to a very small minority. For example, in one local authority, 82% of respondents were in favour of extending community partnership pilots to other parts of the borough; 26% of those in support said they would personally be interested in getting involved. The level of actual involvement was 2% of eligible residents (Page, 2005, quoted in Richardson, 2008a).

One community development worker in a deprived area of a large city noted, "To be honest, when I go home I don't join the residents' association where I live; I want to go to the pub or watch *Coronation*

Street, and the vast majority of the population still want to do that. It's not my job to ... force people that do want to do that into becoming community activists" (Durose, 2007). Practitioners have noted the general decline of certain forms of participation: "local people don't get the training in how to be active anymore, because trade unions, political parties and churches where you used to learn those skills are declining membership wise" (Durose, 2007).

Another argument why a 'civic' rationale might not be as important as an 'economic' one for citizens is that people care more about value for money than opportunities for participation. Survey evidence from 15,000 households in deprived areas shows that satisfaction with the local authority was strongly linked with the perception of value for money public services and less strongly linked with the perception of being able to influence decisions and of opportunities for participation (Page, 2007).

The 'social' rationale around citizen-centred services is already in line with citizens' preferences. Extensive research has shown that impersonal, patchy, untailored and uncoordinated service provision compounds service users' lack of status and power to command a response (PCPS, 2004; Richardson, 2008a).

A 'civic' rationale for neighbourhood working is critical

We have suggested that a focus on the 'political', 'economic' and 'social' goes some way to meeting citizens' needs and preferences. The reasons why a civic rationale is still critical to these other agendas are that:

- representative democracy is not yet robust enough for citizens to feel completely willing to trust local government to get on with things;
- decisions designed to improve delivery are made by local government, but do have a significant impact on citizens, whose views – when offered – are not always taken on board, leading to dissatisfaction;
- civic goals are part of the stated aims of neighbourhood working, but local structures do not always respond in an appropriate way to citizens who do come forward.

Gaps in representative democracy

As decision-making structures in local government have changed, some councillors have felt pushed out (Gains, 2006; see also Stoker et al, 2006). One commentator described these councillors as 'wounded lions', "their powers might be draining away but it [isn't] advisable to try and take them on" (Taylor, 2005b, p 1). However, nationally there is already some evidence that non-executive councillors are enjoying their enhanced community leadership role, including working more closely with the community and voluntary sectors (Rao, 2005). There have been positive outcomes for neighbourhoods, service delivery and citizen engagement/local democracy. In our own research we collected many examples of stronger representative democracy and councillors linking to communities and citizens. However, even this progress does not negate the need for a stronger civic society. *quite !*

One councillor summed up their view of the relative roles of elected members and citizens:"The man on the street [says] we elect Councillor [X] and he gets paid to do it. We don't want to go to meetings, if we've got a good councillor we don't worry. If you do your job regularly [as a councillor] there is no interest [by citizens]. It depends on the issue, but usually there's not a clamour. People expect councillors to deal with it" (Richardson forthcoming). Yet, this argument is in direct contradiction to evidence of citizens' own views. In the local government module of the British Social Attitudes Survey 1998, 88% agreed with the statement 'local councils would make better decisions if they made more effort to find out what local people want', with only 7% who felt that 'local councillors should just get on and make the important decisions themselves. After all, that's what we elected them for' (Chivite-Matthews and Teal, 2001).

The public are unclear about what councillors' roles are and do not see councillors as representative (White et al, 2006). There is still a dislocation between local elected representatives and their constituencies. Citizens are not completely willing to trust local government to make decisions on their behalf. Fifty-five per cent of respondents agreed with the statement that elected members 'tend to lose touch with people pretty quickly' (Chivite-Matthews and Teal, 2001). Cynicism about local democracy got worse between 1994 and 1998, with the percentage of people agreeing that councillors lose touch up from 47% to 55%, and more people agreeing with the statement 'councillors don't care much what people like me think' (up to 40% from 36% (Rao and Young, 1995; quoted in Chivite-Matthews and Teal, 2001). Sixty-three per cent said that they would trust councillors 'only some of the time/almost never' to make important decisions (Chivite-Matthews and Teal, 2001).

There is national survey support for the idea that a small group of 12 to 15 'ordinary local people chosen at random' (Chivite-Matthews and Teal, 2001) would make better decisions about the neighbourhood than local government. This is a relatively strong response, that the respondents in that survey would rather trust people chosen at random than their elected members to 'come to the best view' about something like 'a proposal for a major new building development in your neighbourhood'.

Community groups in neighbourhoods have expressed concern over the remoteness of local elected members and the failure of local elections to provide an adequate mechanism for local accountability in practice (Richardson, 2008a). Many community activists involved in tenants' and residents' associations (TARAs) argue that, while some councillors are 'aggressive community champions', others struggle to engage constructively with citizens taking on a more participative role (Durose and Lowndes, 2008). In one of our research areas, councillors had taken a 'backseat' role in neighbourhood working and neighbourhood structures had been consciously depoliticised because of resident and elected member recognition that residents in that neighbourhood were wary of structures that were seen as 'political'.

Resentment from communities

The lack of impact or change created through citizen input and consultation has left citizens feeling cynical and resentful about their role in local governance. Many areas determined by the government to be deprived have been the subject of several, arguably failed, rounds of government intervention and regeneration. These previous initiatives have been widely criticised as tokenistic in their attitudes to empowering citizens. As such citizens are both cynical and sophisticated in their attitudes towards attempts at engagement; citizens in such areas are seen as suffering from 'consultation fatigue', 'burnout' and 'consultation sickness'. As one community development worker in a deprived neighbourhood noted, "there's been consultations on everything but quantity does not necessarily mean quality, some of the consultation has left communities resentful, that would be to put it mildly" (Durose, 2007). Another community development worker commented that the community's attitude is "why are you asking us?", assuming that their input is not going to be reflected in the change and decision making that happens, and arguing that there needs to be "a link between asking and doing" (Durose, 2007).

Local governance needs to deliver on its aims to empower

In some of the areas we studied, there were questions over whether local authorities and their partners had the authority or capacity to redesign services. One voluntary sector actor commented that the council is committed to community engagement, but "they don't know how to do it well" (Durose and Lowndes, 2008). Community engagement strategies: are dependent on individuals; are naive about the potential timescales involved; can be "incredibly controlling"; show a lack of strategy about bringing groups together; fail to do basic work like needs analyses; often do not act proactively and so are accused of "navel gazing" (Durose and Lowndes, 2008).

There are a minority of citizens who do want to take on an active role in their community and participate in decision making. Having requested that citizens do take part, local government is then often unwelcoming of those active citizens' contributions. These individuals are often described as 'the usual suspects'. The impression given is that their participation is somehow not representative, real or legitimate. One senior officer in a large metropolitan authority commented that: "they [officers and councillors] feel like they have to control that process [of community participation] and are 'blinkered' about the possibilities of a positive contribution; when community groups dissent they go from being 'members' of the community to 'usual suspects' and dismissed". This point is illustrated in the comments of a senior officer in the same locality:

> 'I am not sure why any local person would want to come to council meetings and discuss issues that maybe or maybe not affect their own lives ... perhaps we should be suspicious of them; those groups that purport to be umbrella groups are often no nearer to the community than we are ... some groups are great, some are representative, but some that purport to do so are not ... there is a difference between a community meeting and meeting people from the community.' (See Durose and Lowndes, 2008)

There is a widespread concern about the degree to which community activists are representative – for example, worries about 'small unrepresentative cliques dominating' (Aspden and Birch, 2005: 64). In some cases there can be an element of politicking involved. Throwing the legitimacy of community opinion into doubt can also be part of not taking people seriously and refusing to share power and responsibility with local residents. Some have pointed out that the representativeness of community groups is questioned more when people disagree with their views (Taylor, 2005a). Where local governance makes such a dismissive or unwelcoming response to active citizens, this can create disincentives within the system for both parties.

Most do not get actively involved. However, for those who would want to get involved, the opportunities available within neighbourhood working do not necessarily fit their preferences for flexible, low-intensity ways to input. For example, in one local authority, 20% of residents said they would like to have more say in how their local services were run but were not necessarily interested in coming to events or meetings (Burton et al, 2004 quoted in Richardson, 2008a).

Neighbourhood working structures can fail to allow for citizens' own preferences to be engaged on specific issues that are relevant for them. Local government has been dismissive of citizens who, quite legitimately, engage when decisions directly affect them, but then withdraw having satisfied their interests. For example, one community development worker commented on the "magnolia mentality", referring to the shade of paint many new or refurbished properties are decorated in; many people only want to be involved until they benefit from their own engagement. It is not clear why professionals perceive this as a negative process. Neighbourhood-based working is often linked to a wider programme of area-based regeneration. It is widely acknowledged that communities should 'take ownership' of the regeneration process and become actively involved in the decision-making process. However, the significant physical change that the regeneration of an area can bring is often emotional and traumatic, and as such it is difficult to sustain a level of involvement once no clear funding is attached to the process. Individuals can also suffer from 'burnout' and perhaps it is not realistic to expect such an intensity of involvement over the longer term.

Conclusion

The key emphasis for local government in the last decade has been to improve efficiency and effectiveness in service delivery through operating at the neighbourhood level. Some progress has also been made in recognising and pursuing the 'social' rationale for neighbourhood working, emphasising joined-up citizen-centred services. Despite significant teething troubles with the 'political' rationale, there are emerging signs that progress is being made on improving access and accountability in decision making. It is with the 'civic' rationale for neighbourhood working – empowering citizens – that local authorities have particularly struggled. We argue that this does matter and that neighbourhood working that simply improves or tailors service delivery or strengthens the role of councillors is insufficient to meet 'civic' aims for neighbourhood working.

This chapter shows complexity in creating a balance of scale for neighbourhood working that suits both local government and citizens. It illustrates the difficulties of achieving change in organisations, in political leadership and in citizens themselves. There are some system failures: to welcome citizens when they do get engaged; to offer opportunities that deliver citizens with genuine spaces to play new roles; to be fully responsive to citizen feedback; and to offer engagement opportunities that match citizen preferences. New Labour's policies marked a new high water mark for neighbourhoods as a site for policy action and governance, but it is not clear that there was substantive buy in to neighbourhoods as a site for empowerment.

Now, ten years on, the government's focus on 'neighbourhood policy' is operating in a different context from 1997. The focus on community empowerment now, as evidenced in the recent CLG White Paper (CLG, 2008), is not spatially located. There are questions over whether neighbourhood initiatives have been successful and concerns that regeneration has not reached the hardcore of excluded citizens. Investment from central government into citizen engagement in neighbourhoods has now tailed off, with the hope that statutory bodies at a local level will commit to their own policy innovations as and where necessary; it is up to localities to decide if and how they deliver neighbourhood working. Even if neighbourhoods slipped out of focus in terms of national-level policy and funding, it is likely, given the institutional arrangements established at the neighbourhood level by local authorities, the neighbourhood would persist as a site for local policy action and intervention.

While neighbourhoods may go in and out of fashion in terms of policy, the neighbourhood is an enduring site that citizens identify with, if defined in appropriate ways. However, the evidence is that, without sufficient attention to empowering citizens, neighbourhood working may not endure, to the cost of all stakeholders.

References

Aspden, J. and Birch, D. (2005) *New localism: Citizen engagement, neighbourhoods and public services – evidence from local government*, London: ODPM.

Barrett, A.L. and Campbell, K.E. (1992) 'Sources of personal neighbourhood networks: social integration, need or time?', *Social Forces*, vol 70, no 4, pp 1077-100.

Barrett A.L. and Campbell, K.E. (1993) 'Neighbourhood networks of blacks and whites', unpublished manuscript.

Barrett A.L., Campbell, K.E. and Miller, O. (1991) 'Racial differences in urban neighbouring', *Sociological Forum*, vol 6, no 3, pp 525-50.

Blunkett, D. (2003) *Active citizens, strong communities: Progressing civic renewal*, London: Home Office.

Burton, P., Goodlad, R., Croft, J., Abbott, J., Hastings, A., Macdonald, G. and Slater, T. (2004) *What works in community involvement in area-based initiatives: A systematic review of the literature* (Home Office Online Report 53/04), London: Home Office.

Chaskin, R.J. (1998) 'Neighbourhood as a unit of planning and action: a heuristic approach', *Journal of Planning Literature*, vol 13, no 1, pp 11-30.

Chivite-Matthews, N.I. and Teal, J. (2001) 1998 *British Social Attitudes Survey: Secondary analysis of the local government module*, London, DTLR.

CLG (Communities and Local Government) (2006a) *Strong and prosperous communities: The local government white paper*, London: HMSO.

CLG (2006b) *Exemplars of neighbourhood governance*, London: HMSO.

CLG (2007) *Statistical release citizenship survey: April-June 2007, England and Wales*, London: CLG.

CLG (2008a) *Communities in control: Real power, real people*, London: CLG.

CLG (2008b) *Annex A: The PLace Survey Questionnaire* (www.communities.gov.uk/documents/localgovernment/doc/880053.doc

Corry, D. and Stoker, G. (2002) *New localism: Refashioning the centre–local relationship*, London: New Local Government Network.

Durose, C. (2007) 'Beyond "street level bureaucrats"? Re-interpreting the role of front line public sector workers', unpublished doctoral thesis, University of Manchester.

Durose, C. and Lowndes, V. (2008) 'Explaining neighbourhood approaches to urban regeneration in Manchester, UK: a multi level analysis', paper presented to APSA Conference, Boston, 6-8 September 2008.

Gains, F. (2006) *New council constitutions: A summary of the ELG Research Findings*, London: CLG.

Jacobs, J. (1994) (originally published in 1961) *The life and death of great American cities*, Harmondsworth: Penguin.

Kearns, A. and Parkinson, M. (2001) 'The significance of neighbourhood', *Urban Studies*, vol 38, no 12, pp 2103-10.

Kotecha, M., Graham J. and Cebulla, A. (2008) *Feeling able to influence local decision making: Understanding, barriers, facilitators and strategies for increasing empowerment*, London: CLG.

Lowndes, V. and Sullivan, H. (2008) 'How low can you go? Rationales and challenges for neighbourhood governance', *Public Administration*, vol 86, no 1, pp 53-74.

Miliband, D. (2006) Speech to the National Council of Voluntary Organisations, 21 February

ODPM/ Home Office (2005) *Citizen engagement and public services: Why neighbourhoods matter*, London: ODPM.

Page, B. (2005) *How can we make local community involvement work?* (presentation slides), London: MORI.

Page, B. (2007) 'Frontiers of local government performance: an inconvenient truth', presentation by Ipsos MORI Public Affairs.

PCPS (Policy Commission on Public Services) (2004) *Making public services personal*, London: National Consumer Council.

Power, A. (2004) *Neighbourhood management and the future of urban areas* (Case Paper 77), London: London School of Economics and Political Science/Centre for Social Exclusion.

Rao, N. (2005) *Councillors and the new council constitutions*, London: ODPM.

Rao, N. and Young, K. (1995) *Competition, contracts and change: The local authority experience of CCT*, York: Joseph Rowntree Foundation.

Richardson, L. (2004) *Summary report on a think tank on low demand for housing* (CASE report 22), London, London School of Economics and Political Science.

Richardson, L. (2006) *SWOT assessment of succession strategy for Blacon Together*, London: LSE Housing.

Richardson, L. (2008a) *DIY community action: Neighbourhood problems and community self-help*, Bristol: The Policy Press.

Richardson, L. (2008b) *Votes and voices: The complementary nature of representative and participative democracy*, London: NCVO/LGA.

Richardson, L. (forthcoming) *Neighbourhood working in the North West*, Manchester: University of Manchester.

SEU (Social Exclusion Unit) (2000) *National strategy for neighbourhood renewal: Framework for consultation*, London: HMSO.

SEU (2001) *A new commitment to neighbourhood renewal: National strategy action plan*, London: HMSO.

Stoker, G., Gains, F., Greasley, S., John, P. and Rao, N. (2006) *Councillors, officers and stakeholders in the new council constitutions: Findings of the 2005 ELG Sample Survey*, Manchester: University of Manchester.

Taylor, M. (2005a) *Willing partners? Voluntary and community associations in the democratic process*, Swindon: ESRC.

Taylor, M. (2005b) 'Councillors and community advocates', Policy and Expert Workshop on Citizen Participation and Neighbourhoods, Office of the Deputy Prime Minister, 23 May (unpublished notes and presentation slides).

Taylor, M. and Wilson, M. (2006) *The Importance of neighbourhoods: Tackling the implementation gap*, York: Joseph Rowntree Foundation.

White, G., Dickinson, S., Miles, N., Richardson, L., Russell, H. and Taylor, M. (2006) *Exemplars of neighbourhood governance*, London: CLG.

Young Foundation (2005) *Seeing the Wood for the Trees: The evolving landscape for neighbourhood arrangements*, London: Young Foundation.

FOUR

Urban housing market restructuring and the recasting of neighbourhood governance and community

James Rees

Introduction

Housing has long been recognised as crucial in influencing patterns of social interaction and community formation in the UK. The late 1990s witnessed the growth of a stark national imbalance with 'overheated' housing markets in the South of England and 'low demand' for housing in parts of the North. The policy response to the issue of low demand was to create a Housing Market Renewal (HMR) programme, whose central task was to restore sustainability to inner urban housing markets. The approach adopted by most of the nine HMR 'Pathfinders' was to seek to *transform* affected neighbourhoods — essentially a process of outward-looking and strategic restructuring/ re-envisioning of the fundamental rationale for neighbourhoods and places — with reference to the parallel process of urban economic restructuring. Equally central to restructuring was the aim of bringing new (wealthier, economically active) residents into such neighbourhoods, an aim that stems from a number of related rationales, to ostensibly create what, in central government parlance, are often termed 'mixed communities'.

The problem of 'low demand' for particular housing types and neighbourhoods emerged in the late 1990s and was manifested in very low house prices, dereliction and in some cases near abandonment of neighbourhoods in the inner urban parts of most major cities in Northern England and the Midlands (Nevin et al, 2001). Growing alarm in housing practitioner circles was allied to research by academics and consultants, creating an 'evidence base' for a policy response (Holmans and Simpson, 1999; Nevin et al, 2001). Low demand for housing was understood as resulting from a combination of demographic changes (regional migration, suburbanisation and counter-urbanisation) flowing from economic restructuring, as well as, more controversially, the argument that there have been changes in residential preference, in particular away from traditional pre-1918 terraced housing to larger modern dwellings with gardens (Cameron, 2006). Nine HMR Pathfinders were established after funding was announced in the 2002 Comprehensive Spending Review and the policy was launched in the Sustainable Communities Plan (ODPM, 2003).

This chapter draws on extensive empirical research conducted around the HMR process in East Manchester between 2004 and 2008 (Rees, 2007; Durose and Lowndes, 2008). East Manchester has seen intensive regeneration activity since the mid-1990s, including HMR activity. It is shown that, at the neighbourhood level, housing restructuring is led from above, principally by the local authority and its partners (for example, housing associations, the private sector). The policy-making framework is strongly influenced by wider strategic concerns, such as national policy on social housing, which has largely constricted investment in social housing and supported the creation of market-orientated housing in inner urban areas, but also a concern to create neighbourhoods and a housing offer that supports economic development of the city. There is, therefore, a gap between a governance model of strategic 'top-down' housing/neighbourhood restructuring and the concerns and priorities of longstanding local citizens, despite strong claims that regeneration genuinely consults with these existing residents. There are real concerns that the type of housing market restructuring outlined above may disperse or displace existing residents and communities; enhance conflicts between different social groups; or, alternatively, simply fail in its stated aim of creating new *functioning* communities. It is appropriate to ask whether urban housing market restructuring is antithetical to social cohesion and genuinely sustainable urban social regeneration.

Housing Market Renewal in Manchester: the strategic rationales

The Manchester Salford Housing Market Renewal Pathfinder (MSP) was one of the first Pathfinders to be established in 2003 and covers a large portion of the inner part of the Greater Manchester conurbation. The broad aim of the Pathfinder was to restructure the housing market, through a combination of selective demolition, refurbishment and assemblage of land for new house building; and create 'sustainable' neighbourhoods and communities (MSP, 2003). By the time of a 'scheme update' in 2005, the Pathfinder was, at least in discursive terms, taking a more bullish approach, which emphasised the role of the housing stock holding back the economic competitiveness of the city region and the Pathfinder's role in turning this around (MSP, 2005). The fundamental problem lies squarely in the housing stock and neighbourhood environments of Manchester: 'Manchester has the lowest proportion of owner occupied stock outside London and much of this is terraced housing' (MSP, 2003: 11). This is a problem that has vexed Manchester City Council (MCC) for decades: that the structure of housing provision, intimately related to social composition, is highly skewed. The boundaries of the local authority are tightly drawn, leading to an almost perceptible sense of injustice that the much vaunted 'renaissance' of the city centre has benefited suburban in-commuters and those in the city-regional catchment area, a population who remain stubbornly out of reach for fiscal purposes. MCC is responsible for a highly deprived population across much of its administrative area. Understanding this context is crucial to understanding the approach taken to restructuring within the Pathfinder area.

This is particularly highlighted in the case of East Manchester, the area where MCC has focused its regeneration efforts since at least the late 1980s when it began to pursue a strategy initially focused on sport-led regeneration, which culminated in the hosting of the 2002 Commonwealth Games (Cochrane et al, 1996; Ward, 2003). After 1997 a slew of New Labour area-based initiatives were channelled into the area, but most significant was the establishment of an urban regeneration company (URC), New East Manchester (NEM). The key aim of NEM was to double the population of the area – through the creation of 12,500 new homes – which inevitably means bringing people into the area by providing the type of housing and neighbourhoods that more affluent economically active residents would 'buy into' (NEM, 2001). HMR funds built on this and essentially allowed MCC/NEM to pursue this 'transformational agenda' more rapidly.

While this strategy is complex, the important point is that the regeneration aims in East Manchester 'read up' to the overarching aims of MCC for the city as a whole. Hence, in terms of principles for the renewal of individual neighbourhoods, a key aim is the restructuring and rebalancing of skewed physical attributes of the housing market. Small, predominantly 'front-of-pavement' terraces make up nearly 60 per cent of the stock – twice the national average – and a key aim is to reduce this proportion. In addition, HMR intervention will bring about a clear 'change in the tenure mix from social and private rented housing to owner occupation through the attraction of additional owner-occupiers, the clearance of obsolete stock and the retention of existing owner-occupiers' (MSP, 2003: 16-17).

This strategy of physical intervention – which guides the redevelopment of individual neighbourhoods – is married to an agenda of social transformation, sometimes implicit, but which can be described as being about creating mixed communities or 'bringing people in'. These strategic aims are led by NEM and its partners. The exact interventions carried out vary between neighbourhoods depending on conditions and the ability of the public sector to intervene – a somewhat opportunistic strategy. For instance, some neighbourhoods, considered to be functioning well, particularly with already high proportions of owner-occupation, will stay much the same. Others will see sustained efforts to bring about large-scale physical transformations, which implicitly involve changing the character and social composition of such areas. They are 'outward-looking' developments, which clearly aim to bring people into the area to repopulate and transform the social functioning of the area (Hastings, 2003; Katz, 2004). A key argument employed by regeneration officers is that this represents a rejection of previous 'patch and mend' policies of refurbishment: policies that were primarily focused on local needs. The new neighbourhoods are 'market orientated' – evidenced by a stress on quality, design and, not least, price; and depend on provision by the private sector. Meanwhile, mechanisms are in place to reprovide for existing residents, who, it is argued, will benefit from greatly improved housing conditions and neighbourhood environments.

In neighbourhoods where significant remodelling is planned or under way, there will be quite radical physical transformation of the built environment, involving new housing types, layouts and, by extension, the way in which neighbourhoods function and for whom. A striking example is New Islington, formerly an extremely run-down council estate called the Cardroom – which suffered from social problems and high crime, and was in very low demand. The area has undergone redevelopment as a *Millennium Community*, with input from leading architects and planners, in consultation with existing local residents. The plan involves a massive restructuring of the environment and housing stock of the area through the demolition of most of the low-density Radburn layout council housing and its replacement with large apartment buildings set within a new canal waterfront layout. Residents who wished to stay were assured a 'right to return' and were consulted on the design of new social housing within the scheme, which was carried out by a leading architect practice and developed by a local housing association (HA). This therefore creates a mixed community of existing residents and incomers. Nevertheless, when the remodelling is complete the social housing will be a relatively small component of the new neighbourhood. The new image of the neighbourhood will be one of inner city living in waterfront apartments for a wealthy clientele – a significant social transformation. The tenure profile will be fundamentally restructured, going from almost 97 per cent council housing to approximately 95 per cent privately owned, the remaining 5 per cent being provided by the HA. Indeed, there is likely to be a net reduction in the number of social housing units in the neighbourhood.

A similar process has happened in the Beswick neighbourhood further out from the centre to the East. Beswick had long suffered from concentrated social deprivation and the housing stock was dilapidated and in low demand, and the environment was pocked with sites of previous rounds of demolition. The neighbourhood was the focus of a New Deal for Communities scheme from 1999 and planning for housing redevelopment was well advanced by the time that HMR arrived. The redevelopment was guided by an aim to create a 'critical mass' of private housing in the neighbourhood, in response to an understanding, shared with private developers, that previous attempts to supply private sector housing had failed because they were piecemeal and their small scale failed to create longer-term change in the area. Hence the new housing attempts to break from the past in terms of format: a mixture of low-rise housing in 'city-blocks' with gated rear drives and gardens, and apartments, many in an 'innovative' design to create something of a 'wow factor'. Existing residents of social or private housing subject to demolition would be retained – either in new private housing through assistance packages or they would be 'reprovided' with HA accommodation within the development – which aimed for 'seamless tenure'. The intention is, however, to re-image and remove the stigma of the area, to create a large area of 'normal' owner-occupied housing for economically active residents, particularly families.

It is clear that these plans – particularly to reduce concentrations of social housing and promote owner-occupation – rely on a number of social rationales that are often less explicit and look back to a shared understanding within the local governance arena of what has 'gone wrong' in the past in East Manchester. In the case of New Islington, publications related to the Millennium Community stress historical problems such as the failure of the low-rise and low-density estate to support public and private services in such inner urban settings (Urban Splash, 2004). Narratives about problems with crime and other implicit understandings of the operation of neighbourhood effects are also prevalent. Redevelopment is seen as an opportunity to break up 'monolithic' and stigmatised social housing areas and their associated concentrations of poverty. In explicitly social terms, it effectively creates a bulwark or 'critical mass' of market housing, leading to a more 'normal' housing market that will attract and retain a new population of higher-income residents. Strategically, it is envisaged that remodelling of different neighbourhoods will create a differentiated patchwork of market-orientated housing, moving the area away from its traditional function of mass industrial era working-class housing, more recently interspersed with council estates.

Accompanying these 'backward-looking' rationales for restructuring, which essentially amount to an understanding of what went wrong, are a number of 'forward-looking' rationales used to justify the transformational approach and envisaged social change, based on a vision of how these neighbourhoods will function better in the future. These rationales are genuinely multifaceted if often implicit: that is, they are rarely, if ever, explicitly stated in documents produced in connection to the regeneration process. Instead, they are rooted in the *experience*, and *shared narrative*, of regeneration officers, council leadership, and politicians. Where such narratives are more openly stated they are ostensibly framed in terms of the aim to create mix and choice in the housing market, and socially in terms of the sustainable communities that it is thought will flow from that.

The more implicit drivers include, first, the aim to repopulate the area, thereby reversing historical population loss – but more specifically to attract and retain economically active and higher-status residents. Re-establishing a 'critical mass' of people, it is argued, will create the demand for services, both public and private, while more assertive middle-class residents will demand improvements to services such as education and the police, but also place less demands on traditional welfare services. This calls on a shared belief in the role of neighbourhood effects, so that improvements to services as well as the general neighbourhood environment will benefit existing residents also. In the envisaged socioeconomically mixed neighbourhoods, more direct peer (or role model) effects might operate: for instance increased pressure on young people to enter employment, or reduced acceptance of negative behaviours (again, the existing community is seen as deficient). Notably, the academic literature on neighbourhood effects argues that such effects are hard to identify, and even more difficult to operationalise in policy (Atkinson and Kintrea, 2002; Allen et al, 2005). Although such a strategy raises the spectre of social engineering, what local policy makers envisage is a gradual process whereby increased diversification in neighbourhoods leads to a more 'normal' residential neighbourhood that is self-sustaining and requires less intensive public sector input. As noted earlier, an economic development rationale underlies all of this and should not be downplayed. The conurbation's housing offer has increasingly been seen by the City of Manchester as crucial in underpinning further economic regeneration and development (CRDP, 2006; MSP, 2005). The wider regeneration of East Manchester is one key lynchpin in this strategy.

Urban housing market restructuring versus community aspirations

As the previous section has outlined, the process of urban housing market restructuring enacted in East Manchester involves, inter alia, the creation of aspirational, market-orientated housing in neighbourhoods that are explicitly aimed at new incoming residents, with the intention of effecting a social transition. There will be a transition in the type, form and mixture of housing types, the balance of tenure, and the way security is provided and the neighbourhood is managed. The new neighbourhoods will have a very different aesthetic feel and function to their previous incarnation – through public sector pump-priming and private sector investment the hope is that they will set off an 'upward neighbourhood trajectory' – producing inner-urban neighbourhoods that attract and retain more economically active residents. This agenda is driven by policy makers located within MCC and NEM, and the strategy prioritises the aspirations and needs of wealthier incoming residents above the needs of existing residents. Table 4.1 shows briefly these 'outward-facing' remodelling rationales for the two neighbourhoods already discussed.

As these two brief examples illustrate, neighbourhoods will undergo a transition as they are redeveloped – indeed, the neighbourhoods will take on a 'life of their own' through private sector input and marketing, beyond the initial impetus provided by public sector input into planning and facilitation; thus, the actual market trajectory of such places is quite uncertain. The symbolic change can also be discerned in the way neighbourhoods are marketed to potential new residents, re-imaged as part of trendy 'city living', for example. The key point though is the contrast with community-led regeneration or with traditional collective housing provision (Harloe, 1995). Both the aesthetics of the image of the neighbourhoods and the concrete characteristics of the places – their urban 'feel' – are attuned for their attractiveness to different social groups. This often works on an opportunistic basic,

Table 4.1: 'Outward-facing' remodelling rationales

	Former character	Character of remodelled neighbourhood	Idealised incoming resident
New Islington (Edge of city centre)	Low-density council estate. Low demand, poor environment. High deprivation.	Radical new development, environment. Chic, trendy, high design. High-density, large apartment blocks.	Upwardly mobile young families; urban dwellers but 'tired of city centre'.
Beswick (Inner city, accessible)	Patchwork of terraces and council estates. Poor environment. High deprivation.	Modern 'eye-catching' design. Medium-density 'family' housing and apartments.	Family housing. 'Ordinary'; middle class families. Extension of city-centre living.

by remodelling neighbourhoods where there is an opportunity and supporting upmarket infill developments on brownfield sites. It aims to turn East Manchester from a patchwork of long-established industrial-era neighbourhoods, with particular communities that relate to each other in an inward-looking manner, to a more differentiated pattern of neighbourhoods with new functions.

Tenure is important within this because it is so intertwined with social composition. The supply of social housing will not be expanded and will gradually shrink as a proportion of the East Manchester housing stock as restructuring progresses. NEM argues that:

> 'We are selling to families, not creating housing to rent ... shifting the balance away from social tenure to owner-occupation – that's the nature of the beast ... people aspire to owner-occupation regardless of what background they come from, so it's about greater choice for everyone.' (NEM officer)

This goes to the top of the council, where leaders argue that local governance is for shaping the future needs of the city as a whole, rather than espousing a paternalist 'looking after one's own' philosophy:

'Within the city, local government should try and create places that people choose to live in; it's not about the people who live there: they have no choice! ... 'affordable' does not mean more local authority housing, Manchester needs that like it needs a hole in the head: "There you go, have a free house for 20 years, stay in bed, stay on benefit."' (Senior officer, MCC)

There is a strong sense of the need to promote 'normal' neighbourhoods, rather than pursuing a form of local governance that is seen as pandering to a residual population without potential for economic involvement. Instead it is argued that greater opportunities for owner–occupation will benefit the existing population because it meets their demands for greater choice and quality of housing in the owner–occupied sector, and satisfies the aspirations of local people to own a house in the area. All in all, this forms a powerful agenda within the overall restructuring process led by NEM. Local citizens have very little input into its strategic formulation and it is far from clear that many existing residents support this agenda. As noted earlier, underpinning all of this is a strong rationale of changing the City's fiscal standing. The extent of citizen involvement in this agenda is strongly circumscribed and, in East Manchester, is largely restricted to consultation and involvement in the design of housing for reprovision for existing residents, and to an extent consultation on the future of the neighbourhood environment. Indeed, there is clear evidence of discontent among residents who expected, or felt they were promised, a regeneration process more attuned to meeting their needs and many signs of tensions in the neighbourhood planning led by MCC involving consultation with residents of the area.

In the neighbourhoods discussed above, there are numerous examples of tensions that arose during the neighbourhood planning process that highlight the gap between these professional and existing citizen agendas. The style of the consultation over design could be summarised as one that involved residents but carried them along in a preferred direction. The need was expressed, from a professional point of view, to challenge residents' 'expectations' and to get them to think beyond traditional aspirations for their housing and neighbourhoods. In New Islington, planners, housing providers and particularly architects spoke of needing to 'challenge' and 'push the boundaries' of residents' aspirations for the new housing and residential environment during the consultation process, a process made much of in promotional literature for the area (Urban Splash, 2004). Some residents involved in consultations were taken on tours of new housing regeneration schemes in Britain and the Netherlands in order to achieve this. But, as one of the architects noted, residents had their own agency and strength:

> They were mostly Mancunians who didn't really like Urban Splash's kind of chic modern design. (Quoted in Rose, 2006)

> 'We expected residents to be excited by open-plan designs for their houses but they were having none of it. They said to us: "we don't want our lounges to smell of cooking!"' (Speech at National Housing Federation national conference, 2004)

This stands to symbolise the clash of creative aspirations for New Islington with local desires for, on the whole, better traditional housing and a secure environment (see also Karn, 2006). But there were more far-reaching clashes. Most residents eschewed the chance to take new apartments, meaning the replacement social housing was not in the centre of the redevelopment:

> 'Residents didn't quite realise what was changing. They wanted to be at the heart of the development but the heart was changing – the centre of gravity was moving towards the apartments and waterside.' (HA interviewee, 2005)

> 'The tenants have won the battle to get their family houses, but in doing so have created – for want of a better term – ghetto sites. Everyone's going to know where the social tenants are.' (HA interviewee, 2005)

This certainly calls into question any claims that residents are 'in the lead'. Clearly there was a balancing act between consulting residents and driving through the schemes whose vision was largely set from the beginning by professional agendas.

Many residents in East Manchester were scornful of the way consultation was conducted, both in terms of design and layout of housing, and in general. Many had negative attitudes towards the types and form of new housing, particularly towards the design of some of the housing and a marked hostility to apartments:

> 'I know a lot of our residents on [a nearby area] steering group just are horrified by the Beswick properties. So, where I would think that they would think:"wow it's new, it looks completely different" [in fact] some of them are still lobbying for their own properties to be done up.' (HA employee)

Often the conflict over new housing revealed deeper tensions about the NEM agenda and the perception by residents of what were key local needs:

> 'When we started [with HMR] we wanted bungalows – for the elderly and disabled people ... are we getting any? No "they're not viable" ... Every meeting I went to after that I was:"What about the bungalows?" [The reply was] "Well, there's not much call for it", so I thought:"I thought you'd talked to everyone!"' (Resident representative)

Certainly, residents do win some battles, and often present a strong voice, but nevertheless the disjuncture between the restructuring agenda and resident expectations is real and appears to have fostered a sense of cynicism from residents towards the redevelopment. Another flashpoint was the price of new housing, which some residents rightly suspected was pitched at incomers:

> 'Well once again the community of Beswick has been led up the garden path by the city fathers ... The cheapest house in the first phase was £138,000, that's three-bed with courtyard parking ... This is Beswick we are talking about not Wilmslow ... we are being forced out to make room for the yuppies as they are the only people that will be able to afford to live in Beswick.' (Resident comment, www.eastserve.com/forum, 2004)

Nevertheless, there is often strong resident support for aspects of the new housing designs such as security gates in new 'city block' designs – essentially gated communities (Blandy et al, 2003). Again, this reinforces the point that within the overall renewal process there is a degree of genuine consultation and resident involvement, particularly in relation to detailed design and reprovision of housing, through neighbourhood planning, visits to individual residents and general communication methods. Some things were up for negotiation, but even so the consultation is uneven and circumscribed.

What perhaps comes across most clearly from much of the evidence discussed here is the sense that local citizens felt disempowered by the sense that the wider renewal process was 'predetermined' and out of their control:

> 'At least with New Deal it was resident-led, we could go in there and kick off and they had to listen to us. Housing Market Renewal is an entirely different animal!' (Former resident representative)

> 'It could have been done so much better [the consultation process in New Islington], but it didn't take into account the views of the residents concerned, so it's no surprise quite a few walked out.' (Local councillor)

As has been pointed out in the preceding discussion, there is convincing evidence that it was indeed the case that the direction of change – in all large-scale matters – was set by policy makers and professionals. What is also interesting is that the level of outright conflict between citizens and the local governance 'architecture' is relatively small. In East Manchester, this kind of consultation might be characterised as a strategy of absorbing dissent and conflict, and it is argued here that NEM is skilled at dealing with and 'absorbing' resident opposition, especially when viewed in the light of other Pathfinder areas that have been unable to contain highly contentious issues, particularly around demolition. One possible explanation for this is the history of neighbourhood-level working through New Deal for Communities – the physical presence of MCC staff in the area allowed residents to "see the whites of our eyes", as one officer put it – but there are other Pathfinder areas, and indeed several high-profile NDC programmes around the country, which became bogged down in conflict with community representatives, activists and the community at large. Again, what seems more striking is a particular style of interaction between local governance and citizens in East Manchester: the selective use of different types of consultation in appropriate circumstances; enlisting tenants' and residents' groups to inform and negotiate problematic issues with citizens; but perhaps equally importantly a sidelining of more direct forms of confrontation or ignoring the mere quiet antipathy of some citizens.

What is less clear is whether there was a real alternative to the strategy followed by NEM. This is important because it may be argued that an elite/professional-led strategy was defensible in order to address the strategic problems – outlined above – that MCC believed were facing Manchester. Closely related to this is the question of whether citizens, whether included in consultation or not, alienated or not, will ultimately benefit from the far-reaching changes under way in the area. In many respects these questions must be left hanging, since it will be some years before the consequences in terms of population change and cultural transformation are fully realised and a fuller evaluation can be made. Nevertheless, the following concluding comments suggest some ways in which the overall project can be justified while pointing out that risks for citizens should be more fully thought through.

Conclusion

The redevelopment of housing and neighbourhoods within Housing Market Renewal neighbourhoods in East Manchester amounts to a sustained process of *urban housing market restructuring*, closely allied to a wider local governance strategy of assisted economic restructuring and development around new employment sites, sporting facilities and investments in transport and the environment. Stark calculations have been made by the City. Its tightly drawn boundaries and large deprived communities have prompted it to pursue a strategy of bringing in wealthier and at the least economically active residents in order to 'rebalance' its fiscal profile – the regeneration of East Manchester presents an opportunity. The HMR Pathfinder, one part of this local governance structure, is aiming, through remodelling, to change the raison d'être of neighbourhoods and their associated place characteristics, not least in order to attract new residents. For example, much new housing is marketed as part of an 'inner-city living' circuit to a very different target audience.

Underlying this urban housing market restructuring process are deeper shifts in governance that, at least within Manchester, have been under way for some time. In concrete terms, the implementation of HMR has involved a shift in emphasis from local needs and expectations about housing towards the creation of market-orientated housing and neighbourhood environments that are fitted towards the needs of *potential* incoming (and by extension more economically active) middle-class residents. For existing citizens who have been actively involved in regeneration, they have experienced a difference between 'community-led' neighbourhood renewal of the early Blair years and its successor – a more strategically directed restructuring process that by its nature casts them in a relatively weak and sometimes excluded position. But it also represents a deeper shift, from a local municipal and paternalist state – in its own way often deaf to the concerns of local citizens, but grounded, known, and democratically accountable – to a governance style that is more complex, networked, entrepreneurial and, particularly in the sphere of housing, market-led. Despite the strategic steer of the local authority, many local outcomes will ultimately be dependent on the operation of the market.

This fundamental shift, both in existing citizens' relationship with the local authority (and in some cases its partner agencies) and in their cultural and traditional ties to their neighbourhoods, can itself be seen as an unwelcome outcome. More concretely, there may be very real changes in the way long-term residents relate to their neighbourhoods, and neighbours, which gradually undermines one of the traditional strengths of the area: its community ties and social capital. On the other hand, local people had little control over the slow process of industrial decline that undermined social cohesion and drove population loss, and it can be argued that the governance approach outlined here was an adequate, indeed necessary, response to these challenges. Nevertheless, this governance strategy has other attendant and more insidious risks, which have not always been acknowledged by those on the privileged side of the local governance divide.

Even at this relatively early stage, a variety of mechanisms that may cause a progressive displacement of longstanding residents from the area can be discerned. As has been pointed out, this will never be a uniform process: many local citizens retain a place in the ongoing regeneration; and some individuals will benefit while others may feel they have lost out. Table 4.2 outlines in schematic form a variety of scenarios or trajectories that may arise and result in different forms of displacement. Broadly speaking, the introduction of more 'up-market' housing and the fostering of an upward neighbourhood trajectory may result in existing residents being priced out of the area. This gentrification scenario has been highlighted by many urban researchers, but it is unclear whether an assessment of the impact on social mix can be made for many years, or whether a distinction should be drawn between those directly displaced and those who leave the area willingly as a result of market changes. The reduction of social housing may have similar effects, reducing opportunities for affordable housing and the ability of longer-term residents to stay in the area. Again, displacement may not be direct in the short term but, rather, will have longer-term impacts on social mix and balance, possibly tending towards a social

Table 4.2: Possible displacement scenarios

Policy aim	Intended effects/ motivation	Unintended/ ambiguous effects	Displacement effect
Housing improvement, retention of residents, increased social mix.	Benefit to existing community and incoming residents.	a) Increased housing costs. b) Social and community fragmentation.	Incremental. Highly variable between individuals. Choose or compelled to leave?
Removal of poor housing, reduction of poverty concentration/ social housing estates.	Market recovery, increased social mix, 'sustainable community'.	a) Newly desirable social stock, increased waiting lists. b) Right to Buy removes social stock.	Gradual reduction in social stock and affordable housing. 'Displacement' of future/ potential low-income residents.
New-build housing, promotion of owner-occupation.	Increased housing choice and social mix.	a) Stock taken by investor-buyers. b) Increase in private-rented stock. c) Absentee landlordism.	Vacant new-build stock? Transitory population. Unbalanced.
Action on anti-social behaviour, neighbourhood management.	Improved security for existing residents, secure 'regeneration gains', reduced stigma, 'safe for incomers'.	Direct displacement.	Some direct 'hard-edged' displacement,

monoculture, the opposite of the stated aims of 'mixed communities' policy. Third, there may be a more 'hard-edged' displacement of those seen as antithetical to the regeneration process through anti-social behaviour policies, policing and increased securitisation of housing and neighbourhoods. Many well-established residents may be party to this process of exclusion.

This is grist to the mill of those who see it as a process of 'social cleansing' or at the least a process of local state-led gentrification (Allen, 2008; Lees et al, 2008). However, it is important to balance this with a recognition of the constraints and challenges that face the City of Manchester, and in particular the undoubted need to react to the profound economic restructuring of recent decades, which undermined the economic rationale for entire industrial districts such as East Manchester, a decline that set in train demographic shifts and social problems that led eventually to the phenomenon of low-demand housing in the late 1990s. Further detailed study of the suggested displacement trajectories in areas such as East Manchester that have undergone these significant local governance shifts would be extremely valuable.

References

Allen, C. (2008) *Housing market renewal and social class*, London: Routledge.

Allen, C., Camina, M., Casey, R., Coward, S. and Wood, M. (2005) *Mixed tenure, twenty years on – Nothing out of the ordinary*, Coventry: CIH.

Atkinson, R. and Kintrea, K. (2002) 'Area effects: what do they mean for British housing and regeneration policy?', *European Journal of Housing Policy*, vol 2, no 2, pp 147-66.

Blandy, S., Lister, D., Atkinson, R. and Flint, J. (2003) *Gated communities: A systematic review of the research evidence* (CNR Paper 12), Bristol: Bristol University.

Cameron, S. (2006) 'From low demand to rising aspirations: housing market renewal within regional and neighbourhood regeneration policy', *Housing Studies*, vol 21, no 1, pp 3-16.

Cochrane, A., Peck, J. and Tickell, A. (1996) 'Manchester plays games: exploring the local politics of globalisation', *Urban Studies*, vol 33, no 8, pp 1319-36.

CRDP (City Regional Development Programme) (2006) *Manchester City Region: Accelerating the economic growth of the North*, (www.thenorthernway.co.uk/downloaddoc.asp?id=276, accessed 22 June 2009).

Durose, C. and Lowndes, V. (2008) 'Explaining neighbourhood approaches to urban regeneration in Manchester, UK: a multi level analysis', paper presented to American Political Studies Association Conference, Boston, MA, 4 September 2008.

Harloe, M. (1995) *The people's home? Social rented housing in Europe and America*, Oxford: Blackwell.

Hastings, A. (2003) 'Strategic, multilevel neighbourhood regeneration: an outward-looking approach at last?', in R. Imrie and M. Raco (eds) *Urban renaissance? New Labour, community and urban policy*, Bristol: The Policy Press, pp 85-100.

Holmans, A. and Simpson, M. (1999) *Low demand – Separating fact from fiction*. Coventry: Chartered Institute of Housing for the Joseph Rowntree Foundation.

Karn, J. (2006) *Narratives of neglect: Community, exclusion and the local governance of security*, Cullompton: Willan.

Katz, B. (2004) *Neighbourhoods of choice and connection: The evolution of American neighbourhood policy and what it means for the United Kingdom*, York: Joseph Rowntree Foundation.

Lees, L., Slater, T. and Wyley, E. (2008) *Gentrification*, New York: Routledge.

MSP (Manchester Salford Housing Market Renewal Pathfinder) (2003) *Prospectus*, Manchester: MSP.

MSP (2005) *Scheme update*, Manchester: MSP.

NEM (New East Manchester Ltd) (2001) *New East Manchester: A new town in the city. Regeneration framework*, Manchester: Manchester City Council.

Nevin, B., Lee, P., Goodson, L., Murie, A. and Phillimore, J. (2001) *Changing housing markets and urban regeneration in the M62 Corridor*, Birmingham: Centre for Urban and Regional Studies.

ODPM (Office of the Deputy Prime Minister) (2003) *Sustainable communities: Building for the future*, London: HMSO.

Rees, J. (2007) 'Housing Market Renewal: gentrification or mixed sustainable communities?' unpublished PhD thesis, University of Manchester.

Rose, S. (2006) 'Give us a frill', *The Guardian*, 17 April.

Urban Splash (2004) *New Islington, Manchester's Millennium Community*, Manchester: Urban Splash.

Ward, K. (2003) 'Entrepreneurial urbanism, state restructuring and civilizing "New" East Manchester', *Area*, vol 35, no 2, pp 116-27.

FIVE

Citizen aspirations: women, ethnicity and housing

Bethan Harries and Liz Richardson

Introduction

Housing is one of the key goods that citizens consume and which fundamentally affects their lives and well-being. The provision and supply of housing in the UK is largely market-led, but local governance institutions play a key role in shaping supply. Decisions about what sort of housing is provided, for whom and where, are being made by local governance actors. This chapter explores what and how data is collected in order to make those decisions, and questions whether this intelligence matches what citizens themselves want. What is at stake for governance and citizens is whether major investment in a critical aspect of people's lives – their homes and neighbourhoods – will actually give people what they want.

Housing policy is focused on increasing housing supply, improving existing neighbourhoods, managing community relations and increasing consumer choice. In order to deliver these policies effectively, it is more important than ever to understand how people make choices about where they live, who makes these choices and what those choices are for different groups of people. This chapter explores the extent to which local governance actors understand these choices and meet the needs of citizens – in particular, the needs of two 'types' of citizens, women and minority ethnic communities. It does this through an examination of local policy relating to housing and ethnically mixed neighbourhoods, and by drawing on empirical data from a recent study published by the Joseph Rowntree Foundation and the Chartered Institute of Housing (see Harries et al, 2008).

There is an underlying assumption made by institutions that there are marked differences in citizen aspirations along ethnic lines. Local governance actors concerned with equality and community cohesion bolster this assumption when developing strategies to address these concerns in relation to where people live. Local authorities have, for example, developed black and minority ethnic (BME) housing strategies that seek to meet culturally specific needs of minority households, with an emphasis on needs that differ from the 'mainstream'. At the same time there is an increasingly explicit government agenda to create ethnically mixed neighbourhoods across the UK, evident in policy initiatives both at local and national level. This drive towards ethnically mixed neighbourhoods suggests that there is ethnic segregation, that this is bad and that there is a need to create more (ethnically) diverse communities in order to improve neighbourhoods and foster 'community cohesion'. The intersection of the housing market and ethnic and religious diversity has been particularly pertinent, with certain groups perceived to be self-segregating.

Evidence has shown that some minority ethnic groups have experienced and continue to experience inequitable housing outcomes (Harrison and Phillips, 2003). In particular, British south Asian households are over-represented in overcrowded and low-value housing in the lower end of the private housing market, concentrated in urban, often deprived locations, but are under-represented in social housing. However, these patterns describe the results of historical trends and do not necessarily reflect the choices or preferences of south Asian households. There is now a twin pattern of dispersal and concentration of minority ethnic groups (Lupton and Power, 2004). There is evidence that suggests a trend towards suburbanisation among minority ethnic communities (Bains, 2006), with Pakistanis and Bangladeshis actively seeking dispersal to better areas (Modood et al, 1997), and that, in some areas, there are increasing numbers of people from minority ethnic groups moving to social housing estates that are predominantly white (Blackaby, 2004).

Our research challenges assumptions that underlie current policy based on household surveys. In determining what citizens want, the way that local government gets its intelligence has inadvertently led to a skew towards male perspectives and a focus on the needs of first-generation migrant households. Policy has treated citizens as passive recipients of policy. A failure to incorporate data on aspirations has meant that local policy has not related to citizens either as informed consumers with choices (albeit constrained) or as people with lifestyles to which their housing is centrally linked. In addition, it aims to fill a gap by exploring aspirations of women from different backgrounds about where they want to live (in relation to housing, tenure and neighbourhood). This chapter draws on evidence from a recent study of white and south Asian (second-generation, born or educated in the

UK to migrant parents) British women in the UK and raises questions about the validity of current understanding of citizens' needs. By shifting the focus onto women and second-generation migrants, the research highlights the need for a broader perspective of householders and how they make decisions, and a more flexible understanding of 'minority' needs.

The research method

The study is based on semi-structured interviews with 94 white and south Asian (Bangladeshi and Pakistani) British women from three districts in the UK: Birmingham, Bradford and Tower Hamlets. We employed strategic sampling to enable us to reflect women who are from different types of households (especially tenure and location) and that would help us to make comparisons and to build and test theories based on empirical trends to help understand different patterns of settlement. We targeted women aged 20-45 in an attempt to capture women who were likely to have developed housing aspirations and be broadly at similar life stages (for example, of working age, child-bearing age). The study aimed to capture the views of women from varying socioeconomic backgrounds and from different housing and household types. It also aimed to engage the views of south Asian women who had moved in line with recognised historical settlement patterns, and more recent trends of suburbanisation and changes on social housing estates outlined above. We thus targeted three area types – neighbourhoods described locally as:

- having a relatively high concentration of south Asian residents;
- housing estates that have a concentration of white British residents and that have seen recent increases in numbers of south Asian residents;
- suburban or 'gentrified' areas.

This chapter discusses the findings of our research in relation to the policy context and highlights a number of challenges for local governance actors.

Understanding what people want

Central and local government has not traditionally had a fine-grained understanding of housing aspirations. National and local housing policy has tended to focus on tackling housing 'need' at the extreme end (for example, homelessness), rather than on how to help people achieve their aspirations. Meanwhile, private developers and house builders are able to sell properties and make profits, and satisfy the needs of many sections of the market, particularly middle- and high-income families with children. However, this sort of market information offers only a partial picture of people's housing aspirations and is limited in several ways. It is clearly 'producer-led' and biased in favour of the interests of producers of housing rather than being clearly wants-driven, focusing on the interests of the housing owners or tenants. It is based on the sorts of better-off households that developers would most like to sell to and on a mainstream 'mass market' that is more economical to build for.

Local government used to play a light-touch role in long-term land-use planning and had a largely reactive role in decisions on individual developments. Local authorities' strategic housing planning role was reshaped and enhanced from 2000. This reshaped role included responding to an expectation from central government that councils would carry out 'proper needs assessments and stock condition surveys to underpin their housing strategies' using the guidance provided (DETR, 2000). Local authorities responded and started to collect data and analyse it in a consistent and uniform way. Housing needs surveys offered a rich new source of data. In the first few years they were still primarily focused on housing needs rather than aspirations, and many were aspatial – they did not discuss neighbourhoods or locations. They focused largely on numbers of units, housing type and tenure rather than on the full range of aspects of a home that might be salient to the potential householder. As one report on the 2002 London Household Survey put it:

> Local authorities and housing associations keep very little concrete information on the locational aspirations or expectations of social housing tenants. The emphasis instead is on the nature of existing need and the appropriate type of dwelling to meet that need. (Whitehead and Cho, 2004: 5)

Local governance intelligence has largely derived itself from a combination of household surveys that focus on the head of household (usually male) and other research, such as focus groups and key stakeholder consultation (for example, with BME organisations). This has inadvertently led to a skew towards male perspectives and a focus on the needs of first-generation migrant households. Another issue has been the use of housing needs surveys. The use of housing needs surveys to gather better data on the needs of minority ethnic households is recognised as a step forward. However, while the term 'needs' suggests a citizen perspective, in reality these surveys are focused largely on housing numbers rather the needs or aspirations as expressed by the householder. Needs surveys 'read off' what citizens might want from their demographic characteristics and income levels. In doing this, local government has in effect treated citizens as passive recipients of policy.

This lack of understanding of local housing markets and aspirations on the part of those responsible for local areas is changing. The recent emphasis on a 'place-shaping' role for local government (Lyons, 2007) is an illustration of some of the shifts in thinking that are taking place. It recognises that local government needs to play a more significant and proactive role in terms of understanding local housing markets and local housing aspirations, and to use this information to intervene or manage housing across sectors and tenures. This is even more critical given the current housing growth agenda, with the current government target to create 200,000 additional homes per year by 2016 including new social rented homes (House of Commons and ODPM, 2006), and the promotion of home-ownership options to people on lower-incomes. It is also important in the rejuvenation of existing areas, particularly in Housing Market Renewal areas where attempts are being made to understand housing markets, aspirations and thinking across tenures (Livesey Wilson Ideas Management, 2005). A focus in housing policy since the mid-1970s on increasing consumer choice (DETR, 2000; Stephens et al, 2005) across a range of housing options also means that there is a need to appreciate how people make choices, what those choices represent and how to genuinely meet people's preferences.

Minority ethnic needs as different from the 'mainstream'

The 'race equalities' agenda in the housing field accelerated from the 1990s, particularly following the MacPherson Report on the Stephen Lawrence Inquiry in 1999 and the Race Relations Act Amendment in 2000. This resulted in a raft of documents identifying housing needs of minority ethnic groups or laying out ways that these needs should be assessed and taken into consideration, mostly in the social housing sector (see, for example, Blackaby and Chahal, 2000; DTLR, 2001; Housing Corporation, 2001; NHF, 2002). A good-practice guide to black and minority ethnic (BME) housing strategies found that 55% of authorities had made some assessment of the housing requirements of BME communities in the previous three years (Blackaby and Chahal,

2000). A review of BME housing policy in social housing in 2003/04 noted that there had been considerable work at national level and at regional level by the Housing Corporation and housing associations, and that the shift from local to regional housing strategies provided an opportunity for a strategic focus on BME needs, although housing associations did not feel that the Housing Corporation should be more *proactive* in this area (Hann and Bowes, 2004).

A large part of the impetus behind this work was to encourage housing agencies to be more aware of 'difference', open up services to groups in need who had not accessed support and offer more 'culturally sensitive services' (Housing Corporation 2001; NHF, 2002). Resulting policies constructed the needs of BME citizens as different from the mainstream. These include the need for:

- larger homes for overcrowded Asian families with extended or multi-household families (DTLR, 2001; NHF, 2002; Leeds Housing Partnership, 2004; Ipswich Borough Council, 2005; Northampton Borough Council, 2006; Roberts et al, 2006) and conversion of small terraced homes into larger family houses (NHF, 2008);
- culturally sensitive housing design – for example, kitchen storage to accommodate large quantities of rice and oil (NHF, 1998);
- financial support – for example, for private sector housing improvements that accommodated the needs of specific ethnic groups, such as by offering interest-free loans (DTLR, 2001);
- faster development of appropriate solutions for BME households, such as Sharia-compliant mortgages (Stockport Metropolitan Borough Council, 2004; NHF, 2008);
- development of culturally sensitive housing design – for example, two reception rooms when required, that is on cultural or religious grounds (Roberts et al, 2006);
- provision of adjacent allocation for multi-generational households in social housing (Leeds Housing Partnership, 2004; NHF, 2008).

The development of minority ethnic housing strategies in the early 2000s reflects recognition of past neglect of the specific needs of minority communities. However, assumptions that Asian families prefer multi-generational households and 'Asian' neighbourhoods are being challenged (Bains, 2006). A second generation of British Asian households is now of an age to be making housing choices and there is recognition that, consequently, market intelligence needs to be updated.

> ... we need to remember that BME housing needs and aspirations will change as new generations grow up ... Our evidence base needs to reflect those changes over time. (DTLR, 2001, p 14)

Our study aimed to contribute to understanding of these 'changes over time' through an exploration of second-generation south Asian citizens. The following sections summarise our findings and discuss what this evidence means for governance and public policy.

Housing aspirations of the 'new generation'

The majority of the women we interviewed were married and nearly all had children. Despite efforts to speak to women from a broad range of socioeconomic backgrounds, most were in skilled or professional employment. Most of the women already owned their homes, were not overcrowded and had housing aspirations beyond meeting basic housing need. The most basic conclusion of our work was just how similar the women's housing preferences and aspirations were across ethnic groups, as has been found elsewhere (Beider et al, 2007). There was nothing surprising about their housing and neighbourhood aspirations – people wanted to live in a 'nice' house in a 'nice' neighbourhood with 'nice' neighbours. What this meant at an individual level varied according to individual taste and circumstance, but significantly, women framed many of their aspirations in relation to their family, putting their children's needs at the foreground of their reasons for wanting to live in a particular type of house or neighbourhood. For example, women with younger children had similar priorities in terms of a decent, safe and clean place, well-performing schools, shops and facilities close by, a large house with a garden and a sense of community.

We had set out to determine the extent to which the aspirations of the south Asian women we spoke to differed from the 'mainstream', or perhaps more accurately how they differed from the white British women we spoke to. Put simply, then, the most (un)remarkable finding is that we were unable to identify differences in aspirations according to ethnicity. What is surprising is how far away this picture is from many broad-brush housing strategies. That is not to say that proximity to cultural and religious spaces was not important but that was not a driving aspiration. For example, when asked directly about the importance of being near cultural facilities, many women said that things such as mosques and Halal food shops would always be accessible by car and consequently did not affect residential preferences:

> I can get in the car and I can drive wherever I want to drive
> and buy whatever I want ... these aren't barriers for me. I'd
> like to live where I want to live and then go and buy, shop
> where I want to shop ... and bring it home and live like I
> want to really. (Woman of Pakistani heritage)

Our findings are at odds with many of the BME housing strategies
outlined above and from the understandings of many working in the
field based on accurate data, but perhaps data from very different types
of ethnic groups and households. This suggests that there is a clear
gap between decisions being made in local governance by institutions
and the preferences of citizens. We suggest that the disparity between
our findings and local government's understanding of BME citizens'
needs, reflected in their housing strategies, may be indicative of change
across generations as suggested by the DTLR in 2001 (cited above).
We did not set out to gather data on first-generation migrants and
the following does not intend to substitute for a comparative analysis
across different generations of migrants. However, the perceptions of
the south Asian British women we interviewed and the differences they
outlined between themselves and first-generation migrants provide an
interesting perspective on change.

The south Asian women in the study often contrasted their own
aspirations to the perceptions of their parents and other first-generation
migrants' aspirations. First-generation migrants (including their parents)
were said to be inhibited by language barriers and a 'fear of the unknown',
and consequently tended to settle in particular neighbourhoods because
of existing social networks, shops and amenities that catered to their
needs. Second-generation women described themselves as having
greater flexibility in the options open to them because of increased
social mobility (gained from education and employment) and physical
mobility (gained from access to personal transport):

> So all these people are spreading, but that's kind of second
> generation and third generation. First generation are staying
> put because they don't you know ... they're just scared of
> what's out there really. (Woman of Pakistani heritage)

The study was also concerned with how aspirations might translate
into action and in particular we wanted to explore the extent to which
women were involved in decision making in the household. South
Asian women are customarily portrayed in roles limited outside the
home (Coleman and Salt, 1992) and unfairly depicted as victims of

repressive cultures (Burr, 2002; Phillips 2007). The notion that south Asian women are quiescent was also one that we came across during the course of our research. We were painted a picture by individuals from several organisations, including Asian women's organisations, of shy and reserved women who were unlikely to speak to strangers. It has been argued that second-generation Asian women do not conform to this stereotype (Werbner, 2004) and certainly the image of passive women was not something we came across during the interviewee recruitment process, including when knocking on doors. Further, we found that the women we interviewed (both white and south Asian) were central in the household decision-making process. They talked about making decisions alone or with their partner, by taking into consideration their own needs and the needs of their children.

By chance, during the course of our study, we interviewed several women who had come to settle in the UK as spouses. When asked about the decision-making process in their household, they described how they had gradually taken over responsibility for household decisions from their British-born husbands once they had learnt the language and become more familiar with the systems of the UK. These women (all Pakistani-born) also reported a preference when they first arrived to live in neighbourhoods where there were relatively large populations of Pakistanis but described how this too had changed over time, particularly once they had learnt English. This data came from only a small number of women but, together with the perceptions of the second-generation women, they may shed some light on the transmission of stereotype and on the changes that take place across different generations of migrants. However, research with both first- and second-generation migrants would have to be undertaken in this area.

Aspirations and ethnically mixed neighbourhoods

A debate has been taking place in academia and more informally in local policy making around some of the spatial aspects of minority ethnic housing choices and outcomes. There is a literature on the neighbourhood preferences of south Asian households that suggests kith and kin ties and proximity to culturally appropriate services are important and consequently drive housing choice (Lakey, 1997). The housing pathways available to south Asian communities have thus continued to be seen as restricted to a narrow set of options, because of their strong ties to specific neighbourhoods, that tend to be dominated by certain types of housing that are affordable. The underlying argument is that residential segregation is partly a function of the preferences and market decisions of south Asian households themselves – that those households are 'self-segregating'. However, there is also a significant debate around these propositions, with some well-known writers such as Ludi Simpson arguing that the 'legend' of self-segregation is a myth (Simpson, 2004). Simpson et al (2007, p 6) usefully distinguish between two processes of clustering along 'racial lines':'benign' processess of positive reinforcement which will 'continue to produce areas of different ethnic composition'; and 'dysfunctional' processes, such as inequalities in the housing market or racist practices, which prevent integration.

Much of what the women we interviewed said about first-generation migrants supported the notion that first-generation households were drawn to certain neighbourhoods because of ties to social and kinship networks, and amenities associated with culture and religion. However, as shown above, these concerns were not at the forefront of aspirations and indeed decisions of the second-generation women we interviewed. In addition, when we explored the idea of an aspirational neighbourhood with them, we found there was an overall compelling preference for mixed neighbourhoods by both white and south Asian British households who wanted their children to grow up in multi-ethnic areas.

We were conscious when asking women about mixed neighbourhoods that they might feel compelled to react in a particular way. However, responses were not simply a case of people saying the 'right thing' – some of the women said they had moved deliberately to make sure their children went to mixed schools and others were actively using this criterion in making housing choices. There was a compelling preference for mixed neighbourhoods among both white British and south Asian households because they wanted their children to grow up in multi-ethnic areas. The overwhelming majority said that they thought ethnically mixed neighbourhoods were a positive thing, and conversely that segregated or mono-cultural neighbourhoods created 'dangers' for society as a whole. Living in a mixed neighbourhood was said to generate, or potentially generate, better understanding of different cultures, more respect for other cultures and greater tolerance.

Preferences for ethnically mixed neighbourhoods were good, both for society, and for driving women's personal housing aspirations. Women particularly wanted their children to experience a diverse society and go to multi-ethnic schools:

I think mixed areas are the best thing especially if you've got children, just exposing them to different cultures and influences is important so that as they grow up they are confident in dealing with other people no matter what ethnicity they are. I would always choose to live in a mixed area. (Woman of Pakistani heritage)

Don't the government bang on about this community cohesion and stuff like that? ... You're mixing with other people so you have an understanding of what other cultures are about. They also importantly have an understanding of what your culture's about but I mean I certainly wouldn't want my son to go a predominantly Asian school or to go to a predominantly white school. I would want him to be able to mix with all different children from all different backgrounds. (Woman of Bangladeshi heritage)

This is an interesting finding given that evidence from the 2001 Census shows there are high levels of segregation in both schools and neighbourhoods, with consistently higher segregation for South Asian pupils than for other groups – for example, black pupils. Children are also more segregated in school than in their neighbourhood (Burgess et al, 2005).

Most women in our study chose the benefits of suburban neighbourhoods of higher performing schools and bigger homes with more private and communal green space, despite regrets over the lack of community and other benefits. This was strongly driven by their life stage, to protect their children and offer them what they thought were the best life chances. One of the concerns they expressed was that of their children approaching adolescence and needing more space and distance from negative peer influences. Consequently, city or inner city areas were sometimes described as stopgaps for single women or couples without children, while more affluent areas were places to settle or make a long-term investment and raise a family.

For south Asian women there were additional reasons for wanting to move out of neighbourhoods that had relatively high Asian populations. To begin with, these neighbourhoods were associated with deprivation and problems such as lower standards of accommodation and higher crime rates. The natural aspiration was therefore to move 'out' to more affluent areas; the same reasoning was given by the white British participants who lived or had lived in these areas. In addition, south Asian women wanted to move out of these neighbourhoods when they perceived them as constrictive and intrusive 'closed communities' that housed nosey neighbours. This was described as a greater problem for women than men as they were said to be under greater scrutiny and more susceptible to gossip. The women said it was particularly a problem when certain lifestyle choices such as going to university and being single did not 'fit in' with what was deemed acceptable by others and particularly by older and first-generation migrants. This led some to describe a sense of exclusion:

> 'I feel now I'm not even in my own country and I was born in Birmingham ... this is my town, I don't come from Mirpur, I was born in Birmingham, this is my town.'
> (Woman of Pakistani heritage)

However, for many, the differences that they described between different generations of migrants were rooted in class difference. These women described first-generation migrants who lived in these neighbourhoods as of 'a certain socioeconomic background and of a certain level of educational attainment', as living in a 'time warp', people who maintained gender stereotypes and were resistant to change.

Helping citizens achieve their aspirations

Women from both ethnic groups had similar aspirations and consequently they confronted similar mainstream housing markets with similar levels of frustration. They faced similar affordability problems because of the state of UK house prices. How, then, did they navigate these difficulties in order to achieve or get closer to their aspirations? In addressing this question, again, we were interested to find out whether there were identifiable differences between the ethnic groups.

There were no discernible differences between the women from different ethnic groups and the means they pursued to achieve their housing goals. There was an overwhelming preference for owner-occupation and women employed similar strategies to get on the property ladder. For example, despite preferences to leave areas with higher concentrations of BME residents, women (white and south Asian) often chose to buy in these neighbourhoods because they were affordable and provided a first step on to the property ladder. Extended families are most often associated with the south Asian community. Many of our interviewees had lived with their parents or in-laws for a short time but the majority lived in nuclear families and expressed a preference for doing so. They described their choice to live with parents or in-laws in the same way that many of the white British women did – for example, between jobs or between university and work, in order to save money to get their own home. In addition, both white and south Asian British families were equally likely to get help from family and avoid estate agents fees wherever possible.

In our interviews we wanted to know what women thought of initiatives to help people onto the property ladder. The National Housing Federation, among many others, has recommended that Sharia-compliant mortgages be made widely available (NHF, 2008). However, among the Muslim women in our study, there was little interest in Sharia-compliant mortgages because they were perceived to be expensive, inflexible or "not necessarily Islamic". While the NHF and some local authorities, such as Stockport Metropolitan Borough Council, consider the development of Islamic mortgages as 'essential' to meet the needs of BME households, our findings suggest that this may not be the case for second-generation south Asian Muslim women.

How local governance can help create the 'right' mix

Several women blamed past central and local government policy for deliberately creating segregated communities or aggravating the problem of segregation. For example, there was a strong perception on the part of both the south Asian and white British women that social housing allocations were linked to ethnicity. White British women described local authorities prioritising housing allocations to south Asian households, while south Asian women talked about Asian households being offered only 'Asian' areas. Women said that genuine mixing should happen "organically", rather than being "manufactured". Drawing on their own experience, they described how community tensions had been exacerbated by insensitive regeneration and housing development decisions, or at least the negative unintended consequences of those decisions. Examples given, described poor relations between established white British and established south Asian communities, but women also discussed the potential for tension between established communities of all ethnicities and newly arrived migrants. Housing is one of the key scarce resources around which, competition between groups often centres (Hudson et al, 2007). Given this, a challenge will be to ensure that strategic investment decisions and neighbourhood interventions by local authorities and housing providers cater for the needs of both established and newly arriving communities.

A mixture of incomes, ages, households and housing types was said to be key to generate genuinely ethnically mixed communities, as they would naturally attract householders from different ethnic groups. Many women, both white and south Asian, expressed nervousness about living in newly mixed neighbourhoods, particularly if they would be in the minority. For example, south Asian women were concerned they might not be welcome in a newly mixed neighbourhood and had perceptions that some all-white areas were 'no-go' areas for Asian households. Meanwhile, some white British women were concerned they would stand out in all-Asian areas and similarly talked about 'no-go' areas. Women suggested interventions to encourage ethnic mix. These included the following.

- *Rehousing some existing residents into new housing*: as opposed to moving minority ethnic groups into new housing alongside older, poor-quality housing dominated by white British residents.
- *Rethinking faith schools*: said to further segregate communities by discouraging mix from an early age.
- *Managing the process of change*: helping existing communities adapt to change when new residents move in.
- *Providing mixed-tenure schemes*: to encourage a social mix and make poorer areas more attractive for all.

Women made a distinction between 'mix' and truly integrated communities. For example, a neighbourhood that had people from different backgrounds living in it was not considered to be mixed, if, those populations lived in small segregated pockets. Many of the women emphasised that the degree and type of ethnic mix was critical. They argued against a crude definition of mix, as, simply having a small number of people from one ethnic group living among another single ethnic group. Their definition of an ethnically mixed neighbourhood was that no single group would dominate and that there would be a number of ethnic groups. This would require more than just 'white plus BME' and included the need for a balance – for example, within the single official category of 'Asian', between different countries and regions on the Indian sub-continent, and between different classes.

Conclusion

In this chapter we have looked at significant governance decisions around major investment and key shaping of the housing market by local institutions. We have argued that this intervention in critical aspects of peoples lives – their homes and neighbourhoods – does not deliver what some groups of citizens want. In order to deliver this key set of social and urban policies effectively, local governance needs to take better account of the fact that women make these choices as well as men within households, that women base their choices on their identities as mothers as much as their ethnic and cultural identities, and that the choices for second-generation south Asian women are not hugely dissimilar to those for white British women of the same age.

Our conclusions on housing aspirations and local policy are that policy makers need to adopt more flexible BME housing strategies that take into consideration the demands of different generations of minority ethnic households. We are not advocating a dismissal of ethnic and culturally sensitive approaches to policy making; it is necessary to avoid housing strategies that would reinforce inequitable or dysfunctional outcomes and to take account of the experiences of minority households when formulating policy and strategy. However, we do argue that there is a need for local authorities to rethink how they understand the aspirations of minority ethnic groups and women in the housing market.

Translating complex sets of citizens' preferences and market decisions into real practice is a tough job. One consequence of this complexity is that governance actors latch onto particular policy ideas. For example, a popular sign of 'cultural awareness' for many housing providers in the 1990s was the recognition that Muslim families would refuse a property if the toilet faced Mecca (for example, see Ecotec, 2006). This one crude but genuine example may be a sign of culturally sensitive housing provision, but was not the priority or preference of the women in our study. The 2000s' version of well-intentioned but limited cultural understanding is the current emphasis by institutions on Sharia-compliant mortgages, which our research suggests are nowhere near as popular with consumers as policy makers believe. These examples are given not to be facetious, but to illustrate how difficult and complex it is to embed genuinely sophisticated and nuanced understandings of citizen preferences among practitioners and policy makers.

Other research has identified similar patterns of age and generational structures affecting housing and residential mobility (see, for example, an ongoing project: Regenerating Urban Neighbourhoods (RUN), Local Government Research Unit). These changes take place over many years. The development of BME housing strategies itself took several years to accomplish; adapting strategies for new aspirations will also take time. It is perhaps a feature of local governance structures, particularly for decisions on significant large-scale policy areas, that there will inevitably be a time lag for decisions to catch up with changes in consumer preferences. If this is the case, it raises questions about how 'future-proof' or forward-looking strategies are, or, can be.

Housing strategies need to understand the needs and aspirations of different market segments or different sorts of consumers. Our research confirms we need to ask to what degree 'the emerging generation of new households will base mobility decisions on rather different criteria to their parents' when looking at the housing aspirations of established minority ethnic communities (Cole, 2007). Some have argued that the way in which south Asian communities are portrayed in the media is somewhat outdated, looking back, rather than focusing on the emerging realities of the 21st century (Bains, 2006). Our research concluded that the second-generation south Asian women in the study had aspirations more akin to the white British women of the same age than to their mothers. One of the implications of this research is that the way that minority ethnic communities are understood in housing strategy is not only somewhat outdated on occasion, but also insufficiently stratified. It needs to take more fully into consideration the significant differences between established and newly arrived communities, and between first and second generations within different ethnic groups, and at changing decision making within minority ethnic households.

Institutions trying to make governance decisions about housing have seen citizens in terms of their ethnic group. They made an association between ethnicity and cultural preferences. What we found was that, when thinking about how and where they wanted to live, the women did not construct themselves in terms of their ethnicity. Instead, they were operating either as 'ordinary' consumers in a mainstream British context (for example, preference for houses over the more European apartment, desire for gardens, emphasis on safety, dislike of the inner city, etc), or in their identity as mothers. What they wanted for their children was more important than the fact they were Bangladeshi British or white British.

Local governance actors have made some positive steps towards a better understanding of citizens as informed consumers making choices and trade-offs rather than passive recipients of needs-based provision: as people who consume housing in physical spaces (neighbourhoods), which requires a spatial component to housing strategy; and as people operating with a wider set of lifestyle desires, which housing reflects and expresses. However, there is clearly more work to be done by local agencies on their 'residential offer' to adapt policy and delivery approaches to align more closely with citizen aspirations. More effective interventions need to be made by local institutions when attempting to create more ethnically mixed communities to avoid the sorts of negative unintended consequences the women had experienced. The challenge for local governance is to make strategic investment decisions that facilitate good relations between different ethnic groups.

One issue is how the relationship between local governance structures and citizens is taken forward. Indeed, arguably, one of the things that led to the emphasis on discussions about difference in the 1990s was the dominance of minority ethnic lobbying groups as the main conduit between housing strategists and providers, and citizens and consumers. Given the continuing preference for owner–occupation, most citizens will relate to policy decision on housing across all tenures through the market. Therefore, citizens may need to relate to local governance structures on an individual basis – for example, through market research, which may avoid the construction of citizens into groups with assumed cultural preferences.

References

Bains, J. (2006) *Futures housing: Housing needs choices and aspirations of South Asian communities in the West Midlands 2020*, Birmingham: Ashram Housing Association.

Beider, H., Joseph, R. and Ferrari, E. (2007) *Report to North East Assembly BME housing issues*, Birmingham: CURS.

Blackaby, B. (2004) *Community cohesion and housing: A good practice guide*. London: Chartered Institute of Housing and the Housing Corporation.

Blackaby, B. and Chahal, K. (2000) *Black and minority ethnic housing strategies: A good practice guide*. London: Federation of Black Housing Organisations and the Housing Corporation.

Burgess, S., Lupton, R. and Wilson, D. (2005) 'Parallel lives? Ethnic segregation in schools and neighbourhoods', *Urban Studies*, vol 42, no 7, pp 1027-56.

Burr, J (2002) 'Cultural stereotypes of women from South Asian communities: mental health care professionals' explanations for patterns of suicide and depression', *Social Science and Medicine*, vol 55, no 5, pp 835-45.

Cole, I. (2007) *Shaping or shadowing? Understanding and responding to housing market change*. York: Joseph Rowntree Foundation.

Coleman, D. and Salt, J. (1992) *The British population: Patterns, trends and processes*. Oxford: Oxford University Press.

DETR (Department of the Environment, Transport and the Regions) (2000) *Quality and choice: A decent home for all, the way forward for housing*. London: DETR.

DTLR (Department for Transport, Local Government and the Regions) (2001) *Addressing the housing needs of black and minority ethnic people*, London: DTLR.

ECOTEC (2006) *Manchester city region: Demand and aspirations of minority ethnic communities*, Manchester: ECOTEC.

Hann, C. and Bowes, E. (2004) *The Housing Corporation's BME housing policy: assessing its impact*, London: Managing Diversity Associates.

Harries, B., Richardson, L. and Soteri-Proctor, A. (2008) *Housing aspirations for a new generation: Perspectives from white and south Asian British women*, London/York: Chartered Institute of Housing/Joseph Rowntree Foundation.

Harrison, M. and Phillips, D. (2003) *Housing and black and minority ethnic communities: Review of the evidence base*, London: Office of the Deputy Prime Minister.

House of Commons and ODPM, Housing, Planning, Local Government and the Regions Committee (2006) *Affordability and the supply of housing: Third report of session 2005-06, volume 1*, London: HMSO.

Housing Corporation (2001) *The big picture: Meeting the needs of black and minority ethnic communities*, London: Housing Corporation.

Hudson, M., Phillips, J., Ray, K. and Barnes, H. (2007) *Social cohesion in diverse communities*, York: Joseph Rowntree Foundation.

Ipswich Borough Council (2005) *Housing strategy 2006-2009*, Ipswich: Ipswich Borough Council.

Lakey, J. (1997) 'Neighbourhoods and housing', in T. Modood, R. Berthoud, J. Lakey, J. Nazroo, P. Smith, S. Virdee and S. Beishon (eds) *Ethnic minorities in Britain: Diversity and disadvantage. The fourth national survey of ethnic minorities*, London: Policy Studies Institute.

Leeds Housing Partnership (2004) *Improving housing, empowering communities: A BME housing strategy and action plan for the Leeds Housing Partnership 2005-2010*, Leeds: Leeds Housing Partnership.

Livesey Wilson Ideas Management (2005) *Dreaming of Pennine Lancashire*, Accrington, Lancashire: Elevate.

Lupton, R. and Power, A. (2004) *Minority ethnic groups in Britain* (CASE-Brookings Census Briefs 2), London: Centre for Analysis of Social Exclusion.

Lyons, M. (2007) *Lyons Inquiry into Local Government. Place shaping: A shared ambition for the future of local government*, London: HMSO.

Modood, T., Berthoud, R., Lakey, J., Nazroo, J., Smith, P., Virdee, S. and Beishon, S. (1997) *Ethnic minorities in Britain: Diversity and disadvantage: The fourth national survey of ethnic minorities*, London: Policy Studies Institute.

NHF (National Housing Federation) (1998) *Accommodating diversity: Housing design in a multi-cultural society*, London: NHF.

NHF (2002) *Race equality code of practice for housing associations*, London: NHF.

NHF (2008) *Black and minority ethnic communities and housing in the East Midlands: A strategy for the region*, London: NHF.

Northampton Borough Council (2006) *BME housing strategy 2007-2011*, Northampton: Northampton Borough Council.

Phillips, A. (2007) *Multiculturalism without culture*, Princeton, NJ/Oxford: Princeton University Press.

Roberts, C., Moon, S., Gulliver, K., Pocock, R. and Shaikh, B. (2006) *BME housing strategy research report 2006*, Wolverhampton: Wolverhampton City Council.

Simpson, L. (2004) 'Statistics of racial segregation: measures, evidence and policy', *Urban Studies*, vol 41, no 3, pp 661-81.

Simpson, L., Ahmed, S. and Phillips, D. (2007) *Oldham and Rochdale: Race, housing and community cohesion*, Manchester: Cathie Marsh Centre for Census and Survey Research.

Stephens, M., Whitehead, C. and Munro, M. (2005) *Evaluation of English housing policy: Lessons from the past, challenges for the future for housing policy*, London: ODPM.

Stockport Metropolitan Borough Council (2004) *Stockport strategic housing: Housing strategy 2005-2008*, Stockport: Stockport Metropolitan Borough Council.

Werbner, P. (2004) 'Theorising complex diasporas: purity and hybridity in the south Asian public sphere in Britain', *Journal of Ethnic and Migration Studies*, vol 30, no 5, pp 895-911.

Whitehead, C. and Cho, Y. (2004) *Affordable housing in London: Who expects to move and where?* (Housing Corporation Sector Study 39), London: Housing Corporation.

SIX

Can we promote cohesion through contact? Intergroup contact and the development of community cohesion

Matthew J. Goodwin[1]

Introduction

Recent years have seen an upsurge of interest in the effects of immigration and increased ethno-cultural diversity. As in countries elsewhere, in the UK policy makers and practitioners face a number of challenges that are multidimensional in nature. In the wider national and international context, new migration patterns, rapid demographic change and the arrival of super-diversity highlight the evolving nature of diversity in contemporary Britain and raise important questions over the extent to which local authorities are able to bring together increasingly diverse and often transient groups around a set of shared values and sense of belonging. Linked closely to these broader trends are more specific challenges such as multilingualism and the proliferation of transnational networks, all of which require national and local government to think in different ways about how best to effectively encourage and support relationships between different ethnic groups. Meanwhile, at the micro-level, a further challenge centres on the changing perceptions and attitudes of citizens toward immigrants, minority ethnic groups and increased diversity more generally. Confronted with the arrival of new migrants and changing neighbourhoods, some citizens perceive ethnic 'out-groups' as posing a threat to the socioeconomic resources and cultural values of the native 'in-group'. A sense of anxiety over the allocation of scarce resources and perceptions of ethnic threat and competition appear to be important drivers of prejudice and anti-immigrant hostility (for example, McLaren and Johnson, 2007). Such views seem to owe less to concern over personal well-being than a sense of anxiety over the 'threat' that immigrants and minority ethnic groups (though increasingly Muslims) pose to the *collective* in-group. A corollary issue centres on the specific challenge posed by organised extremist movements, which seek to mobilise support by embellishing these perceptions of a threatened way of life (see Eatwell and Goodwin, 2010). Researchers, policy makers and practitioners face the task of understanding what produces these psychological states and also what tools might be used to combat them.

Confronted with those challenges above some have argued that the traditional model of multiculturalism in Britain offers an inadequate response in that it has prioritised what differentiates one ethnic group from the next at the expense of promoting commonalities that bind different groups together. At the same time, there has emerged a broader debate over the effects of increased ethnic diversity – for example, on levels of social capital (Putnam, 2007), trust (Alesina and Ferrara, 2002) and civic engagement (Costa and Kahn, 2003).[2] The aim of this chapter is not to contribute directly to these debates. Rather, our aim is to examine more closely one approach that has gained considerable currency in the discussion over how best to effectively respond to those challenges above. Proponents of what can be loosely termed the 'contact approach' stress the important role of promoting and creating opportunities for contact and social interaction between different ethnic groups as a means to reduce prejudice and anxiety while fostering tolerance, cross-cultural understanding and 'cohesive' local communities more generally. Following the urban disturbances in Bradford, Burnley and Oldham in 2001 and the subsequent discussion over citizens leading 'parallel lives', numerous reports and recommendations have emphasised the role of intergroup contact (or 'meaningful interaction') as a crucial mechanism through which local authorities can encourage attitudinal and behaviour change. This discussion, however, has largely glossed over the underlying theoretical and empirical base on which the contact approach stands. More broadly, the debate over 'community cohesion' has tended to focus on questions that centre on citizenship, governance and participation rather than the mechanics of intergroup contact, an area that has traditionally been the domain of social psychologists. As advocates of contact theory note, the task of understanding how and why intergroup contact works is an important prerequisite to the development of more effective interventions (Tausch and Hewstone, 2008). Yet, in the debates that surround community cohesion, there have been few attempts to root this discussion more firmly in the evidence base.

The chapter is organised as follows. First, it provides a brief overview of the concept of 'community cohesion' and the role of group contact within this field. It then turns to investigate the wider theoretical and empirical base that underpins the contact approach. Finally, the chapter raises several questions concerning the implementation and effects of contact-based interventions.

The concept of community cohesion

The concept of community cohesion emerged following urban disturbances in parts of northern England in summer 2001. Concern over the existence and effects of spatial and social segregation led some to argue that the traditional model of multiculturalism had done little to bring different ethnic groups together around a set of shared values and sense of belonging (though see Finney and Simpson, 2009). In contrast, in economically deprived boroughs such as Burnley, the past emphasis on diversity policies combined with area-based regeneration had encouraged different groups to organise and demand what limited resources were available, inadvertently reinforcing perceptions of ethnic competition and a form of 'tribal thinking' through which groups were encouraged to 'look after their own' (Cantle, 2001: 10). In the aftermath of these events, some began to argue that Britain possessed a weak sense of what citizenship should entail and that more effort should be devoted to developing a stronger understanding 'of what our collective citizenship means, and how we can build that shared commitment into our social and political institutions' (Blunkett, 2001: 2). The critique of Britain's traditional approach to race relations has since gathered considerable pace to the extent that some, as others observe, have seemingly begun to 'dance on the grave of multiculturalism' (Johnson, 2008: 4). Political elites have referred to multiculturalism as one of 'five barriers of division' and as an approach 'which focuses on what divides us rather than what brings us together'.[3] Others suggest that past conceptions of multiculturalism 'led not to integration but to segregation' and 'allowed groups to live separately with no incentive to integrate and every incentive not to'.[4]

In place of the earlier understanding of multiculturalism has emerged the concept of community cohesion, which (argue its advocates) seeks to promote a more inclusive notion of citizenship, identity and belonging, and the development of integrated communities that while they are ethno-culturally diverse are grounded in a set of shared values and understandings. According to the report of the Commission for Integration and Cohesion (CIC, 2007: 38), community cohesion is 'the process that must happen in all communities to ensure different groups of people get on well together; while integration is principally the process that ensures new residents and existing residents adapt to one another'. While there is a clear need for greater conceptual clarity of terms such as 'cohesion' and 'integration', the definition advanced by the CIC (Box 6.1) highlights current thinking in terms of what constitutes a cohesive and integrated community.

Box 6.1: Definitions of integration and cohesion

An integrated and cohesive community is one where:
- there is a clearly defined and widely shared sense of the contribution of different individuals and different communities to a future vision for a neighbourhood, city, region or country;
- there is a strong sense of an individual's rights and responsibilities when living in a particular place – people know what everyone expects of them and what they can expect in turn;
- those from different backgrounds have similar life opportunities, access to services and treatment;
- there is a strong sense of trust in institutions locally to act fairly in arbitrating between different interests and for the role and justifications to be subject to public scrutiny;
- there is a strong recognition of the contribution of both those who have newly arrived and those who already have deep attachments to a particular place, with a focus on what they have in common;
- there are strong and positive relationships between people from different backgrounds in the workplace, in schools and in other institutions within neighbourhoods.

Source: CIC (2007: 42).

Consistent with Labour's emphasis on local responsibility, cohesion policy has increasingly assumed a local focus, stressing, for example, the need for 'tailored and bespoke local activity to build integration and cohesion' (CLG, 2007: 4). Local arenas of interaction such as schools, the workplace and public spaces thus become central and local authorities assume a prominent role in the implementation and delivery of cohesion-based strategies. From this perspective, it is only at local level 'that leaders can understand in detail the profile of the population, the changes that are taking place ... [and] where specific initiatives can be crafted and delivered' (CIC, 2007: 4). In short, community cohesion 'is something that can only be understood and built locally' (CLG, 2008: 9).

Critics of the emergent framework, however, argue that community cohesion exaggerates differences of ethnicity (for example, Robinson, 2005), directs a discourse of blame towards British Muslim communities and new migrants (for example, Worley, 2005), is akin to assimilationism and holds little regard for the diversity of social context or underlying socioeconomic inequalities (for example, Back et al, 2002; Cheong et al, 2007). This latter emphasis on the importance of structural factors is supported by findings that similarly question the growing tendency to downplay the importance of socioeconomic variables. For example, based on the 2001 Citizenship Survey, the study by Letki (2008: 122) argues that the main factor undermining neighbourly interactions is not racial diversity but rather socioeconomic status: '[T]o maintain social solidarity and community cohesion twenty-first century Britain needs more social and economic equality, rather than more cultural unity'.[5] Yet, while community cohesion may well have been 'founded on the principle that it is insufficient to focus entirely on socioeconomic disadvantage and ignore the belief systems upon which it depends' (Cantle, 2008: 14), advocates of the new approach have been careful to note that the task of promoting a sense of belonging and diversity 'has to stand alongside more traditional approaches to equality' (Cantle, 2008: 17) and that 'having some values in common does not mean sharing all values' (Cantle, 2008: 18). Whether geared towards individuals, the organisations and communities in which they are embedded or the wider national community, cohesion-based initiatives should focus on developing commonalities in the socio-cultural sphere *as well as* socioeconomic equality.

While this debate has become increasingly polarised what has remained constant is an emphasis on the importance of group contact and interaction. Though encompassing longer theoretical roots, the concept of community cohesion was effectively 'born' amidst the events of 2001 and subsequent evidence of residential and educational segregation. One report drew attention to the existence of separate educational arrangements, community and voluntary bodies, employment, language, places of worship and socio-cultural networks and noted how many communities operated 'on the basis of a series of parallel lives', which 'often do not seem to touch at any point, let alone overlap and promote any meaningful interchanges' (Cantle, 2001: 9). In later years, others similarly suggested that some districts in Britain 'are on their way to becoming fully fledged ghettoes' (Phillips, 2005). Segregation was identified as a central contributory factor to the existence of negative stereotypes, intergroup tension and the reinforcement of group boundaries:[6]

> Little or nothing had been done to break down the barriers
> between the communities, to promote interaction and
> mutual trust and understanding – prejudices were allowed
> to fester with little leadership at either local or national level
> to promote a positive view of diversity. (Cantle, 2008: 10)

Implicit in much of the discussion thereafter is the assumption that
contact-based interventions are a useful 'tool' that can be used to
reduce prejudice, anxiety and perceptions of ethnic competition while
improving community relations and the 'cohesiveness' of local areas
more generally. Recommendations put forward by the CIC (2007: 111)
stressed the need 'to improve the value of the everyday interactions that
take place in the four spheres ... [schools; the workplace; public spaces;
and sports, culture and leisure] whilst also creating opportunities for
new ones to be taken up'. Others have likewise argued that national
and local government should examine more closely ways to promote
'contact and interaction between people from different backgrounds to
break down barriers'. In turn, group contact 'should reduce prejudice
and challenge stereotypes, creating the conditions through which an
inclusive understanding of local identity can develop' (Rogers and
Muir, 2007: 5-9).[7] Such interventions will assume a local focus and
in this respect local authorities are especially well situated to promote
contact and interaction. More recently, this focus has been extended to
include universities and colleges that are advised to 'set up inter-faith
and inter-cultural dialogue and interaction' as one means to counter
the appeal of violent extremism (DIUS, 2008: 11). In more concrete
terms, the proportion of people 'who have meaningful interactions
with people from different backgrounds' is now one of three national
indicators used to measure the cohesiveness of local communities
(CLG, 2008a).[8] Nor is this approach unique to the English urban
context but rather reflects a broader policy trend. Debates over how
best to encourage conflict resolution in areas such as Northern Ireland
have similarly centred on the need to promote contact between
Catholic and Protestant communities (for example, Hewstone et al,
2006). Meanwhile, the European Commission named 2008 the Year
of Intercultural Dialogue and stressed the important role of dialogue
in attempts to 'foster European identity and citizenship'.[9]

It is difficult to imagine how social trust, a shared future vision, sense
of belonging and recognition of the value of ethno-cultural diversity
would be possible were members of different ethnic groups not to
make contact and interact with one another. Linked to this point is
evidence indicative of the potential *negative* effects that arise from

an absence of contact and interaction. Misinformation about other ethnic groups, anxiety over group encounters or a lack of contact may encourage the development of negative attitudes and render citizens increasingly susceptible to exclusionary campaigns. For example, one study of support for the extreme right British National Party (BNP) suggests that, while the party tends to recruit support in districts with large minority ethnic (although particularly Pakistani and Bangladeshi) communities, 'its strength seems to be concentrated in wards where white residents are less likely to encounter members of ethnic minority groups than other whites in their district; i.e., in white enclaves within ethnically diverse cities' (Bowyer, 2008: 617).

While it is crucial not to downplay the importance of surrounding socioeconomic structures there is a large body of research to support the proposition that intergroup contact exerts positive effects (see below). One study finds that citizens who talk regularly to their neighbours are not adversely affected by the racial and ethnic diversity of their surrounding area with the implication being that social ties can help overcome the feeling of being threatened by diversity (Stolle et al, 2008). Analysis of the 2005 Citizenship Survey similarly reveals that having friends from ethnic groups other than one's own is a strong positive predictor of cohesion and that part of the positive effect of diversity is a result of increased proportions of inter-ethnic friendships (Laurence and Heath, 2008: 7). As these authors note, 'increasing diversity leads to more cohesion as the likelihood of inter-ethnic interaction ("mixing") increases and the formation of primary and secondary bonds between different groups develop'. Increased contact, it is suggested, reduces the likelihood of negative perceptions, misinformation and rumours from becoming embedded in the fabric of local communities. More recent findings from the Citizenship Survey (April to June 2008) reveal that 76% of respondents felt they belonged strongly to their neighbourhood, an increase of 6% since 2003 (CLG, 2008b). The proportion of people who agree that their local area is a place where people from different backgrounds get on well together has also risen, from 80% in 2003 and 2005 to 84% in April-June 2008. In terms of reported contact, 82% of respondents mix socially at least once a month with people from different ethnic or religious backgrounds (an increase from 80% in the period 2007-08).[10] Young people are especially more likely to mix socially with people from different backgrounds, with 96% of 16-24 year olds mixing in this way compared with 53% of citizens aged 75 years or over. Based on this data, contact with others from different backgrounds is more likely to take place at the shops (63%), at work, school or college (54%) and in pubs, clubs, cafes or restaurants (47%).[11]

Yet one important aspect that should not be downplayed concerns the quantity and quality of contact and the question of whether more simplistic or superficial forms of contact are being translated into more substantive interactions. While providing some insight into the frequency of contact between members of different groups those findings above actually tell us little about the nature of intergroup contact and the extent to which citizens perceive this to be a positive or negative experience.[12] For instance, compared to those findings above, only 37% of respondents mix socially with individuals from a different background in their or another person's home (CLG, 2008b). This question of the quality of contact is also evident in findings highlighted by the CIC (2007: 110-11). Outside of the workplace and schools only 20% of respondents in one survey experienced daily or weekly social contact with members of other ethnic groups and only 16% experienced contact in their own or another person's home. Though citizens often interacted in schools and the workplace these chance interactions often fell short of more meaningful forms of interaction.

One study that highlights the particular complexities of group contact is Daly's (2007) examination of group interaction in an area of refugee resettlement in the West Midlands. Rather than contemporary forms of belonging superseding traditional bonds the study found instead that individuals often defined themselves and others according to ethnic and cultural bonds. Meanwhile, at the meso-level, community groups and organisations similarly tended to be culturally specific:

> Community relations mainly occurred at a surface level and significant separation was apparent between different cultural groups, not in terms of the 'parallel lives' discussed by Cantle (2005), but more in terms of a superficial harmony and reluctance to tackle issues. (Daly, 2007: 9)

Though new migrants often progressed economically, they mixed little outside of their own ethnic in-group and, though long-term citizens appeared well integrated into mainstream structures, they often remained socially and economically isolated from other residents. In other words, contact 'mainly occurred at an informal, individual and superficial level without leading to meaningful relationships across difference or attitude changes' (Daly, 2007: 6). Like others, Daly linked examples of prejudice and negative stereotypes to the absence of meaningful forms of contact and opportunities to interact:

... the ability to facilitate meaningful inter-group contact and dialogue, address issues and tensions, challenge myths and prejudices, resolve conflict and encourage participation and co-operation towards shared goals were all identified as critical for local cohesion practice. (Daly, 2007: 9-10)[13]

The next section turns to examine the evidence base that underpins the contact approach. The study of contact theory has produced a vast academic literature and, as proponents of community cohesion have noted, the recent emphasis on interaction is based on this specific theoretical tradition (Cantle, 2008: 15).

Contact: a theoretical overview

According to the contact hypothesis, when intergroup contact takes place under certain 'optimal' conditions it can lead to a reduction in prejudice, anxiety and perceptions of ethnic threat while encouraging the development of more favourable attitudes towards different ethnic groups and their members. Research into this proposition and the effects of contact builds on the work of early studies that produced promising results (for example, Stouffer, 1949). For example, following desegregation in the US, Merchant Marine Brophy (1946) found a relationship between the number of voyages white peoples took with black peoples and more positive racial attitudes. Similarly Kephart (1957) found that white police officers who worked alongside black colleagues were less opposed to working alongside black partners, taking orders from black superiors and recruiting black peoples to join their police district. More specifically, however, the contact hypothesis is linked to Allport (1954) who suggested that the positive effects of contact occur under a set of four 'optimal' conditions:

- equal status between groups in the situation;
- cooperation between the groups or the pursuit of common goals;
- the avoidance of competition among the groups;
- the contact 'intervention' is legitimised through institutional support.

In setting out these conditions Allport (1954) sought to challenge the notion that simple encounters between different groups were sufficient to reduce prejudice and improve relations (Nagda et al, 2006: 440).[14] One earlier piece of research supportive of Allport's theorising was an experimental study of racially prejudiced white adults in the American

South who worked alongside black and white co-workers under the specified conditions. Not only did participants report more favourable attitudes towards their black co-workers but they also continued to express lower levels of prejudice several months later (Cook, 1978).[15] Following such studies both the contact hypothesis and the effects of contact-based interventions have received considerable attention (for reviews see Stephan and Stephan, 2001; Tausch et al, 2005; Pettigrew and Tropp, 2006). There is now a large body of research that supports the notion that intergroup contact (particularly when taking place under those optimal conditions) reduces prejudice, perceptions of ethnic threat and feelings of anxiety over interactions with members of other groups (Emerson et al, 2002: 747). Importantly this evidence base also draws on various methodological traditions, such as experimental and longitudinal research. A meta-analysis of over 500 studies demonstrated convincingly that contact-based interventions are an effective tool in the reduction of prejudice (Pettigrew and Tropp, 2006). This research base tells us that contact exerts positive effects by providing information and opportunities to learn about other ethnic groups (for example, Eller and Abrams, 2004), reducing anxiety over encounters with others (for example, Paolini et al, 2004) and depending on the quality and quantity of contact countering perceptions of ethnic threat and competition (for example, Stephan et al, 2000). Evidence also suggests that contact might produce not only positive change in respect to attitudes but also the development of an overarching identity (Pettigrew, 1998) and can exert positive effects in different social contexts. For example, in areas with a history of intergroup conflict such as Northern Ireland, research demonstrates that contact can assume an important role by encouraging trust and forgiveness between Catholics and Protestants with experience of sectarian violence (see Hewstone et al, 2006; Tausch et al, 2007). Alternatively, contact in school settings has been shown to be an effective mechanism for countering negative stereotypes and prejudice. One study investigated the effects of segregated and integrated education on political attitudes and, despite methodological limitations, provides promising evidence that individuals who experience more integrated education hold more favourable attitudes and are more likely to abandon biased views in favour of a more neutral position (Hayes et al, 2007; also Dixon and Rosenbaum, 2004).

Contact and community cohesion

While the contact approach is supported by a large body of evidence, it poses a number of challenges for policy makers and practitioners.

Within contact theory there remain a number of important but as yet largely unresolved questions, most of which are often glossed over in the current discussion over the importance of contact to the development of cohesive local communities. What type of contact should be promoted? In what context should contact-based interventions be implemented? To what extent are interventions evaluated? And to what extent can we expect group contact to result in behaviour change?

In terms of the first, contact theory has devoted considerable effort to investigating the conditions under which contact exerts positive effects as well as the factors that mediate this process (see above for reviews). The general consensus is that intergroup contact exerts particularly powerful effects when it takes place under optimal conditions, namely equal status among the groups involved, cooperation and the pursuit of common goals, an absence of competition and the provision of institutional support. More broadly contact appears particularly constructive when it moves beyond 'initial acquaintanceship' towards the development of closer and longer-term relationships (Pettigrew, 1998: 76). As noted by Nagda (2006: 557), cross-cultural understanding and a reduction in prejudice does not simply emerge 'from working, living, or playing together with people who are different from oneself'. Existing initiatives often gloss over this important distinction between the quantity and quality of contact. Recalling an earlier critique directed towards work in Northern Ireland (Niens et al, 2003), too often studies appear content to note that contact has actually occurred while ignoring the more important questions of how contact was experienced (that is, was it positive or negative?) and whether participants were able to interact about issues that 'really matter'. For example, one recommendation is a nationally sponsored 'community week', which entails a celebration of the history and diversity of local areas and street parties that will 'demonstrate what neighbourhoods and local people have in common' (CIC, 2007). Recognising and supporting ethno-cultural diversity is clearly an important task and may on its own foster greater interest in interaction with others (Tropp and Bianchi, 2006). However, there is also a risk that simplistic or superficial encounters might produce the opposite effects by further entrenching pre-existing negative stereotypes and prejudice (see also Amin, 2002: 969; Vertovec, 2006: 26). If the experience of contact was negative or if contact was superficial and lacked intimacy then attitudes towards other ethnic groups might actually worsen. As noted by Amir (1976: 276), 'Casual contact typically has little or no effect on basic attitude change. When such contact is frequent, it may even reinforce negative attitudes, especially when it occurs between non-equal status groups.' By downplaying or ignoring sensitive and value-laden topics, failing to provide new information or encouraging group contact in unsupported arenas interventions may inadvertently confirm initial suspicions and reinforce feelings of anxiety and ethnic threat. To return to Allport (1954: 276), contact must 'reach below the surface in order to be effective in altering prejudice'.

A second challenge centres on the context in which contact-based interventions take place. Societal, regional and even local contexts may all undermine the likelihood of those key conditions above thereby constraining opportunities for constructive contact. For instance, research in Quebec and Northern Ireland highlights the potential danger of interaction being reduced to constrained discussion that tends to avoid divisive concerns and issues (Taylor et al, 1986 cited in Pettigrew, 1998: 78). Areas where intergroup relations are strained or areas that have a history of intergroup conflict may have to move beyond a one-size-fits-all approach and celebratory initiatives towards developing deeper and more sustained forms of engagement that 'involve more than just talk' (Nagda, 2006: 571). One example is the Good Relations Project in the borough of Burnley in Lancashire, which aims to promote intergroup understanding and respect through facilitated dialogue sessions. These sessions were initially supervised by Mediation Northern Ireland (MNI), an organisation with experience of sectarian conflict in Northern Ireland. This particular programme engages individuals and organisations from across the borough, including for example representatives of the extreme right British National Party (BNP).[16]

A third challenge concerns the need for robust evaluation. In the more general debate over community cohesion, published advice and examples of best practice typically lack rigorous evaluation (Temple and Moran, 2005: 11). Similar questions emerge over the extent to which contact-based interventions and their effects are adequately evaluated. The academic study of contact theory has tended to eschew 'real-world' settings in favour of laboratory experiments. In large part this has been due to the difficulties associated with bringing together an adequate number of people in real life contexts (Niens et al, 2003). Academic studies themselves have also often been weakened by methodological problems. A review of almost one thousand contact-based studies found that few were actually able to speak convincingly to the questions of whether, why and under what conditions contact actually works (Paluck and Green, 2009, forthcoming).[17] Closely linked to this point is the issue of participation. Citizens who are more prejudiced than others will typically avoid contact and interaction with members of other ethnic groups. As a result, though interventions often claim to exert positive effects, it may be that the opposite causal sequence is operating in that more prejudiced citizens are avoiding attempts to bring them into contact with other ethnic groups (Pettigrew, 1998: 69). It is therefore important that interventions overcome selection bias and attempt to engage citizens from all groups and communities.

A final question centres on whether contact can actually result in behaviour change. While numerous studies provide evidence in support of the notion that contact can lead to more positive perceptions, attitudes and emotions, much less is known about the effect of contact on actual behaviour. In short, evidence that demonstrates that contact can affect the behaviour of citizens towards the out-group is sparse or non-existent (Taush and Hewstone, 2008). An important question therefore is whether contact interventions per se are capable of producing behaviour change and, if so, whether such change is longer-term and is able to extend beyond the immediate intervention.

Conclusion

Implicit in much of the recent debate over community cohesion is the assumption that promoting contact between different groups is an important tool in the reduction of intergroup hostility, prejudice and feelings of anxiety over scarce resources. However, and as others observe, much of this debate has tended to focus more on desired outcomes or indicators than on what contact interventions practically entail at local level (Daly, 2007: 14). As detailed above, there is a large body of research to support the basic notion that contact between different groups, when implemented under certain conditions, can exert positive effects. However, within this wider evidence base, there remain important and largely unresolved questions concerning the specific type of contact, the settings in which it takes place, who should be involved, how the effects of contact are evaluated and whether the effects of contact-based interventions are capable of extending beyond attitudes towards changing behaviour. While each of these avenues requires further research, much of the current emphasis on contact, interaction or meaningful interchanges fails to acknowledge the complexities associated with implementing contact-based interventions. Though researchers, policy makers and practitioners have tended to talk past one another there is a clear need to develop a more holistic response in order to strengthen our understanding of intergroup contact and its role in future attempts to encourage the development of cohesive local communities.

Notes

[1] The author would like to express his thanks to the Economic and Social Research Council (Grant ref: PTA-026-27-2117).

[2] For studies that similarly question the effect of diversity on social capital and 'civic' attitudes more generally see, for example, Aizlewood and Pendakur (2005); Anderson and Paskeviciute (2006); Glaeser et al (2000); Leigh (2006).

[3] David Cameron identified 'five barriers of division': extremism; multiculturalism; uncontrolled immigration; poverty; and inequality in education. See Cameron (2007).

[4] 'Wanted: a national culture – multiculturalism is a disaster', Jonathan Sacks, *The Times*, 20 October 2007.

[5] For a similar argument in the British case see Laurence and Heath (2008).

[6] It is important, however, to note evidence that does not support the 'doom-laden view of increasing segregation and the threat of ghettos' (see Simpson, 2007: 423).

[7] The promotion of group contact is one of three ways identified by Rogers and Muir (2007) that the state can attempt to foster cultural and attitudinal change. The other two approaches include: fostering a set of shared values; and encouraging the development of shared civic identities.

[8] The other two indicators are: the percentage of people who believe people from different backgrounds get on well together in their local area; and the percentage of people who feel that they belong to their neighbourhood.

[9] Available online (www.interculturaldialogue2008.eu).

[10] As noted by DCLG (2008b: 9), survey respondents are asked how many times they mix socially with people from different ethnic and religious groups to themselves in different areas of their lives. Mixing socially is defined as 'mixing with people on a personal level by having informal conversations with them at, for example, the shops, your work or a child's school, as well as meeting up with people to socialise'. However, it excludes 'situations where you've interacted with people solely for work or business, for example just to buy something'. This measure of mixing socially was first introduced in 2007-08.

[11] There have been some statistically significant changes in terms of where social interaction occurs between 2007–08 and April–June 2008. Respondents in the latter survey are more likely to mix socially at the shops (+ 4%), in pubs, clubs, cafes and restaurants (+ 4 per cent) but are less likely to interact during formal volunteering (–3%).

[12] On this point though applied more generally to the academic literature see Niens et al (2003).

[13] Furthermore, Daly (2007: 14) notes how there is a 'surprising lack of research focusing on the actual interaction of individuals'.

[14] It is important to note that underneath the broader contact hypothesis are several divergent models. For a summary see Niens et al (2003) or those reviews highlighted in the text.

[15] A more recent example is an experimental study that randomly assigned white teenagers to either racially homogeneous (that is, all white) or heterogeneous camping expedition groups (Green and Wong, 2008). Examining the effects of contact under most of those optimal conditions outlined above (that is, equal status, common goal of survival, authority support), the study found that after one month white teenagers from heterogeneous groups reported significantly less aversion to black people than teenagers from the homogeneous group. It should be noted, however, that the study is limited in that it had a sample size of only 54 students and, reflective of the wider literature on contact theory, did not explore behavioural outcomes.

[16] 'Truth and reconciliation: mediation skills built up during Ulster's sectarian conflict may defuse tension between Asians and whites in English towns', *The Guardian*, 12 December 2007.

[17] It is important to note that the review by Paluck and Green (2009) focuses more on prejudice-reduction strategies in the real world (for example, the workplace) as opposed to the literature on contact. Paluck and Green also review studies that are not specifically contact-based (for example, intercultural training).

References

Aizlewood, A. and Pendakur, R. (2005) 'Ethnicity and social capital in Canada', *Canadian Ethnic Studies*, vol 37, no 2, pp 77–103.

Alesina, A. and Ferrara, E. (2002) 'Who trusts others?', *Journal of Public Economics*, vol 85, no 2, pp 207-34.

Allport, G. (1954) *The nature of prejudice*, Reading, MA: Addison-Wesley.

Amin, A. (2002) 'Ethnicity and the multicultural city: living with diversity', *Environment and Planning*, vol 34, no 6, p 959-80.

Amir, Y. (1976) 'The role of intergroup contact in change of prejudice and ethnic relations', in P.A. Katz (ed) *Towards the elimination of racism*, Oxford: Pergamon Press, pp 245-308.

Anderson, C.J. and Paskeviciute, A. (2006) 'How ethnic and linguistic heterogeneity influence the prospects for civil society: a comparative study of citizenship behaviour', *Journal of Politics*, vol 68, no 4, pp 783-802.

Back, L., Keith, M., Shukra, A. and Solomos, J. (2002) 'New Labour's white heart: politics, multiculturalism, and the return of assimilation', *Political Quarterly*, vol 73, no 40, pp 445-54.

Blunkett, D. (2001) 'Blunkett calls for honest and open debate on citizenship and community' (www.number-10.gov.uk/news.asp?newsID=3255).

Bowyer, B. (2008) 'Local context and extreme right support in England: the British National Party in the 2002 and 2003 local elections', *Electoral Studies*, vol 27, no 2, pp 611-20.

Brophy, I.N. (1946) 'The luxury of anti-Negro prejudice', *Public Opinion Quarterly*, vol 9, no 4, pp 456-66.

Cameron, D. (2007) *Bringing down the barriers to cohesion* (http://conservativehome.blogs.com).

Cantle, T. (2001) *Community cohesion: A report of the independent review team*, London: Home Office.

Cantle, T. (2005) *Community cohesion: A new framework for race and diversity*, Basingstoke: Palgrave Macmillan.

Cantle, T. (2008) 'Parallel lives – the development of community cohesion', in N. Johnson (ed) *Citizenship, cohesion and solidarity*, London: Smith Institute, pp 10-21.

Cheong, P.H., Edwards, R., Goulbourne, H. and Solomos, J. (2007) 'Immigration, social cohesion and social capital: a critical review', *Critical Social Policy*, vol 27, no 1, pp 24-49.

CIC (Department for Communities and Local Government) (2007) *Commission on Integration and Cohesion – Our shared future*, London: CIC.

CLG (Communities and Local Government) (2008a) *Cohesion delivery framework: Overview*, London: CLG.

CLG (2008b) *Citizenship survey: April–June 2008, England*, London: CLG.

CLG (2006) *2005 Citizenship survey: Community cohesion topic report*, London: CLG.

Cook, S.W. (1978) 'Interpersonal and attitudinal outcomes in cooperating interracial groups', *Journal of Research and Development in Education*, vol 12, no 1, pp 97-113.

Costa, D.L. and Kahn, M.E. (2003) 'Civic engagement and community heterogeneity: an economist's perspective', *Perspectives in Politics*, vol 1, no 1, pp 103-11.

Daly, C. (2007) 'Exploring community connections: community cohesion and refugee integration at a local level', *Community Development Journal*, advance accesss (http://cdj.oxfordjournals.org/cgi/content/full/bsm026v1).

DIUS (Department for Innovation, Universities and Skills) (2008) *The role of further education providers in promoting community cohesion, fostering shared values and preventing violent extremism*, London: DIUS.

Dixon, J.C. and Rosenbaum, M.S. (2004) 'Nice to know you? Testing contact, cultural and group threat theories of anti-Black and anti-Hispanic stereotypes', *Social Science Quarterly*, vol 85, no 2, pp 257-80.

Eatwell, R. and Goodwin, M.J. (eds) (2010: forthcoming) *The new extremism in twenty-first century Britain*, London/New York, NY: Routledge.

Eller, A. and Abrams, D. (2004) 'Come together: longitudinal comparisons of Pettigrew's reformulated intergroup contact model and the common ingroup identity model in Anglo-French and Mexican-American contexts', *European Journal of Social Psychology*, vol 34, no 3, pp 1-28.

Emerson, M.O., Kimbro, R.T. and Yancey, G. (2002) 'Contact theory extended: the effects of prior racial contact on current social ties', *Social Science Quarterly*, vol 83, no 3, pp 745-62.

Finney, N. and Simpson, L. (2009) *Sleepwalking to segregation? Challenging myths about race and migration*, Bristol: The Policy Press.

Glaeser, E.L., Laibson, D.I., Scheinkman, J.A. and Soutter, C.L. (2000) 'Measuring trust', *The Quarterly Journal of Economics*, vol 115, no 3, pp 811-46.

Green, D.P. and Wong, J.S. (2008) 'Tolerance and the contact hypothesis: a field experiment', in E. Borgida (ed) *The political psychology of democratic citizenship*, Oxford: Oxford University Press.

Hayes, B.C., McAllister, I. and Dowds, L. (2007) 'Integrated education, intergroup relations and political identities in Northern Ireland', *Social Problems*, vol 54, no 4, pp 454-82.

Hewstone, M., Cairns, E., Voci, A., Hamberger, J. and Niens, U. (2006) 'Intergroup contact, forgiveness and experience of "The Troubles" in Northern Ireland', *Journal of Social Issues*, vol 61, no 1, pp 99-120.

Johnson, N. (2008) 'Introduction: the state of cohesion policy', in N. Johnson (ed) *Citizenship, cohesion and solidarity*, London: The Smith Institute, pp 4-9.

Kephart, W.M. (1957) *Racial factors and urban law enforcement*, Philadelphia, PA: University of Pennsylvania Press.

Laurence, J. and Heath, A. (2008) *Predictors of community cohesion: Multi-level modelling of the 2005 citizenship survey*, London: CLG.

Leigh, A. (2006) 'Trust, inequality and ethnic heterogeneity', *The Economic Record*, vol 82, no 258, pp 268-80.

Letki, N. (2008) 'Does diversity erode social cohesion? Social capital and race in British neighbourhoods', *Political Studies*, vol 56, no 1, pp 99-126.

McLaren, L. and Johnson, M. (2007) 'Resources, group conflict and symbols: explaining anti-immigrant hostility in Britain', *Political Studies*, vol 55, no 4, pp 709-32.

Nagda, B.A. (2006) 'Breaking barriers, crossing boundaries, building bridges: communication processes in intergroup dialogues', *Journal of Social Issues, vol 62,* no 3, pp 553-76.

Nagda, B.A., Tropp, L.R. and Paluck, E.L. (2006) 'Looking back as we look ahead: integrating research, theory and practice on intergroup relations', *Journal of Social Issues*, vol 62, no 3, pp 439-51.

Niens, U., Cairns, E. and Hewstone, M. (2003) 'Contact and conflict in Northern Ireland', in O. Hargie and D. Dickson (eds) *Researching the Troubles: Social science perspectives on the Northern Ireland conflict.* Edinburgh: Mainstream.

Paluck, E.L. and Green, D.P. (2009) 'Prejudice reduction: what do we know? A critical look at evidence from the field and the laboratory', *Annual Review of Psychology*, vol 60, no 3, pp 339-67.

Paolini, S., Hewstone, M., Rubin, M. and Pay, H. (2004) 'Increased group dispersion after exposure to one deviant group member: testing Hamburger's model of member-to-group generalization', *Journal of Experimental Social Psychology*, vol 40, no 5, pp 565-89.

Pettigrew, T.G. (1998) 'Intergroup contact theory', *Annual Review of Psychology*, vol 49, pp 65-85.

Pettigrew, T. and Tropp, L. (2006) 'A meta-analysis test of intergroup contact theory', *Journal of Personality and Social Psychology*, vol 90, no 5, pp 751-83.

Phillips, T. (2005) 'After 7/7: sleepwalking to segregation', speech, 22 September (www.cre.gov.uk)

Putnam, R. (2007) 'E pluribus unum: diversity and community in the twenty-first century. The 2006 Johan Skytte Prize Lecture', *Scandinavian Political Studies*, vol 30, no 2, pp 137-74.

Robinson, D. (2005) 'The search for community cohesion: key themes and dominant concepts of the public policy agenda', *Urban Studies*, vol 42, no 8, pp 1411-27.

Rogers, B. and Muir, R. (2007) *The power of belonging: Identity, citizenship and community cohesion*, London: Institute for Public Policy Research.

Simpson, L. (2007) 'Ghettos of the mind: the empirical behaviour of indices of segregation and diversity', *Journal of the Royal Statistical Society*, vol 170, no 2, pp. 405-24.

Stephan, W.G. and Stephan, C.W. (2001) *Improving intergroup relations*, Thousand Oaks, CA: Sage.

Stephan, W.G., Diaz-Loving, R. and Duran, A. (2000) 'Integrated threat theory and intercultural attitudes: Mexico and the United States', *Journal of Cross-Cultural Psychology*, vol 31, no 2, pp 240-9.

Stolle, D., Soroka, S. and Johnston, R. (2008) 'When does diversity erode trust? Neighbourhood diversity, interpersonal trust and the mediating effect of social interactions', *Political Studies*, vol 56, no 1, pp 57-75.

Stouffer, S.A. (1949) *The American soldier*, Princeton, NJ: Princeton University Press.

Tausch, N., Kenworthy, J.B. and Hewstone, M. (2005) 'Intergroup contact and the improvement of intergroup relations', in M. Fitzduff and C.E. Stout (eds) *Psychological approaches to dealing with conflict and war, Volume Two*, Westport, CT: Praeger, pp 67-108.

Tausch, N. and Hewstone, M. (in press) 'Intergroup contact and prejudice', in J.F. Dovidio, M. Hewstone, P. Glick and V.M. Esses (eds) *Handbook of prejudice, stereotyping and discrimination*, London: Sage.

Tausch, N., Hewstone, M., Kenworthy, J., Cairns, E. and Christ, O. (2007) 'Cross-community contact, perceived status differences and intergroup attitudes in Northern Ireland', *Political Psychology*, vol 28, no 1, pp 53-68.

Taylor, D.M., Dube, L. and Bellerose, J. (1986) 'Intergroup contact in Quebec', in M. Hewstone and R. Brown (eds) *Contact and conflict in intergroup encounters*, Oxford: Blackwell, pp 107-18.

Temple, B. and Moran, R. (2005) *Learning to live together: Developing communities with dispersed refugee people seeking asylum*, York: Joseph Rowntree Foundation.

Tropp, L.R. and Bianchi, R.A. (2006) 'Valuing diversity and interest in intergroup contact', *Journal of Social Issues*, vol 62, no 3, pp 533-51.

Vertovec, S. (2006) *The emergence of super-diversity in Britain* (Compas Working Paper No. 25) (www.compas.ox.ac.uk).

Worley, C. (2005) '"It's not about race. It's about the community": New Labour and "Community Cohesion"', *Critical Social Policy*, vol 25, no 4, pp 483-96.

SEVEN

New migrants, citizenship and local governance: 'Poles' apart?

Leila Thorp

Introduction

'I work, I pay my taxes, I have a right to live here like everybody else.' (Polish migrant woman interviewed by Rageh Omaar for Channel 4 *Dispatches: Immigration: the inconvenient truth*, 21 April 2008)

'Four out of five migrants take more from economy than they put back' (Headline of article by James Slack, *Daily Mail*, 29 August 2006)

The question as to whether new migrants have a right to be engaged in British politics and society on an equal basis has been hotly debated in the media. This chapter moves away from the normative positions behind these headlines to consider ways in which such politics are played out on the ground at the local level. More specifically within the context of this volume, the chapter questions whether Polish migrants (as the largest group of UK new migrants) are included in the renegotiation of citizenship and local governance? The chapter considers this question by exploring to what extent, and on what terms, Polish migrants are invited to the negotiation table. In particular the chapter will consider the way in which the transient existence and limited citizenship of new migrants impacts on the possibilities for their inclusion. As will be discussed, the literature suggests that factors relating to the social and formal status of new migrants place serious restrictions on inclusion in the political and social practices of citizenship. The effects that such factors have on new migrants' inclusion are discussed. In addition to this it is suggested that the dynamics of the governance arrangements and the locality in which new migrants find themselves is significant when considering such effects in relation to the political engagement of new migrants.

The chapter is structured as follows: First, the rationale behind this topic and the debates in the literature around citizenship and local governance as they relate to new migrants are discussed. Next, the contours of the research project will be described, before the final two sections set out both the challenges and opportunities for inclusion in citizenship and local governance engagement that currently exist at the local level.

Globalisation, citizenship and local governance

Policy makers have increasingly recognised the challenges to citizenship that the phenomenon of globalisation presents. Challenges include: the extent and levels of diversity among the population (referred to as super-diversity); greater population movement caused by mass migration and/or churn and the accompanying social dislocation; the fact that people perceive themselves in relation to a range of different identities (multiple identities); and the role of technology in enhancing transnational networks of communication (transnationalism) (CIC, 2007).

For local authorities wishing to engage with their communities, this reality presents new challenges. As Nicola Bacon and Geoff Mulgan, from the Young Foundation note, 'councils can no longer think of a simple division between the minorities and the majority: instead they have no choice but to deal with quite messy differentiated patterns of assimilation, integration and strongly asserted difference' (De Groot and Mason, 2008: 18). Moreover, in particular local circumstances (for instance, of scarce economic resources and lack of familiarity with new migrants), the issues described above can cause heightened insecurity among the host population and potentially harmful schisms (CIC, 2007: 22-33). Thus, government is increasingly asking local authorities to lead on building relations between these populations in order to ensure stability and cohesion.

New migrants, and in particular Polish migrants, have been seen to be at the forefront of these challenges in recent years. Estimating the number of new migrants is notoriously difficult. In 2008, using worker registration statistics, IPPR research (perhaps tellingly entitled *Floodgates or turnstiles?*) found that 665,000 Accession 8 (A8 – The Czech Republic, Estonia, Hungary, Latvia, Lithuania, Poland, Slovakia and Slovenia) and Accession 2 (A2 – Romania and Bulgaria) nationals were resident in the UK, an increase of 550,000 since the borders were opened in 2004 (Pollard et al, 2008). Polish migrants were the biggest nationality within this group and have since become the single largest foreign national group resident in the UK, which represents a significant change to the UK demographic. Although the number of new migrants now entering the UK has started to slow, the IPPR research has estimated that the current stock is likely to remain constant or to fall only slightly in years to come (Pollard et al, 2008). Thus, challenges of citizenship in relation to new migrants are likely to remain for local governance actors for the foreseeable future.

New migrants as locally engaged, cosmopolitan citizens?

Historically, citizenship has been understood as a contract between ruler and ruled within a polity. This delicate balance ensured that the tyranny of rule could not predominate. The contract primarily consisted of rights and duties attached to formal citizen status. However, with the work of T.H. Marshall it was increasingly recognised that formal status alone was not necessarily enough for an individual to be able to enact citizenship rights. Marshall (quoted in Yuval-Davis et al, 2007) extended the notion of citizenship to define it to be: 'full membership in a community with all its rights and obligations'. Marshall's ideas reintroduced Aristotle's concept of 'well-being' to underscore political interest recognition. In order to engage in the general standard of well-being in a community, one must first feel a sense of belonging to a given community in that there should be no barriers to access in terms of discrimination. The limits of the community, its general standard of well-being and what are effectively barriers to access are continually contested as the substantive meaning of citizenship is (re)defined through practices (for an overview of the problems attached to this definition see Prior et al, 1995).

In the era of globalisation, the traditional ideas of citizenship within a polity and how collective interests are recognised both politically and socially are increasingly being challenged. In sociology several authors are concerned with how multiple identities and increasing diversity can be reconciled within a complex society (Hall, 1992; Hall and Du Gay, 1996). A growing number of feminists have been concerned with how group rights and practices can be questioned when oppressive at the same time as being championed when liberating women (Phillips, 2007), while, in politics, some authors have been preoccupied with considering the most appropriate means of political representation for such complexity within a global polity (Held, 1992). Debates have covered a large number of perspectives and literatures, but in general terms it can be said that they have converged on discussing the need for a different form of citizenship that reflects and supports global changes; for many this has been the idea of cosmopolitan citizenship (Beck, 2002). Cosmopolitan citizenship is the idea of a cultural citizenship where individuals are able to imagine, through encountering in dialogue with others, alternative ways of living and rationalising; to incorporate these into their own sense of being. This moves away from the idea of fixed traditions or identities as the basis of self-esteem and social development. Instead globalised identities seem possible and more relevant as a shifting, fluid notion underpinned by basic human values of respect and sociability. Despite the relevance of the global context, however, it is at the local level that many see these identities as best reinforced and politically engaged (Held, 1992). This chapter considers the relevance and effects of this form of identity for local governance and citizenship. The discussion takes place within the broader focus on Marshall's citizenship as inclusion in social and political practices.

Policy and new migrants

The challenges of globalisation and new identities have triggered a number of policy responses relating to 'community cohesion', debates over the nature of Britishness and British values (Goodwin, this volume) and faith group engagement (Chapman, this volume). The 'new migrant' is in many ways a symbolic construct of these debates in the way that they are, more than most, not politically or socially bound within a nation state. This factor was explicitly recognised in the Commission for Integration and Cohesion (CIC) *Our shared future* report of 2007. The CIC was set up by the government to consider how community cohesion could be promoted nationally. At the time, the influx of new migrants was a prevalent concern in the media and for many authorities, and thus became a key consideration for these commissioners (presentation by CIC member, 22 November 2007, Derby Community Safety Partnership). The definition that the commission came up with in terms of community cohesion reflected these concerns as well as reinforcing a cosmopolitan notion of citizenship (see Goodwin, this volume).

The CIC report focuses squarely on the idea of 'shared futures' to include new migrants in a notion of citizenship (in place of shared traditions/pasts). This is described in the policy literature as the development of a locally shared vision to be enacted through participatory dialogue, the benefits of which should be shared out so as to enhance community solidarity and engagement (LGA, 2002; CIC, 2007). In addition to this, general community cohesion policy aims to develop shared values via personal/community development; social inclusion by supporting individual needs and opportunities; and by using myth busting to dispel corrosive social divisions.

However, in policy terms, community cohesion has two dimensions as it specifically relates to new migrants. Alongside an acceptance of new migrants as citizens in terms of participation, there is an obligation on the new migrant to 'integrate' before participation can take place. In this way the commission made a distinction between a phase of integration and cohesion in relation to new migrants. The first phase is incumbent on new migrants learning the political and social norms (such as rules of queuing or rubbish collection procedures), rights and services (health services, employment rules) and language (for communication) of the UK through initiatives like welcome packs (CIC, 2007: 67-75). In addition to this duty on new migrants, community cohesion places on the host population duties of 'hospitality' and 'mutual respect' towards newcomers. According to the report, this underlines the importance of civility to one another, including towards those who 'have strong local attachments or who are strangers locally' (CIC, 2007: 41).

In summary, the policy initiative of community cohesion extends the notion of the community of citizens to include those with very limited formal citizenship rights. The general standard of well-being is being defined as active engagement in forging a shared future of place, through dialogue with others to reach consensus at the local level. Moreover, barriers to a sense of belonging are said to be removed through a basic level of mutual understanding. This is specifically ensured through integration on the part of new migrants and hospitality as respect on the part of the host population, while the other more general community cohesion measures later apply as a second stage to this process.

Critics of the policy of community cohesion find problems with this approach in general terms (see Goodwin, this volume for more details). However, to date, little work has been done to explore the way in which the policy has been played out on the ground in relation to a group such as new migrants (notable exceptions in relation to other groups are McLoughlin, 2005; Thomas, 2006). This chapter goes some way towards addressing this gap.

Furthermore, the chapter asks what the policy mechanisms are through which such engagement is taking place in terms of our understanding of governance? As set out in the government 2006 White Paper (DCLG, 2006), in recent years there has been a move towards increasing community-led initiatives at the neighbourhood level to empower citizens (Durose and Richardson, this volume). At the same time as this, new citizen-centred forms of governance have been put in place, particularly in relation to services (Barnes et al, 2008).

Recent policy suggests that there is a new emphasis on 'place' as opposed to neighbourhood, which has accompanied developments in community cohesion (CIC, 2007). In parallel to this, the idea of place shaping came out of the Lyons Inquiry of 2007 and suggests that local authorities need to take a lead on supporting the active engagement of citizens within a context of increasing diversity. Lyons' (2007) notion of place shaping is proactive, with the local authority acting as a 'convener', which involves being able to: 'identify a direction of travel, articulate a sense of the future, and enthuse others to be part of a common mission' (Lyons, 2007: 5.26). Place shaping in this meaning is about creating a sense of general well-being through the use of opportunities, events and dialogue that Lyons saw as needing to be reflected within governance arrangements such as: local area agreements (LAAs), local strategic partnerships LSPs and community strategies. The idea of the 'well-being' of a place has also been linked to that of social capital in policy documents (ODPM, 2005; CLG, 2007). In this way, places are seen as comprised of fluid networks and cross-boundary relationships, which, through their realisation, generates a sense of commitment to a place and its well-being. The challenge of defining the limits of the local community of citizens in order to promote local autonomy has, however, not been completely removed by the focus on widespread engagement, as will be discussed in later sections. Thus, the IDeA-Solace Foundation has suggested that place shaping, when pursued as a strategy alongside community cohesion, also needs to incorporate a strong equalities dimension in order to ensure full participation (De Groot and Mason, 2008).

It may be too early to consider the full impact of the notion of place shaping on local authority's work in relation to new migrants. But we can ask how it is currently being conducted in terms of citizen mechanisms for engagement and consider the future direction of these developments. The literature concerned with governance developments more widely has raised several questions about the participatory or representational forms of engagement for such governance forms to work (see Barnes et al, 2008). To date, however, there has been little work conducted on how these factors are being played out within the wider context of a policy of community cohesion and new migrants (one notable exception is the work by Blake et al, 2008). This chapter will therefore be able to offer new insights into this particular area of local governance citizen engagement.

Research and methods

The aim of the research was to assess to what extent, and in what way, Polish migrants were included in any renegotiation of governance and citizenship. In particular the research was interested in understanding more about how the transient existence of new migrants and their limited citizenship status impacted on the possibilities for inclusion in local governance.

In order to answer these questions a small-scale research project was undertaken primarily in the spring-summer of 2008 in the East Midlands. This involved six in-depth, qualitative interviews with local governance actors in two authorities, participant observation at two regional events for policy makers and practitioners working with new migrants, and participation at strategy group meetings. During attendance at events and meetings, insights were gained through the collection of ethnographic materials on various initiatives to support other data. Where explicitly referred to in the analysis provided basic information is given, as in the case of interviews. Only where documentary sources were provided explicitly to the researcher, are they included as refernces in the bibliography. The events included presentations and workshops with a range of stakeholders and were of a large scale. A number of secondary sources were used to support the analysis that is provided here. Although the focus here is on Polish migrants, some of the secondary literature considers new migrants more generally.

Challenges to the inclusion of new migrants

As discussed in relation to issues of citizenship and new migrants, there are a number of challenges that are perceived to relate to the status of new migrants. Status here refers to new migrants as global cosmopolitan citizens (with a transient existence) and as limited formal and social citizens. Following a brief discussion of the formal limits of the new A8 migrant status, this section explores these challenges in more detail and draws on a mixture of primary and secondary evidence to consider the extent and way that the contours of a new migrant's citizenship is defined through social practices in relation to the policy aims of community cohesion.

New migrants' citizenship status

When eight countries in Central and Eastern Europe and the Baltics joined the EU in May 2004 the citizenship status and potentially the practices of these populations changed. Citizens of the A8 countries became citizens of the European Union, thus allowing them freedom of movement across the EU. A8 nationals have similar rights to people from other European Economic Area/EU countries but there are restrictions on their rights to work or to apply for benefits. These restrictions have been differentially applied since they do not apply to people from Malta and Cyprus, which also joined the EU in May 2004.

Similarly not all countries in the EU opened up their borders to these countries at the time of their entry into the EU. In need of a low-cost workforce to support a growing economy, at this time Britain was one of the first countries to open its borders to the newest members of the EU (Spencer et al, 2007). However, EU membership was not to be equated with full citizenship rights within the UK. Citizenship was differentiated for these EU countries as opposed to those individuals from other groups in a number of ways. Political rights to a vote were not admissible in national elections, but in local or EU elections this group were allowed to vote. Access to social and economic rights was limited to those who could be considered to benefit the wider UK community in terms of either tax revenues or the prevention of illnesses. These included registration with a GP, obligatory worker national insurance scheme registration (with an initial fee payable for administration costs) and most healthcare costs. At the same time, on entry to the UK, the fulfilment of duties as a legal subject were applicable in the same way as civil rights were bestowed on individuals.

Local authorities were issued with guidance that these new EU citizens were not to be supported by 'public funds', although this issue has remained complex and has been elaborated on in an attempt to clarify the situation (Immigration Directorate Instructions, 2005, part of New Migrants Task Group minutes; Leicester City Council, 2008). Other councils have reported confusion over this (for example, Peterborough – see Flynn and Williams, undated). Even greater confusion exists among the wider population, which is made worse by the proliferation of erroneous media stories (Berkeley et al, 2006). Such complexity has not been helped by the fact that in Britain today there are a range of citizens with differing degrees of rights (even from among the EU member states). What has this differential status between individuals meant for the way in which local authorities relate to new migrants as practising citizens resident in a local area in terms of both group recognition and political engagement? This question will be explored in the subsequent two sections.

Community cohesion and the social inclusion of new migrants

A number of factors present both challenges and opportunities for the inclusion of new migrants in relation to community cohesion. These issues relate to belonging and access to social resources. One benefit of categorising issues in this way is that we begin to see the problems of addressing cosmopolitan citizenship in relation to new migrants separately from addressing equality of access to social resources (Marshall's social citizenship).

The literature on new migrants identifies factors that influence belonging as lifestyle, issue-based politics and a transient existence. The most recent wave of migrants to come from A8 and A2 countries are predominantly young people – those aged 16–39 years made up three quarters of the total of this group in 2007 (Pollard et al, 2008). Markova and Black (2007) found that the factors of age and a transient existence meant that new migrants were more likely to get involved in sports clubs than social clubs. Other leisure activities that this group indulged in include: library use (a third); attending concerts, museums or galleries (a half); use of sports facilities (a third); and visits to pubs or clubs (a quarter) (Spencer et al, 2007). These pastimes appear to support the current focus in community cohesion policies. The policy agenda focuses on engagement with a cross-section of individuals at public events or places by utilising the arts or sport as a way of building individual self-esteem and intergroup engagement.

In spite of this, however, there are issues in relation to the time available to new migrants for leisure activities. They are predominantly working in what has been termed 3D jobs ('dirty, dangerous and difficult'). Within this context they often find themselves isolated in ethnic labour markets (Markova and Black, 2007). The low pay and long working hours associated with these jobs have been found to have a significant social impact beyond the workplace (Spencer et al, 2007). New migrants are unlikely to get involved in voluntary activities because of a lack of free time (Markova and Black, 2007). The same authors highlight the workplace as an area currently lacking in community cohesion initiatives, but within which greater possibilities might be achieved in relation to new migrants.

The cultural legacy of communism means that, for many, participating in organised associations or civic action is disliked and avoided. In contrast to this, however, one study identified a willingness among interviewees to get involved with protest actions where considered appropriate to them (Markova and Black, 2007). This, once more supports an emphasis on looser forms of engagement in a similar mode to that of new social movements, which exist through events, dialogue and opportunities rather than membership of formal organisations.

It is widely considered that new migrants are solely interested in coming to the UK to earn money for a short time. Although this is certainly the case for a number of new migrants, the picture is far more complex. Several research reports find different commitments to staying from the outset and, in addition to this, emphasise a mixture of reasons for coming to the UK (Eade et al, 2007; Spencer et al, 2007; Pollard et al, 2008). It has also been noted how a diaspora's sense of home and belonging is always in transit, shifting and differential (Ryan et al, 2008), thus making it difficult to accurately assess permanent commitment to a place. Markova and Black (2007) have suggested therefore that, where achieving community cohesion is concerned, a focus on shared dialogue in place of relations based on common values and more rooted belonging may be more appropriate in the case of new migrants.

Barriers to social inclusion and integration for new migrants can be felt strongly through limited access to social resources. Language proficiency figures prominently in people's ability to meet those from other backgrounds, to gain access to services and employment, and enforce individual rights, especially at work (Spencer et al, 2007). In addition, those who arrive with poor English are least likely to take classes to improve their language. The reasons for this are the financial costs involved and the lack of access to classes in relation to working hours (Spencer et al, 2007). Promotion of English language classes for new migrants in place of translation services has been at the forefront of government community cohesion policy. The question of resources to provide this service has remained a source of contention, however, with the latest initiatives set on employers taking on this responsibility.

In spite of popular myths that East Europeans stick together in their own cliques, individuals may remain socially isolated when they have little English language (Leicester City Council, 2007; Markova and Black, 2007, Ryan et al, 2008). Reasons include class and social differences (this is particularly marked between the first generation of Polish migrants and the current wave), and competition for jobs (both between and among East European nationalities). Ryan et al (2008) reveal that newly arrived migrants, especially those with limited social, economic and cultural resources, often find themselves dependent on ethnic-specific sources of support. They observe how:

> Informal networks of co-ethnics may be their only route to employment, accommodation, practical assistance such as translation and even companionship. [But] This reliance has to be reconciled with wariness, competition and distrustfulness. (Ryan et al, 2008: 680)

The complexity of cohesion issues among new arrivals, as much as between the host population and new arrivals, is little appreciated. In fact, the policy literature focuses instead on new migrants as a collective group, lumping many individuals together, just as much as any collectivity based on ethnicity.

In the case of new migrants, because of their formal status, they are not entitled to access the majority of social services. So the community cohesion principle of ensuring 'equal access to opportunities' is not realisable. Exceptions to this include most health services and mainstream education for children. The lack of access to housing or job support services, however, has effectively marginalised those who find themselves homeless or jobless for any period of time. In London, one survey found that in one week in March 2006 the number of A8 migrants who accessed support from 43 frontline services (outside that of hostels, to which they were ineligible) was 638 out of 4,356 people and, although in some cases the figures of A8 migrants counted only 5% of those entering the service, in others the figure was greater than 50% (Homeless Link, 2006). Other homelessness charities (Shelter, Red Cross and Scottish Council for Single Homelessness) and academic researchers (Spencer et al, 2007) have argued that the situation is in fact worse than anticipated, as severe overcrowding certainly hides a population of 'hidden homeless' among A8 migrants, which, alongside the very poor housing conditions experienced by many, is similarly marginalising. In addition, difficulties meeting housing costs and finding work mean that a majority of new migrants move at least once in the early stages of their arrival (Markova and Black, 2007), which makes settling into any one place more challenging.

Local governance and place shaping

The research project set out to explore the extent and the way in which Polish migrants were included in any renegotiation of citizenship and local governance. The previous section considered the extent and way in which new migrants are able to be included as citizens in full membership of a community in relation to the policy of community cohesion. Building on that analysis, this section will consider the role of local governance arrangements and the policy of place shaping with new migrants. Local governance actors not only act as convenors (in Lyons' terms) but also engage with new migrants to encourage a general sense of well-being of their localities (place shaping) in a number of ways connected to local governance. They construct their relationship through different, but related terms of debate. Local governance actors also act on the basis of specific rationales as to the role that the new migrant should play in a place in relation to the 'common mission' identified by them. The typology shown in Table 7.1 was inductively developed out of my small-scale research project. The general aim behind the research here was to explore the different patterns of engagement and senses of well-being of place in existence at the local level. In any given time and place a mix of these types will be present. The remainder of this section explores these different role types primarily using interviews drawn from two local authority areas, supported by ethnographic fieldwork data from across the East Midlands. Four local authority convenor roles are identified.

Type A reflects a group-based idea of citizenship as found in social citizenship ideas in place of the individual focus found in cosmopolitan notions. However, when the LA is constructed as a corporatist broker, new migrants are perceived as being able to contribute to the well-being of the place by becoming part of the long-term community interest. This sets up a distinction between the long- and short-term residents of a place. A Leicester policy officer stated, "We thought wouldn't it be nice if they started contributing to life in Leicester, we forgot that young people are just interested in travelling the world and earning a quick buck" (interview 1, Leicester). It is also important to note that it is 'community' not 'place' that is key here. For example in Leicester a policy officer commented:

> 'I can go and speak to someone from Poland, for example, but how do I know they are, whether they are representative of that community or talking as regards to their own perspective, their own needs and aspirations that's the difficulty really ... is knowing who they represent.' (Interview 2, Leicester)

Table 7.1: Construction of place-shaping typology

Construction of place shaping	Type A	Type B	Type C	Type D
Convenor role of local authority in locality	Corporatist broker	Pluralist convenor	Professional welfare administrator	National custodian
Rationale for engagement	Long-term community interest	Future socioeconomic development	Humanitarian vs resources available	General risk-assessment
Terms of debate	Local leader	Local knowledge	Customer vs stranger	Informer/learner
Governance spaces	Strategy groups/LSPs	Neighbourhood places/events/e-governance	Statutory agencies/charities	Neighbourhood/community/e-governance
Mechanism for engagement	New Link, Peterborough: service hub, community development workers	East Midlands Rural Arts, Leics citizens' council forum: regional body uses voluntary organisation contacts/e-forum	Leics adult education professional/housing officer: personal	Mapping, Leics community policing, welcome pack: targeted publicity/beat officer relations

New migrants' contributions are therefore organised on ethnicity group grounds and the exploration and development of these cultures of identity are promoted through community development work, where new migrants are prioritised by councils (see Box 7.1). Through this process, groups gain the capacity and leadership to become empowered to enter into the political process. Local community leaders are then able to feed community interests into strategic bodies such as the LSP, or to other strategy groups. The local authority (LA) therefore acts as a broker between the different political interests represented by community groups in forums. There can, however, be problems with this approach, especially in relation to issues of how representative these mechanisms are, alongside the time involved in developing a strong community base to ensure widespread representation (see Blake et al, 2008: 35). For example, Peterborough City Council is often highlighted for best practice. In spite of the acclaim that this approach has received, though, there is little evidence to suggest that the uptake among new Polish migrants has been significant. The community group has a web presence but there are few postings and the site seems to be little used since the organisation was started in 2006. Initial difficulties with this approach seem to include a lack of resources committed to new migrants in any particular city context (for example, Leicester) and/or engagement problems related to the social issues outlined in the previous section (as discussed in Leicester interviews 1 and 2).

Box 7.1: Corporatist convenor: Peterborough new link initiative

Peterborough has set up a one-stop shop for new migrants to access information and services. One aspect of the service offered is:

[A] project ... run by a community development officer based at the centre. It tackled the need to engage with the new communities in a more holistic way and be less reliant on dealings with community 'gatekeepers', who tended to be those who had resided longest and had the best English. To do this we asked new arrivals if they would be interested in getting together with friends to set up a group. This proved to be incredibly successful and twenty groups have been established from among the different nationalities. Although some participants had taken years to consider getting a group together, others ran with the idea much more quickly. The groups have democratically elected representatives and a new arrival forum has been established where ten of the groups are represented and discussions take place on issues around integration and access to services in Peterborough. Our aim is for this group to feed into the Local Strategic Partnership – the multi-agency forum which brings together the different parts of the public, private, community and voluntary sectors to support one another and work together more effectively. This forum has enabled services to access information and advice on how to best meet the needs of the new migrants. (Leonie McCarthey, New Link, Peterborough, quoted in Flynn and Williams, undated)

Type B in Table 7.1 reflects the cosmopolitan sense of citizenship outlined in earlier sections. The pluralist convenor role of an LA relates most closely to the 'place-shaper' role described in both community cohesion and place-shaping policy documents. New migrants are perceived as part of a 'shared future' and are expected to contribute to well-being on this basis. One senior manager commented:

'[We need to be] proactively trying to get people to come to Leicester and Leicestershire, to come and see the benefits of settling here, of working here and bringing families over and these sorts of things, not to do everything as reaction but to be a lot more proactive.' (Interview 3, Leicestershire County Council)

This 'shared future' is perceived in terms of socioeconomic development, thus effectively excluding those new migrants who are not young, educated and interested in supporting the socioeconomic developmental well-being of a place (interview 3 and field notes from Leicestershire).

The terms of engagement take place in relation to what has been termed as 'local knowledge.' Barnes et al (2008: 4) see local knowledge as where 'individuals (...) provide their views and expertise as people who live in a community, have particular needs or interests, or use specific public services'. In relation to place shaping and governance arrangements the authors identify this mode of engagement as being about 'creating understandings through open, informal and deliberative relationships between citizens and professionals, managers and politicians' (Barnes et al, 2008: 4). It is assumed that this process will benefit all parties.

Deliberative forums, citizens' juries and community conferences are ways of bringing together individuals from a range of relevant publics to discuss and debate their needs and possible policy options'

(Barnes et al, 2008: 5). Such deliberative forums frequently take place at neighbourhood level in public arenas such as: schools, sports centres, streets and so on. The focus is on bringing people together for a practical event, not simply on the bringing together. It is accepted that "the notion of just turning up and knocking on the door and saying please speak to us ... you've got to be realistic that doesn't happen" (interview 3, Leicestershire County Council). The aim is for a wide range of participants to attend and, in order that those from minority ethnic groups are present, these may be targeted within a particular area (see Box 7.2).

Examples of deliberative forums, citizens' juries and community conferences

Citizens' Watch Jury, Leicestershire

'We're going to launch a new group of people or project for two reasons. Firstly people will have the authority, capacity to continue to manage and scrutinise organisations and this needs to happen not just sometimes but 365 days of the year, to help us encourage them when they are doing something right and to advise them when they're doing something wrong ... the second aspect is the community cohesion impact, we want to use members of the Citizens' Watch to help progress getting people together ... We've organised an advert asking people who've got that sort of vision to get in touch, but also we're doing a bit of proactive work to encourage communities who may not apply to do so, so we're going to people like Tad in the Polish community to try and get him to encourage people he knows personally to get in touch with us and other individuals already on the Citizens' Jury are also doing this ... the great thing is that it is a citizens-led initiative.' (Senior manager, Leicestershire County Council)

Culture East Midlands/EMDA Culture in Rural Development Programme

We commissioned research in South Lincs and Boston to understand cultural preferences and barriers to access for rural communities. Building on this understanding we completed a number of projects including: a further consultation and sharing event around food where people gathered at a museum to discuss their memories of food and make recipe cards to swap, etc as a public event.

While in Herefordshire villages we worked with a media company (Rural Media) to engage the local villages in a production that told a story of place (Crafta Webb) and within that interwove individuals' stories so as to promote understanding. This brought together all residents (including new migrants) and supported them in a creative venture, which also gained them skills as well as enhancing relations. (Notes from presentation, Culture East Midlands, Loughborough)

Inclusion within the specific social context may also be achieved through working on particular barriers to entry. Leicestershire County Council is considering a fund to support those with specific skills to gain better access to housing and jobs on their initial arrival (A8 migrant group e-notices, 2008). Regional bodies have supported training services for those wishing to start new businesses from among the new migrant population (A8 migrant group e-notices, 2008) and the County has produced a welcome pack where the focus is on providing useful information in order to be able to navigate oneself effectively within a new social and political context. Those in charge commented, "The welcome pack [is] based on the holiday camp sort of thing, you know like when you go to a holiday camp and you get a pack that tells you where the doctors and all that sort of thing is and also based on the fact that the new communities have been producing these sort of packs themselves, and so you think it's a good idea" (interview 3, Leicestershire County Council). This stands in contrast to welcome packs produced elsewhere, where the rationale is one of control and enforcement rather than rights and empowerment.

Type C in Table 7.1 represents a challenge to the narrow legal definition of citizenship described in relation to new migrants' status. This is highlighted as a professional welfare adminstrator role for the LA in place shaping. Two conflicting notions of general well-being are in operation. The first is a humanitarian sense of welfare as a universal right. In this way professionals find it impossible to turn away new migrants who are homeless, or to ignore the pleas for access to English language classes made by a new migrant without language skills who is unemployed. In such cases individuals may be directed to agencies for support (see Box 7.3) or helped by finding discretionary funds to repatriate them or allow access to classes (interview 4, Leicester and event Boston).

Box 7.3: Professional welfare administrator

Housing officer, Leicester:
'Last year I found a young lad sleeping rough outside the council offices. Others had just left him there on their way to work ... but I couldn't see him like that ... I found him a temporary place to stay and then managed to organise the funds to get him a return ticket home ... after that I don't know what happened to him there, we didn't have any contacts to find out, but at least he was at home there hopefully with family and friends around for support and he could speak the language.' (Interview 5, Boston, 2008)

Education officer, Leicester:
'As far as homelessness goes, I've only been able to find them alternative accommodation, or in one case the landlord seemed to be at fault – the landlord had removed the person's possessions and locked the place, that was tied up with a deal that was tied up with the employment situation, so I referred that to the job service partnership. When I was doing this more, I felt I was offering friendly moral support more than any specific entitlements that they might have and that the main short-term objective was to try and get them employment so that they could pay for accommodation and get out of the trap they were in.' (Interview 4, 2008)

Education support officer, Lincolnshire:
'When I have a child who is a high achiever and wants to learn I can't tell them that they have no right to an education!' (Workshop, Boston, 2008)

This role shares an aspect of the cosmopolitan model in that it has at its core, universal human values. However, these are constantly in tension with the national political interest and so, in many cases, the best the professional can do is to remove 'the problem' elsewhere – this equates to a displacement of citizenship responsibility on human terms. The national interest manifests itself in the narrow definition of citizenship that is present in legislative restrictions to access services:

'... up until last September ESOL [English for speakers of other languages] was generally speaking free to residents, then there was quite a messy introduction of fees with the government changing position a number of times, so this meant right up until September the guidelines for this were very confusing and I would say that the motive behind that introduction of fees was the migrant worker. It was an attempt to redirect funding to what was seen as the settled communities, rather than the migrant worker pick up free ESOL.' (Interview 4, education officer, Leicester)

Some consider there to be an additional effect on the relationship between new migrant and local officer under these circumstances. It has been felt that any real sense of solidarity with the individual is denied through the emphasis on such a purely reactive, distant relationship. One Polish homelessness NGO working in the UK (notes from Barka NGO interview, 2007) argues that the professional–organisational approach towards the distribution of services in the UK is not well suited to the needs of the East European migrant because it is not proactive or fraternal. Currently, in their experience, new migrants are related to as 'customers', whereby strict 'boundaries' are created and maintained between the service providers and their clients.

The final type of local governance role with new migrants (Type D) is that of a national custodian. This reflects a narrow idea of citizens where they are seen as having responsibilities in terms of duties and laws, and only limited rights. In this sense engagement with new migrants occurs in relation to a general risk assessment, when they are considered to be of potential threat to general well-being. At the current time, within the context of concerns over Muslim terrorism, a consideration of potential areas of threat is constantly demanded.

The police make a direct link between the preventing violent extremism (PVE) strand of work and their increasing work with new migrants. In relation to direct work around the policy of community cohesion alone this type of work with new migrants was not a priority (interview 6 with senior police officer, Leicester).

The risk-based rationale is apparent in the following discussion of the link between PVE and new migrants:

'Around preventing violent extremism that's the other massive challenge for us because they are linked, there are quite strong links there because if we don't know the communities we've got then that actually is a weakness that those that want to try and forge violent extremism forwards, that's a weakness, that's a chink in the armour that they can get into and we want to be strong enough I suppose, and when I say we, that's across the board to all agencies, we need to have strong enough links with those communities that anybody else who wants to get, for less noble reasons, can't get an 'in' because the link is strong enough already ... We need to provide them with a strong base because if we don't and they feel vulnerable then they'll go to somebody who's offering a way out of feeling vulnerable.' (Senior police officer, Leicester)

The majority of initiatives within this area focus on mapping (see Box 7.4), soft-intelligence gathering or informing citizens about their duties to maintain the general well-being. For example, the police see their role in relation to three aspects: 'tracking where individuals are' and gaining a sense of when a community is forming in a place; targeting the community with information about British police culture and the rules of where they find themselves; and gaining the trust of the community to be able to learn when there are problems and deal with them (paraphrased from interview 6 with senior police officer, Leicester).

Box 7.4: Mapping initiatives

'We need a method to identify people coming in and the issue is it needs to be at quite a local level, but the issue being that you need to track the people from the moment they arrive because whilst you've not got an auditable trail of being able to keep track of the people as soon as there is a break in the chain then you can lose them for ever and never find them ... whilst it's not important on a national level to know everyone that's coming into the country it's important on a local level, so we've got a workable local solution when they come into the city ...

'What we've started to do is we've started to identify what communities we've got and we've tried to use the same sort of methods and IT solutions that all the major industries and supermarkets use out there to actually hotspot all of our communities and that work is going on at the minute.' (Senior police officer, Leicester)

Risk assessment occurs not only in terms of the police. As suggested in previous types, a weighing of the position of new migrants vis-à-vis a threat to the national citizen interest is also taking place in relation to services and additional allocation of resources. One county councillor commented at a workshop on community cohesion and new migrants that these people were only here for a short time, so he didn't think councils should bother about them, as they've no sooner done that and they go back (paraphrased from workshop in Boston, June 2008). At the same workshop, one group when asked to consider strategies for new migrants to gain a sense of 'belonging' debated whether this was something that should first be considered in relation to new migrants and whether in fact helping to make people feel proud of their area should be something that was important first for the host population. In establishing this sense of pride, things like making sure whether those around them spoke English in the street was considered to be a priority (paraphrased from workshop in Boston, June 2008).

Within type D, the individual or group is educated either through a broad-brush approach in schools and community settings or through the use of targeted leafleting or internet information sites. In addition to this, individuals are approached informally for information as to the culture and tensions that are present in their community. In this way community police officers are able to build relations so as to pre-empt any problems occurring. Community police officers are often where possible selected from the particular ethnic group in order to build such relations (paraphrased from interview 6 with senior police officer, Leicester). The identity of new migrants as outsiders here is therefore seen within this framework to be fixed and 'other'. Citizenship is focused on controlling the alien culture here rather than really engaging with new migrants in an equal dialogue.

Conclusion

This chapter considered to what extent and in what way new migrants (and Polish migrants in particular) were a part of both formal citizenship and informal social and political citizenship practices at the present time in the UK. The challenges to informal citizenship as it relates to new migrants were highlighted around cosmopolitan transient identities and a status conferring partial rights differential to others within the wider population.

Local authorities are just beginning to grapple with the challenge of engaging with new migrants as citizens, which is found to be particularly tough given the social status and identity of new migrants. In spite of this, though, the policy of community cohesion would seem to relate quite well to the inclusion of new migrants.

However, both in different places and in the same place, in relation to different areas of governance, it was suggested that the inclusion of new migrants is played out differently. This chapter identified four types of local governance role in relation to the definition of well-being of a place and the new migrants within it. These types all drew the boundaries of inclusion and the exclusion of new migrants in slightly different ways but the common theme throughout was the predominance of new migrants' position vis-à-vis the majority settled population. The position of new migrants in this relationship represents what Yuval-Davis et al (2007) refer to as 'the situated politics of belonging'. This is to say that, in relation to citizenship, there is a weighting of duties as opposed to rights being placed on the new migrant as opposed to the wider population. This does not appear to be simply an initial phase of integration either, but an ongoing, status-related allocated role. Such duties are framed by a variety of notions of 'common mission' or more precisely ideas of general well-being. So, as recognised at the outset of this chapter, policy makers are excluding certain new migrants from participating in the detailed definition and realisation of the mission. The ways in which such exclusion operates at the level of policy implementation include a lack of resource allocation to, or promotion of, policy to engage with new migrants in order to overcome the challenges related to their status. Or exclusion occurs through the shaping of governance spaces in such a way as to engage a certain type of new migrant at the expense of others.

Promoting an active equalities policy towards new migrants (as suggested by De Groot and Mason, 2008) might be one way of countering some of the negative effects found in relation to citizenship inclusion for new migrants. However, the research shows that such policies will need to be considered differently in a range of local contexts and across a range of policy areas and governance spaces in order to be fully successful. Further research is required to explore in more detail the diverse contexts of place and policy implementation that surround the inclusion and exclusion of new migrants.

References

Barnes, M., Skelcher, C., Beirens, H., Dalziel, R., Jeffares, S. and Wilson, L. (2008) *Designing citizen-centred governance*, York: Joseph Rowntree Foundation.

Berkeley, R., Khan, O. and Ambikaipakur, M. (2006) *What's new about new immigrants in twenty-first century Britain?*, York: Joseph Rowntree Foundation.

Beck, U. (2002) 'The cosmopolitan society and its enemies', *Theory, Culture and Society*, vol 19, nos 1-2, pp 17-44.

Blake, G., Diamond, J., Foot, J., Gidley, B., Mayo, M., Shukra, K. and Yarnit, M. (2008) *Community engagement and community cohesion*, York: Joseph Rowntree Foundation.

CIC (Commission for Integration and Cohesion) (2007) *Our shared future*, London: CIC (www.integrationandcohesion.org.uk).

CLG (Communities and Local Government) (2007) *Place matters*, London: CLG.

DCLG (Deparment of Communities and Local Government) (2006) *Strong and prosperous communities*, The Local Government White Paper (Oct) Norwich: Crown Copyright.

De Groot, L. and Mason, A. (eds) (2008) *How equality shapes place: Diversity and localism*, London: IDeA-Solace.

Eade, J., Drinkwater, S. and Garapich, M. (2007) *Class and ethnicity – Polish migrants in London* (Full Research Report ESRC End of Award RES-000-22-1294), Swindon: ESRC.

Flynn, D. and Williams, Z. (eds) (undated) *Towards a progressive immigration policy*, London: Compas (www.compassonline.org.uk).

Hall, S. (1992) 'The question of cultural identity', in S. Hall, D. Held and T. McGrew (eds) *Modernity and its futures*, Cambridge, Polity Press/OUP, pp 273-26.

Hall, S. and Du Gay, P. (eds) (1996) *Questions of cultural identity*, London: Sage.

Held, D. (1992) 'Liberalism, Marxism and democracy', in *Modernity and its futures*, Cambridge: Polity Press/OUP, pp 13-60.

Homeless Link (2006) *A8 nationals in London homelessness services – Executive summary*, London: Homeless Link.

Kleinman, M. (2008) Presentation at 'Sharing best practice in evolving new communities in the East Midlands' conference, Boston, Lincs, 28 June.

Leicester City Council (2007) Reports on A8 migrant workers, Community Cohesion Project Team, March and April.

Leicester City Council (2008) New Migrants' Task Group minutes of meetings, January–September.

Local Government Association (LGA) (2002) *Guidance on community cohesion*, London: LGA.

Lyons, M. (2007) *The Lyons Inquiry into Local Government*, London: The Stationery Office.

McLoughlin, S. (2005) 'Mosques and the public space: conflict and co-operation in Bradford', *Journal of Ethnic and Migration Studies*, vol 31, no 6, pp 1045-66.

Markova, E. and Black, R. (2007) *East European immigration and community cohesion*, York: JRF.

ODPM (Office of the Deputy Prime Minister) (2005) *Vibrant local leadership*, London: ODPM/Local Vision.

Phillips, A. (2007) *Multiculturalism without culture*, Woodstock, NJ: Princeton University Press.

Pollard, N., Latorre, M. and Sriskandarajah, D. (2008) *Floodgates or turnstiles? Post-EU enlargement migration flows to (and from) the UK*, London: IPPR.

Prior, D., Stewart, J. and Walsh, K. (1995) *Citizenship: Rights, community and participation*, London: Pitman Publishing.

Ryan, L., Sales, R., Tilki, M. and Siara, B. (2008) 'Social networks, social support and social capital: the experiences of recent Polish migrants in London', *Sociology*, vol 42, no 4, pp 672-90.

SCSH (Scottish Council for Single Homelessness) (2006) *Homeless A8 migrants – The Scottish experience* (research paper summary report), Edinburgh: SCH.

Spencer, S., Ruhs, M., Anderson, B. and Rogaly, B. (2007) *Migrants' lives beyond the workplace: The experiences of Central and East Europeans in the UK*, York: Joseph Rowntree Foundation.

Thomas, P. (2006) 'The impact of "community cohesion": a case study from Oldham', *Youth and Policy*, vol 93, autumn, pp 41-60.

Yuval-Davis, N., Kannabiran, K. and Vieten, U. (eds) (2007) *The situated politics of belonging*, London: Sage.

EIGHT

Citizens of faith in governance: opportunities, rationales and challenges

Rachael Chapman

Introduction

Debates about the role and place of faith in the public realm are re-emerging in light of contestation surrounding the decline of religion predicted by secularisation theses. Indeed there is evidence suggesting that the interface between the state and citizens of faith and their communities is changing and that faith groups are gaining increased influence and prominence in the public domain within, what has been termed, the post-secular society (Habermas, 2006). As part of this, new opportunities for faith participation in the public realm have emerged, particularly from the early 1990s onwards. These include representation on partnership bodies, consultations and the provision by faith-based organisations of state-funded welfare services and programmes aimed at facilitating community cohesion. Such opportunities have emerged in the context of broader UK government agendas towards partnership, democratic renewal and community empowerment. This, together with concerns over polarisation and religious extremism, led the government to declare an intention to work more closely with faith communities and citizens to facilitate community cohesion, active citizenship and good governance, as well as help prevent violent extremism.

This chapter explores the extent to which there has been a renegotiation of state–faith relations in Britain from the early 1990s onwards and discusses the implications and impact of this for local governance structures, processes and actors. The chapter begins with an overview of faith diversity and secularism in Britain, following which new opportunities for faith engagement in local governance are identified. It then explores the implications and impact of this for local governance processes and actors. In doing so, it discusses the rationales, opportunities and challenges surrounding faith engagement, focusing in particular on issues of power and citizenship. The discussion draws on available evidence from primary and secondary sources, including 44 interviews undertaken between 2005 and 2008 with various actors. These include: national faith leaders and civil servants in the Home Office and the Department of Communities and Local Government (CLG); faith leaders and activists from Christian, Muslim, Hindu, Sikh, Jain, Jewish and Bahá'í communities; members of faith-based organisations; and representatives from the wider voluntary and community sector and statutory bodies, including the local authority and constabulary in Leicester.[1] The chapter concludes by arguing that a renegotiation of state–faith relationships from the 1990s onwards has opened up new opportunities for actors involved in, and affected by, local governance. Through their engagement, faith groups and citizens have increasingly informed and contributed to public policies and service delivery, which has helped facilitate greater policy effectiveness and responsiveness, as well as enhance democratic participation by widening representation and accountability. However, a range of challenges still need to be addressed if such opportunities are to be fully taken up and benefited from.

New opportunities for faith participation

The nature and degree of 'secularism' and multiculturalism creates a unique context in Britain. The UK as a whole is recognised as having a greater degree of diversity of world religions than any other country of the European Union (EU), with this diversity being a strongly visible part of public life (Weller et al, 2007: 21). Christianity remains the predominant religion, with Muslims forming the next largest religious group. There are also relatively large groupings of Hindus, Sikhs and Jews, together with smaller numbers of Buddhists, Bahá'ís, Jains and Zoroastrians (Weller et al, 2007: 21). According to the 2001 population census (National Statistics 2003), 72% of people affiliate themselves with the Christian tradition and a further 5% to a non-Christian denomination (over half of which are Muslims). People of no religion make up 15% of the population. Religious diversity is greatest within some cities (for example, London and Leicester), metropolitan boroughs and towns (Weller et al, 2007: 29). In Leicester, 45% of people identified themselves as Christian, 15% as Hindu, 11% as Muslim and 17% as having no religion (Dinham and Lowndes, 2008: 3).

As with other countries, the role and relationship between the state and faith groups in Britain is complex and has changed over time. Following the Reformation in the 16th century, the Church of England played a central role in exercising social control and in providing education, health and social care. The role of the state was seen to be minimal and regulatory (Taylor, 2004). By the 20th century, the balance shifted towards a more secular welfare state whereby religious organisations became more subordinate and the state played an increasing role as a regulator, funder and then provider. This trend cumulated in the 1940s in the establishment of a comprehensive welfare state, in which the state took major responsibility for welfare. While Christianity no longer had such a central role in shaping political and social policy (Momen, 1999: 480) it continued to have an input in politics through the Church of England bishops' role as lawmakers in the House of Lords and through dialogue between ministers and faith organisations, leaders and citizens on the development of policies and legislation. This, together with the continued significance of faith-based social action and religious affiliation remaining at about three quarters of the population, has contributed to contestation surrounding the decline of religion predicted by secularisation theses.[2]

Added to this complexity is the increasing prominence of religion in public policy discourse and practice from the 1990s onwards. As Smith (2004: 185) notes, religion in the UK has moved up the political agenda and official discourse and policy initiatives structured around the notion of 'faith communities' have emerged. This has opened up new opportunities for faith organisations and citizens to engage in the policy process, through:

- direct engagement and representation of faith communities on strategic and delivery partnerships;
- wider consultations with faith communities by statutory authorities;
- increased partnership with faith groups in delivering public-funded welfare services and initiatives aimed at enhancing social inclusion, community cohesion and preventing violent extremism.

At the local level, direct engagement and representation of faith communities on partnerships has taken place most notably on local strategic partnerships (LSPs). These bodies are required to make specific efforts to involve and consult with faith communities, including in the development of strategic plans such as community strategies and local area agreements (Geddes et al, 2007). A survey in 2004 found that faith representatives were involved in 71% of LSPs and were part of the core membership in 46% of them (ODPM, 2005). Statutory authorities have also been encouraged to engage faith communities in developing local compacts,[3] and to consult with them on various policy issues, including education, community cohesion and the prevention of violent extremism. This has taken place through: standing advisory councils on religious education, which are locally representative faith bodies with a remit to support religious education and collective worship in schools (including on an interfaith basis); local interfaith forums; and neighbourhood-level governance structures and initiatives.

Increased partnership between the state and faith groups is also taking place at the local level through publicly funded welfare services and policy initiatives aimed at enhancing social inclusion, community cohesion and preventing violent extremism. Faith communities are seen by government to 'play an essential role, alongside others, in building cohesion by promoting and supporting a society based on mutual respect and an understanding between people of all faiths and none' (CLG, 2007: 12). The concept of community cohesion came out of an inquiry led by Ted Cantle into the disturbances in a number of British northern towns in 2001, which were perceived to have occurred largely as a result of people living 'parallel lives' (Community Cohesion Panel, 2004). In its most basic terms, the concept refers to supportive communities where everyone feels at home and sticks together regardless of pressures – for example, economic inequalities, ethnic, racial, faith and political (Commission on Integration and Cohesion, 2007). Community cohesion has subsequently developed as a practice-based policy agenda around which the negotiation of individual identity and a local sense of attachment can take place (Lowndes and Thorp, 2008). It is a pre-emptive policy agenda that aims to prevent violence or political unrest before it happens by challenging 'unsociable' attitudes and tackling tensions associated with super-diversity, perceptions of unfairness over public allocation of resources and multiple identities that can lead to individual isolation or prejudice towards others (Lowndes and Thorp, 2008).

To aid the delivery of this policy agenda, the government established the Faith Communities Capacity Building Fund (FCCBF), a £13.8 million grant programme running between 2006 and 2008 to support faith, interfaith and non-faith based groups to build capacity around community cohesion, develop interfaith programmes and promote faith participation in civil society. Similarly, Faiths in Action, a £4 million government grants programme to run between 2009 and 2011, has been set up to promote understanding, dialogue and the development of strong and sustainable partnerships. The fund is open to faith, interfaith and voluntary and community sector organisations, and was set up to support the delivery of the government's strategy: *Face to face and side by side: A framework for partnership in our multi faith society* (CLG, 2008a). Projects funded by the programme are required to address one of the following four priorities set out in the framework:

- developing the confidence and skills to 'bridge' and 'link';
- supporting shared spaces for interaction and social action;
- developing structures and processes that support dialogue and social action;
- improving opportunities for learning that build understanding.

Examples of the types of projects supported by these funds can be seen in Box 8.1.

Box 8.1: Projects undertaken by faith-based organisations in relation to community cohesion

Sikh Community and Youth Service, Nottingham

The Sikh Community and Youth Service in Nottingham received a grant from the FCCBF to 'improve the capacity of the Sikh Community to engage with local authorities, inform future policy decisions and play a fuller part in their local community' (CLG, 2008a: 38). The project achieved this through a number of community events, which facilitated engagement with schools, local businesses and existing community networks. This included a conference event for the public, voluntary and business sectors to discuss how to make diversity work (CLG, 2008a: 38).

Active Faith Commmunities Programme, West Yorkshire

The Active Faith Communities Programme was established in 2002. It aims to build the capacity of faith communities to develop and enhance lives in their neighbourhoods through offering advice, support, mentoring, workshop events and networking opportunities. It received a grant from the FCCBF to run a mentoring project that provided capacity-building workshops and ongoing support to smaller faith-based organisations across West Yorkshire (CLG, 2008a: 83).

Funding has also been administered to Muslim community organisations to develop skills and training projects targeted at marginalised Muslim women and young men as part of the preventing violent extremism strategy. Local forums against extremism and Islamophobia have also been established to encourage grassroots resistance to messages of violent extremism and build relationships between key local partners (CLG, 2008b: 7). These forums are intended to provide a safe space for discussion, feed into local policy making and take forward projects for tackling extremism. Membership of the forums varies in different areas. In Derby, they include representatives from Muslim communities, local authorities and other local partners – for example, the police. The government has also funded the development of community leadership training to support the skills development of Muslim and other faith leaders (see CLG, 2009). Research by Lowndes and Thorp (2008) identifies a range of projects addressing these agendas in the East Midlands region, of which two examples are given in Box 8.2.

Box 8.2: Projects undertaken by faith-based organisations in relation to the prevention of violent extremism agenda

Youth Awards, Leicester

This was a prestigious event at which awards were given to celebrate the positive contributions of young Muslims and community leaders working with young people across the city and county. The event was attended by approximately 800 guests. It was filmed by the BBC and winners received local newspaper coverage. Leicester City Council, through the Mainstreaming Moderation Forum, supported the event since it met with preventing violent extremism aims to: provide positive role models; encourage engagement in volunteering and community activities; build confidence and self-esteem in young people; and combat Islamophobia (Lowndes and Thorp, 2008).

Muslim Women's Empowerment events, East Midlands

The organisation held a number of events, including a conference, open days at an education centre and a multicultural day aimed at engaging and empowering local Muslim women. The events sought to: promote specialist services that cater for the needs of Muslim women; encourage learning about and across diverse cultures and religions; provide opportunities for socialising and Islam education and discussion; and encourage participation in volunteer work and community issues (Lowndes and Thorp, 2008).

As can be seen, state–faith relations have undergone a renegotiation in which faith communities and citizens have been prescribed and have taken up key roles in the development and delivery of local policies, initiatives and governance arrangements. This reflects New Labour's concept of citizenship in which more active and direct forms of engagement from a wider array of groups are being encouraged. The next section explores the implications of these developments for local governance processes and actors in order to better understand the opportunities, rationales and challenges associated with this renegotiation.

Implications of faith engagement for local governance

Opportunities and rationales

Policy rationales for engaging citizens of faith in governance are often unclear. As Dinham and Lowndes (2008: 6) state, 'rationales for faith group involvement have rarely been spelled out; they have been implicit, sometimes contradictory, and often downright opportunistic'. Perhaps reflecting this is the lack of clarity over the role citizens of faith are expected to play in governance arrangements, as has been the case on LSPs, for example (see Escott and Logan, 2006: 6). This lack of clarity led Lowndes and Chapman (2005, 2007) to develop a model identifying three broad rationales for faith engagement. The first, normative rationale, relates to community values and identities, linked to both their spiritual capital and enduring presence within communities. Spiritual capital is defined by Baker and Skinner (2006) as the motivating basis of faith, belief and values that shape the concrete actions of faith communities and citizens. It can provide a theological identity, worshiping tradition, value system and moral vision that underpins religious capital – that is, the concrete actions and resources that faith communities contribute (Baker, 2009). The second rationale – resources – focuses on the resource capacity of faith groups and citizens that form the basis of action and societal contribution. Resources can include: human capital (for example, staff, volunteers, faith leaders, members), social capital (for example, networks of trust and reciprocity), physical capital (for example, buildings) and financial capital (for example, donations and fundraising income). The third rationale – governance – highlights the representative and leadership role of faith groups and citizens both within their communities and within broader networks and partnerships through, for example, direct participation on LSPs.

The importance of each of the above rationales is recognised by policy makers, practitioners and faith communities alike. However, Lowndes and Chapman's (2005, 2007) study and further analysis by Dinham and Lowndes (2008) indicate that these actors understand faith engagement differently and place varying degrees of significance and meaning to the different rationales. National policy maker narratives, for example, tend to emphasise the resources rationale; faith actors, the normative rationale; and local stakeholders, the governance rationale. According to Dinham and Lowndes (2008: 13) the 'resources' narrative of policy makers tends to be instrumental in the sense that it sees faith communities as 'repositories' of resources for addressing issues of public significance, including urban governance in general and the more specific issues of community cohesion and the prevention of religious extremism. This reflects a perception among policy makers of untapped resources in relation to community leadership, representation, knowledge and assets. Policy guidance, for example, recognises faith groups as:

> ... a particularly important method of delivering mainstream services in a culturally sensitive way. Or in more informal ways ... a valuable form of community self-help, through working with the young, older people, lunch clubs or drop in advice centres. (LGA, 2002: 21)

More recent policy statements identify existing and potential social capital resources of faith communities as significant in promoting better and shared understanding between people of different backgrounds, a key aim of the government's community cohesion agenda (CLG, 2008a; see also JRF, 2006). In particular, emphasis is placed on the importance of 'bridging' and 'linking' social capital and on the role of interfaith activities for developing a broader trust network within CLG's *Face to face and side by side* framework for multi-faith partnership published in July 2008 (CLG, 2008a). Faith groups themselves have also acknowledged tendencies towards an instrumental resource-based rationale within policy narratives. As a report by the Commission on Urban Life and Faith (CULF) states:

> From a governmental point of view, the social capital and, specifically, the faithful capital[4] offered by Christian churches and other faith organisations can be seen as both a valuable resource and as a source of discomfiture. Commitment to neighbourhood, long-term presence, strong value base, important community facilities, bridging inter-faith networks – they all offer paths to the grails of 'community cohesion' and urban 'regeneration'. (CULF, 2006: 3)

As Dinham and Lowndes (2008) suggest, this instrumental resource-based rationale of policy makers contrasts with faith actor narratives, in which spiritual capital is emphasised most strongly. In this case, the faith community is seen:

> ... primarily as a place of belief, worship, and fellowship rather than as a repository of resources for the pursuit of policy goals ... their goals are highly variable and derive from the primary fact of being in or of a faith community rather than being policy or socially orientated. (Dinham and Lowndes, 2008: 18)

This religious focus of faith communities and citizens can challenge policy makers and practitioners by vocalising explicit debates about values (for example, around social justice) that are sometimes contrary to those pursued in the more secular public service ethos that entail, for example, competitive market-orientated and short-term performance-driven approaches.

While faith actors and citizens are likely to emphasise spiritual capital as a key motivating force for action, they may also take part in governance in order to secure additional resources (for example, public funding) and political influence. This may in turn assist them in ensuring community needs are met as well as helping them pursue broader social action goals. When asked why faith groups would want to engage in local governance, a trustee of a Jain organisation based in Leicester stated that it is probably because they "know the needs of their membership much better than anyone else". According to one report (Escott and Logan, 2006: 7) membership of LSPs allowed faith representatives to:

- represent particular views and issues of concern to faith communities;
- act as an advocate on behalf of those who are marginalised and who lack a voice;
- ensure that the practical contribution of local faith communities is identified in the formulation and delivery of policy;
- raise issues, give views and make decisions on the basis of their own personal and professional competence, experience and interest.

Another report (Berkeley et al, 2006: 9) found that almost all faith respondents felt that the issues discussed in public partnerships were relevant and important to their local area, indicating that there is something to gain from their participation.

So far, this chapter has outlined various opportunities and rationales for faith engagement from the perspectives of policy makers, practitioners and faith groups. Taken together, faith engagement offers opportunities for faith groups and citizens to inform and contribute to more effective and responsive policies, services, strategies and social action, as well as enhance democratic participation by widening citizen engagement, representation and accountability. This carries with it the potential for enhancing community well-being as well as reducing the isolation of some faith communities and countering the trend towards religious extremism that such isolation can foster (Finneron, 2007). However, achieving these ends and building trust among faith communities that their involvement is worthwhile also implies the need for faith engagement to be empowering as opposed to tokenistic. Empowering communities is a key government agenda as outlined in the *Communities in Control White Paper* (CLG, 2008c). This defines empowerment as a process of 'helping citizens and communities to acquire the confidence, skills and power to enable them to shape and influence their local place and services' (CLG, 2008d: 5).

The next section discusses the extent to which faith groups and citizens have been empowered and the challenges and issues associated with this.

Impact and challenges

There is evidence indicating that faith groups and citizens have been 'empowered' through their engagement, although there are signs that some feel they have little or no impact. In a study by Escott and Logan (2006) in which 57 faith representatives on LSPs were consulted, nearly three quarters felt that their presence made a difference in 'hard terms/ outcomes (for example, influencing the direction of policy, the shape of projects and the provision of services)' (Escott and Logan, 2006: 27). This compares to nine respondents who stated they felt they made little or no difference and a further six who had serious reservations. One key impact that faith representatives reported was in relation to signalling and opening up discussion about a moral and spiritual dimension, both in terms of values and in relation to a concern for justice (Escott and Logan, 2006: 19). As one of the interviewees stated, "I have had some influence in focussing activity on our poorer wards" (Escott and Logan, 2006: 19). Other research by Berkeley et al (2006), reported that 80 per cent of faith representatives consulted on public partnerships felt that their input was taken very seriously or as seriously as other members (Berkeley et al, 2006: 9). However, James (2007) highlights concerns by some faith groups of what they see as the government's 'top-down' approach to faith engagement, in which they feel their participation is tokenistic and superficial (James, 2007: 54).

As with other actors, variability in the degree of influence by faith representatives on partnerships and through other forms of engagement can be explained by a range of complex and interrelated factors. These include their relative skill, knowledge, legitimacy and resources, as well as the composition and dynamics of the decision-making network or engagement opportunity. According to a bishop within the Pentecostal Church, the factors shaping the degree to which faith actors are taken seriously on partnerships are no different to what other organisations face:

> 'I have to argue for my place just like anybody else …
> and can't take it for granted that it is just going to happen.
> However good my intentions and however helpful and
> beneficial what I bring to the table would be, you still
> have to fight your corner. I think some faith-based groups
> do not sufficiently factor in the degree to which you have
> to fight for your bit of cake and think, just because it's
> inherently good in our view, it should just be and that leads
> to a number of disappointments … I just have to earn my
> credibility and it is as I earn this credibility and influence
> by my incremental contributions that people listen.'

The above comment suggests that the skills and capacity of faith groups and citizens, together with their willingness to 'play the game', are key factors shaping the degree to which faith partners are influential. However, concerns have been raised over unrealistic assumptions in policy narratives of the capacity and willingness of faith communities and citizens to mobilise in the pursuit of urban governance objectives. As Dinham and Lowndes (2008) suggest, some faith communities and citizens may be primarily focused on the faith community itself (for example, on the relationships, fellowship, prayer life or spirituality of the community and its members). This focus is not necessarily in line with that of policy makers and other local governance actors whose rationale for engaging faiths relates to improving the quality of urban governance, either in democratic and/or performance terms. In this case, 'the "faithfulness" of faith communities may be of secondary and limited (or even no) significance' (Dinham and Lowndes, 2008: 14).

Even when faith groups are willing to 'play the game' they do not necessarily find the rules favourable. Rules often criticised by faith groups include those around competitive funding, which may lead people to act in ways that are not cooperative or friendly, and a bias in government funding initiatives towards demonstrating 'hard, measurable' outcomes as opposed to 'softer' outcomes that faith groups are renowned for but which are harder to measure. As the bishop from within the Pentecostal Church commented:

> '... very often what you end up doing is applying for those things which can be measured but then seeking to do the things that can't be measured on the back of the money that you've got ... it is certainly the case that faith-based organisations are trying to do far too much for far too little in terms of people and money and very often in terms of accommodation.'

The government's current emphasis on bridging social capital has also been criticised by some faith groups on the basis that too much focus on 'bridging' can weaken the ties that 'bond' people together within faith communities. In other words, the very identity of faith groups may be undermined by too strong a focus on shared identities and values between different communities (see James, 2007).

Tensions can also arise between faith and state actors relating to the positioning of religious beliefs, values and language in the public sphere. An evaluation of the Faith Communities Capacity Building Fund highlights a number of issues, including concerns among practitioners and policy makers of faith groups proselytising, failing to deliver on equalities and using value-based approaches to convert individuals to extremist ideologies (James, 2007: 57). Such issues have been recognised by the Commission for Integration and Cohesion, which recommended that clear guidelines be provided to statutory authorities enabling them to award public service contracts to faith groups without fearing it will lead to proselytising or pressure on service users to accept religious beliefs (James, 2007: 132). On the other hand, interview evidence suggests faith groups can find it difficult to express religious beliefs, values and principles in a secularised policy context because of fear of 'sounding a bit weird' or because they themselves take them for granted. According to one member of the Salvation Army, there is a need to adopt a more 'secularised language' in this context, using terms such as 'honesty, tolerance and the importance of relationships', as opposed to more instinctive Christian language of 'grace, peace, joy and love'. This led to concerns about what is 'lost in translation' and appears to confirm Habermas' (2006) concerns of an asymmetrical burden on faith groups to translate religious reasoning and language into more secular forms. Similarly, the *Faithful cities* report argues that:

> ... the distinct and conflicting language of faith, the values that challenge rather than support government policy, and working styles that fail to mesh with time-limited, benchmark-driven, outcome-required government schemes, all pose a challenge. (CULF, 2006: 3)

Baker (2009) also refers to what he terms 'blurred encounters', in which miscommunications arise from attempts to use shared language and concepts as well as different ones. He suggests the reason for this is that:

> ... faith and non-faith sectors have different understandings and interpretations of key motifs used within government policy, a problem exacerbated by the fact that government interpretations based on secular/modernist assumptions of the importance of neutrality and bureaucratic accountability are usually assumed to be the default ones. (Baker, 2009: 105)

Different faith groups also have varying resource bases, institutional structures, political agendas and interests, all of which shape the nature, extent and potential impact of any engagement. Larger, highly organised and well resourced faith groups, such as Anglican Christians, are, for example, more likely to find engagement easier than smaller traditions such as Jains, Bahá'ís or Zoroastrians (Dinham and Lowndes, 2008: 15). According to a Jain trustee in Leicester, the ability of smaller, non-Christian, faith groups to engage is hindered by lack of time and availability of individuals, paid or otherwise, who can attend meetings during the day:

> 'I find that, from the Christian side, the reverends and the canons and the bishops and the archdeacons are so many and they can always relieve one or two to go and attend meetings; while, with a group like ours, where our total membership in Leicester is 500, it is difficult to attend the numerous meetings and at all times. I think that is probably a factor where you will see that participation by the smaller groups is not taking place.'

The above suggests that diversity, in terms of capacity and willingness to engage, is not always fully understood and/or accommodated effectively by policy makers and statutory partners involved in local governance. A review of policy narratives also suggests that a largely 'top-down' construction of faith identities has emerged that centres on collectives and tends to mask diversity within and between religious traditions and groups (Smith, 2004; Chapman and Lowndes, 2008). Terms such as 'faith communities', 'faith groups' and 'faith-based' organisations are frequently, and often interchangeably, used within policy narratives.[5] Smith (2004: 185) questions whether there is a clear understanding of the notion of 'faith community' and whether government discourse resonates with the understandings of community and identity in major faith traditions. He suggests there may be conceptual and cultural gaps between official and religious discourses and agendas about community whereby a homogeneous reading of the term 'faith community' may 'miss many of the internal divisions of gender, age group, caste, ethnicity, and religious belief, which may fragment and exclude' (Smith, 2004: 200).

Accommodating religious diversity in urban governance is often assumed to take place through the engagement of interfaith organisations and/or multiple single-faith organisations, in which one or two member faith leaders or 'representatives' may sit on a partnership. While this concept of representation goes some way to accommodating diversity, it does not necessarily go far enough in some cases, nor does it entirely fit with how faith groups and citizens see themselves or their role, as the following quotes illustrate:

> 'The term "faith community" is very much a local authority kind of phrase in a sense, because a lot of churches don't see themselves as representative of a faith community; they see themselves as a church. They don't see themselves in the same pot as other faith institutions around.' (Member of a Christian faith-based charity)

> '... representative is the wrong word [on the primary care trust]. Your primary responsibility is to, not so much be a representative, but to be somebody who has the interests of everybody in the community at heart ... [but] as a Christian I've got a keen eye, as I said, for those who are not doing so well.' (Bishop from within the Pentecostal Church)

'... how do I represent all the faith groups? ... If there is something going on in the partnership or one of the subgroups that I am involved in, I need to be aware of how a specific proposal, decision, or policy might impact on each of the eight major faith traditions. Should I consider difficulties or problems are likely to arise, or offence be taken, then I must advise the decision/policy makers accordingly. At the same time, I also need to consider what is in the best interests of all Leicester's citizens.' (LSP faith sector representative, Jewish)

'... faith leaders may not reflect the views of the entire congregation or even a very significant part of that congregation.' (Employee of an organisation in the voluntary and community sector)

Some faith groups have also encountered statutory partners, including diversity officers working within local authorities, with low levels of knowledge about religious diversity. As a member of a Christian faith-based charity commented:

'Their [diversity officers with a faith remit] level of knowledge, even around churches, was low, let alone mosques and Hindu temples. They haven't even been to these places.'

It seems reasonable to suppose that greater policy clarity, guidance and understanding over the role, significance and place of religious beliefs, practices, values and language in the public domain may help overcome some of these tensions alongside other measures (for example, training and improved faith/secular literacy around values, language, beliefs and practices). There are indications that policy debates and action are beginning to take place along these lines. The government is looking to develop a more comprehensive set of guidelines to address funding issues associated with the faith sector (CLG, 2008e: 43). It also announced a three-year package of support aimed at building capacity around community cohesion in its *Face to face and side by side* strategy (CLG, 2008a: 10-11). This includes:

* £7.5 million to help build the capacity of regional faith forums and support local activities facilitating dialogue and collaborative social action between citizens of different faiths and none;

- the development of guidance material to local authorities, community groups and citizens;
- support for web-based resources and sharing of effective practice;
- support of various events to celebrate success and raise awareness.

The government is also committed to a programme of faith literacy in the public sector (CLG, 2008e: 43). This will be important in improving understanding of religious and faith-based organisational diversity, among other things. Baker (2009) suggests faith literacy should facilitate a move beyond functionalist levels of discourse, around 'what to do at a civic function and how to get funding', to one that aids the uncovering of values and visions of those engaged in the public domain. This, he suggests, 'will involve a commitment to a more profound type of literacy involving deep listening to language that expresses core values and visions, and a commitment to the exploitation of the many points of connection and overlap' (Baker, 2009: 120). Faithworks, a Christian organisation seeking to promote unity and partnership within and between faiths and secular authorities and voluntary organisations, also argues that better understanding by government of the motivational nature of faith and the different roles that faith groups play in communities is needed in order to promote integration and community cohesion (Duncan and Madeiros, 2007). Similar calls for better governmental understanding of the ways in which faith-based organisations operate and are motivated were also expressed in interviews with individuals from three Christian faith-based organisations.

Yet, improved literacy should be a requirement not just of state and wider civil society actors. As three interviewees from Christian faith-based organisations suggested, state–faith relations would also benefit from better understanding by faith-based organisations and citizens about how the state works and is structured, and what its agendas are. One of these interviewees also commented that faith-based organisations could also benefit from improved literacy around the availability of support and resources from secular agencies, including those from the wider voluntary and community sector. Many faith-based organisations do not see themselves as part of the wider voluntary and community sector and would not readily access it for support (Finneron, 2007: 41; Jones, 2007: 3). They are not always aware of where to look for support and often turn to organisations and individuals in their own faith traditions because they feel better understood, and seek to avoid perceived misunderstanding and suspicion by secular agencies and partners. This suggests that secular agencies and partners need to be open to learning and understanding distinctive faith-based organisational needs, interests and ways of operating, and faith-based organisations need to become better at articulating to secular agencies "what they are about, who they are, what they stand for and how they behave" (member of a Christian faith-based charity).

Conclusion

As has been shown in this chapter, a significant renegotiation of state–faith relationships has taken place from the 1990s onwards. New opportunities have emerged for faith groups and citizens to participate in public consultations and partnerships, and in the delivery of state-funded welfare services and programmes aimed at facilitating community cohesion. As such, faith communities and citizens have gained increased influence and prominence in the public domain, suggesting we are increasingly living in what has been termed the post-secular society. In doing so, they help facilitate greater policy effectiveness and responsiveness, as well as enhance democratic participation by widening representation and accountability. This has the potential to create a 'win–win' situation whereby policy makers and local governance actors gain from the resources that faith engagement brings (including knowledge, social capital, volunteers and buildings), enabling them to better pursue policy and urban governance goals through a more participatory democratic process; and faith groups and citizens benefit from additional funding and policy influence, enabling them to ensure the needs of others (for example, faith groups, geographical and/or minority communities and the marginalised) are increasingly met through either social action and/or the policy domain. Such a 'win–win' scenario is likely to be strongest where faith and local governance actors have shared goals and where the practice of local governance enables conflict and difference to be discussed and addressed. However, as this chapter has shown, various challenges that bring into question the extent to which the potential beneficial opportunities of faith engagement are being fully realised remain. Such challenges include: improving literacy of the state and faith groups in terms of how they operate, their diversity, motivations and agendas; improved clarity over the roles that faith participants are expected to play; building capacity of faith communities to engage; overcoming fear, suspicion and misconceptions; and ensuring appropriate forms and systems of faith engagement are in place.

There are signs that such challenges are being acknowledged and debated within the policy arena. Moves towards a resolution are likely to involve commitments by the state and faith communities alike, which Baker (2009) suggests should entail 'deep listening' to language that expresses core values and visions. This may require a greater commitment by secular actors to be more accepting and enquiring as to the meaning of religious language, beliefs and principles. In other words, that they 'play their part in the endeavours to translate relevant contributions from the religious language into a language that is accessible to the public as a whole' (Habermas, 2006: 51-2). It may also require a greater commitment by faith groups and citizens to be more open to learning about the state and local governance processes, and better at articulating to secular agencies what they are about and how they operate.

Notes

[1] The interviews were conducted as part of three research projects: 'Faith, hope and clarity: developing a model of faith group involvement in civil renewal' funded by the Home Office (see Lowndes and Chapman, 2005); 'Faith and the voluntary sector in urban governance: distinctive yet similar?' funded by De Montfort University (2007; see Chapman, 2009); and 'Faith based social action: literature review and interview findings' funded by the Faith Based Regeneration Network (see Dinham et al, 2008). The author wishes to thank all those who gave up their time and shared their insights and experiences as part of this research. Special thanks are also due to Dr Leila Thorp, who contributed to some of the thinking and research material on which this chapter is based, and Professor Vivien Lowndes for her feedback and contribution to the research.

[2] Secularisation, a concept with various and contested meanings, broadly encompasses the idea that progress and modernisation will lead to the disappearance of the religious phenomenon. Alexander (2001) identifies three different strands to such claims. The first relates to the process whereby religious thinking, practice and institutions lose their social significance; the second to the decline in religious belief; and the third to the privatisation of religion (Alexander, 2001: 48-55).

[3] Local compacts are agreements drawn up between third sector organisations, local authorities and other public bodies at the local level. They set out a framework for relations and partnership working between the state and third sector in England. They include codes of good practice – for example, on black and minority ethnic groups, consultation, policy appraisal, funding and volunteering.

[4] The *Faithful cities* report (CULF, 2006) uses the term 'faithful capital' to identify two distinguishing elements that faith groups contribute to the public realm – language (for example, concepts such as love, hope, judgement, forgiveness, remembrance and hospitality) and practices (for example, local rootedness, acceptance of failure, genuine participation, working together) (see Baker, 2009).

[5] Work by Lowndes and Chapman (2005, 2007) has been undertaken to unpack these terms. This identifies a range of faith actors embodied in the term 'faith community' and illustrates their potential for contributing to civil renewal and governance.

References

Alexander, D. (2001) *Rebuilding the matrix: Science and faith in the 21st century*, Oxford: Lion Publishing.

Baker, C. (2009) 'Blurred encounters? Religious literacy, spiritual capital and language', in A. Dinham, R. Furbey and V. Lowndes (eds) *Faith in the public realm: Controversies, policies and practices*, Bristol: The Policy Press, pp 105–22.

Baker, C. and Skinner, H. (2006) *Faith in Action: The dynamic connection between spiritual and religious capital,* Manchester: William Temple Foundation.

Berkeley, N., Barnes, S., Dann, B., Stockley, N. and Finneron, D. (2006) *Faithful representation: Faith representatives on local public partnerships: Summary, key findings and recommendations*, London: Church Urban Fund.

Chapman, R. (2009) 'Faith and the voluntary sector in urban governance: distinctive yet similar', in A. Dinham, R. Furbey and V. Lowndes (eds) *Faith in the public realm: Controversies, policies and practices*, Bristol: The Policy Press, pp 203–22.

Chapman, R. and Lowndes, V. (2008) 'Faith in governance? The potential and pitfalls of involving faith groups in urban governance', *Planning Practice and Research*, vol 23, no 1, pp 57–75.

CLG (Communities and Local Government) (2007) *Improving opportunity, strengthening society: Two years on – A progress report on the government's strategy for race equality and community cohesion*, London: CLG.

CLG (2008a) *Face to face and side by side: A framework for partnership in our multi faith society*, London: CLG.

CLG (2008b) *Preventing violent extremism: Next steps for communities*, London: CLG.

CLG (2008c) *Communities in Control White Paper: Real people, real power*, London: CLG.

CLG (2008d) *Communities in Control White Paper: Impact assessment*, London: CLG.

CLG (2008e) *The government's response to the Commission on Integration and Cohesion*, London: CLG.

CLG (2009) *Faith leaders and workers project; Evaluation report*, London: CLG.

Commission on Integration and Cohesion (2007) *Our shared future*, Wetherby: Commission on Integration and Cohesion.

Community Cohesion Panel (2004) *The end of parallel lives: The report of the Community Cohesion Panel*, London: Home Office.

CULF (Commission on Urban Life and Faith) (2006) *Faithful cities. A call for celebration, vision and justice*, London: Methodist Publishing House and Church House Publishing.

Dinham, A. with Chapman, R. and Miller, S. (2008) *Faith based social action and the inter-faith network*, London: Faith Based Regeneration Network.

Dinham, A. and Lowndes, V. (2008) 'Religion, resources and representation: three narratives of faith engagement in British urban governance', *Urban Affairs Review*, vol 43, no 6, pp 817–45.

Duncan, M. and Madeiros, J. (2007), *The integration and cohesion agenda: A Faithworks' perspective*, London: Faithworks.

Escott, P. and Logan, P. (2006) *Faith in LSPs? The experience of faith community representatives on local strategic partnerships*, London: The Churches Regional Network.

Finneron, D. (2007) 'Local governance, representation and faith-based organisations', in V. Jochum, B. Pratten and K. Wilding (eds) *Faith and voluntary action: An overview of current evidence and debates*, London: NCVO, pp 39–42.

Geddes, M., Davies, J. and Fuller, C. (2007) 'Evaluating local strategic partnerships', *Local Government Studies*, vol 33, no 1, pp 97–116.

Habermas, J. (2006) 'Religion in the public sphere', *European Journal of Philosophy*, vol 14, no 1, pp 1–25.

Home Office (2004) *Working together: Co-operation between government and faith communities*, London: The Stationery Office.

James, M. (2007) *Faith, cohesion and community development: An evaluation report from the Faith Communities Capacity Building Fund*, London: Community Development Foundation.

Jones, P. (2007) 'The Guildford Report: governance support needs of smaller and local faith based organisations', an unpublished report to the Governance Hub.

JRF (Joseph Rowntree Foundation) (2006) *Faith as social capital: Connecting or dividing?*, York: JRF.

LGA (Local Government Association) (2002) *Community cohesion – An action guide: Guidance for local authorities*, London: LGA Publications.

Lowndes, V. and Chapman, R. (2005) *Faith, hope and clarity: Developing a model of faith group involvement in civil renewal: Main report*, Leicester: De Montfort University.

Lowndes, V. and Chapman, R. (2007) 'Faith, hope and clarity: Faith groups and civil renewal', in T. Brannan, P. John and G. Stoker (eds) *Re-energizing citizenship: strategies for civil renewal*, Basingstoke: Palgrave Macmillan, pp 163–84.

Lowndes, V. and Thorp, L. (2008) *PVE pathfinder in the East Midlands action research report,* Leicester: De Montfort University.

Momen, M. (1999) *The phenomenon of religion: A thematic approach*, Oxford, Oneworld Publications.

National Statistics (2003) *Religion in the UK*, London: National Statistics.

ODPM (Office of the Deputy Prime Minister) (2005) *Local strategic partnerships: Shaping their future: A consultation paper*, London: ODPM.

Smith, G. (2004) 'Faith in the community and communities of faith? Government rhetoric and religious identity in urban Britain', *Journal of Contemporary Religion*, vol 19, no 2, pp 185–204.

Taylor, M. (2004) 'The welfare mix in the United Kingdom', in A. Evers and J.L. Laville (eds) *The third sector in Europe*, Cheltenham: Edward Elgar, pp 122–43.

Weller, P. (ed) (2007) *Religions in the UK 2007-2010*, Derby: Multi-Faith Centre, University of Derby.

NINE

Citizens' reflections on behaviour change policies

Rebecca Askew, Sarah Cotterill, Stephen Greasley

Introduction

Balancing state intervention and personal responsibility is one of the enduring challenges of public policy. Controversies around the causes and remedies of deprivation, the regulation of public behaviour, the provision of public services and the solutions to collective problems all revolve, to some extent, around finding an appropriate balance between government activism and individual responsibility. One current manifestation of this debate in public policy focuses on attempts to engender 'behaviour change' in a diverse range of policy areas. Although behaviour change policies are not new, there appears to be a momentum in the current effort to turn broad policy discourse about what it is to be a responsible citizen into concrete and deliverable policy programmes (for examples, Halpern et al, 2004; APSC, 2007; Lewis, 2007; Knott et al, 2008; O'Leary, 2008).

 The appeal to policy makers of behaviour change interventions is that they purport to offer solutions where problems seem intractable or where the political and/or administrative costs of alternative policies are too high. However, doubts remain about the efficacy of behaviour change policies, about the administrative capacity of governance to successfully deliver them and about how comfortable we, in a liberal society, should be to accept government interference in citizens' values, attitudes and decision-making processes. If there is more to the behaviour change agenda than think tank noise, these doubts require some examination.

This chapter explores behaviour change policy on the ground, using evidence from four empirical projects conducted by the authors aimed at changing citizen behaviour. The chapter starts by briefly reviewing what is meant by behaviour change policy. It then examines four behaviour change interventions with a particular focus on the citizens'

experience of their interaction with governance networks. It looks at the results of the projects and assesses their efficacy. These examples are used to draw out some key issues in successful implementation of behaviour change policies, exploring questions around the capacity of institutions to deliver policies effectively. We also reflect on whether the interventions can be characterised as empowering or whether citizens are simply being nagged by an overbearing state.

The governance of public behaviour

The label 'behaviour change' has been adopted in the policy literature for a collection of interventions that are based primarily on persuasive mechanisms. All policy tools – taxation, rewards, regulation – seek in some sense to change behaviour, but they do so by altering the incentives and opportunities that individuals face leaving their preferences and capacities unchanged. What is distinct about the current discourse is the attempt to change behaviour by changing people using a variety of methods (Halpern et al, 2004; Lewis, 2007). It is this direct and deliberate attempt to change people that raises some hackles and at the same time recasts the relationship between state action and personal responsibility. Traditionally this relationship is portrayed in either/or terms but, with recent behaviour change policies, state intervention is understood to support personal responsibility.

A range of policy justifications is put forward for focusing on behaviour change (Halpern et al, 2004). Government is less likely to achieve policy goals on employment, crime, health, education, environment, transport and the economy if citizens are passive and disengaged. There is a belief that government can have much greater impact across all these policy areas by engaging service users and others in the planning, design and delivery of public policy (see the literature on active citizenship covered in Brannan et al, 2006). Policy makers also hope to deliver cost savings in the long run by establishing patterns of behaviour that create fewer demands on public services (for example, by improving public health) and ultimately they hope to achieve a less coercive relationship between governance and citizens. This is part of a wider debate about the role of government – whether the state has expanded to take on some responsibilities that should rightly be taken by individuals.

As well as deliberately targeting behaviour change, governance frames the structure of rules and practices in which social behaviour takes place. For example, participation behaviour is affected by 'rules in use', formal and informal institutions and arrangements that shape

'Rule in use'

behaviour (Lowndes et al, 2006b). Too much state monitoring of behaviour can have a counterproductive result, with individuals feeling that they are not trusted and responding by becoming untrustworthy (Ostrom, 1998). If citizens take it for granted that government takes on a lot of responsibility for the common good, they may feel they don't have to make an effort. In short, intentionally or not, the operation of governance exerts an influence over what citizens think and how they behave.

Lewis (2007) discusses in detail the dilemmas of behaviour change policies, noting that people often do not match up to the rational decision makers assumed in some political theory and that this may provide a justification for public action: 'what is important is that the state acts to empower people to make good choices' (Lewis, 2007: 32). In this sense individuals and groups can be said to be empowered when they are helped to develop skills and resources to address problems for themselves. However, empowerment can also be understood in relational terms – an individual or group might be said to be empowered in their relationship to, for example, the institutions of local governance. This second meaning is more closely related to the traditional questions of the politics of public service provision – can service users influence service providers and hold them to account?

meaning of Empowerment

The dual interpretation of empowerment is important. Policy makers sometimes seem to display a certain disappointment in the nation's citizens and 'empowering citizens' in the first sense is sometimes a polite way of saying 'improving citizens'. However, citizens are also sometimes disappointed by the way that public governance operates and empowerment, in the second meaning of the term, refers to their ability to influence public sector provision. These two interpretations of 'empowerment' can capture the simultaneous attempts of governance to influence citizens and of citizens to influence governance.

Behaviour change in practice

In this section we use the experience of participants in four local behaviour change projects to explore the implications of the projects for citizen–governance relations on the ground. The four projects address a variety of behavioural issues from fairly minor shifts in recycling behaviour all the way to engaging substance users with chaotic lives. This variation allows us to look at behaviour change policy across the range of challenges that it is likely to face. What the projects have in common is a partial reliance on persuasion as a mechanism for delivering policy objectives. In each case one of the co-authors worked

relate this to a v. middle class culture of self-improvement (REF?)

with policy makers in the design, implementation and evaluation of the projects – Sarah Cotterill on the recycling and the community participation projects (Cotterill and Richardson, 2009) and Rebecca Askew on the family support and the problem drug use projects (Askew and Richardson, 2008; Askew et al, 2008). The recycling project was evaluated using a randomised controlled trial. The other three projects were design experiments, a method where researchers work closely with policy makers in the design and adjustment of policies; see Brannan et al (2006: 197–8) who argue it to be particularly appropriate for use in policies that require active citizenship.

One of the doubts about behaviour change policies is that they are ineffective. These four projects demonstrate that local behaviour change policies can be effective – the recycling, family support and drugs support projects were successful in encouraging behaviour change and the community participation was successful in generating interest although this was not sustained.

Promoting recycling

The recycling promotion experiment set out to investigate whether doorstep canvassing is an effective way to encourage kerbside recycling. The research took place in a relatively deprived inner-city neighbourhood in the North West of England where a weekly kerbside recycling scheme is provided to 6,580 households by a social enterprise, funded by the local council. Recycling is not too overwhelming a task and beneficial to the environment and public finances, yet at the start of the project only half of households in this neighbourhood were recycling.

There has been considerable experimentation with techniques to increase recycling rates (for example, Timlett and Williams, 2008) and previous research has suggested that a door-to-door canvassing campaign can successfully encourage households to raise recycling rates (Shaw et al, 2007) but this has not yet been robustly tested. Half the streets in the neighbourhood were randomly allocated to a treatment group to be canvassed and the remaining streets received no special attention. A team of four canvassers sought to persuade households to participate in a weekly kerbside recycling collection and to recycle the full variety of materials that could be collected. The intervention tried to influence the habits of households by providing information and encouragement. Canvassers made sure householders were aware of the service by confirming the day and time of collection, explaining the variety of materials that can be recycled. They promoted positive attitudes to recycling and were enthusiastic about encouraging people to take part. They addressed barriers to recycling by providing plastic bags as required and ordering new boxes if they were lost or missing (Shaw et al, 2007). An information leaflet was given to every household.

Measurement of recycling rates were taken before and after the canvassing in both sets of streets, and then repeated three months later. If the intervention worked, there ought to be higher rates of recycling in those streets where the canvassers operated than in those that did not receive a visit. The research provided evidence of an increase in recycling related to the canvassing. Immediately after the canvassing campaign, recycling participation rose by 5.4% among the canvassed streets compared to the control group who had not been canvassed. Three months later the canvassing was still having an effect – albeit a reduced effect – on recycling participation. The recycling rate of the canvassed streets compared to the control group was 1.7% higher than the baseline rates (Cotterill et al, 2009). *not significant !*

may not have been a v. anthropological approach though ...

Community engagement

In its various guises community engagement has been ever present in the policy programmes of Labour governments since 1997. Government has argued that it is associated with improved public services, cohesive communities, revived local democracy, improved well-being and the identification of solutions to difficult problems (CLG, 2008).

Some local authorities, however, find their citizens to be reluctant to become involved and those who are interested tend to be drawn from a small pool. The community engagement design experiment was an attempt to use residents' phone calls to a council contact centre to encourage community action on local issues. Councils' contact centres receive numerous day-to-day phone calls, providing opportunities for local councils to engage with citizens from a wide range of backgrounds, including so called 'hard to reach' groups such as young people, full-time workers and people from minority ethnic communities. Being asked to participate is an important element in becoming involved in civic activities (Verba et al, 1995; Lowndes et al, 2006a). *yes !* The project assessed whether minor adaptations to a council's core operations could help to encourage greater civic activism simply by inviting people to participate.

Residents from one neighbourhood who phoned the contact centre with an environmental enquiry during a seven-week trial period were asked: 'We are currently promoting civic awareness and are looking for people to get involved in improving the area. We want to encourage people to take action on community issues in the area. Would you be interested in finding out more?' Those who said 'yes' were visited by a community worker who discussed the available opportunities and then provided further support as necessary or introduced the citizen to others who could help and support their activity. The neighbourhood has about 4,000 residents, is ethnically mixed and is in the top 30% of most deprived areas in England.[1] It was chosen partly because a range of community groups existed in the area.

The project is still under way at the time of writing so settled conclusions have yet to be drawn. The experience of the first wave of the project is interesting however. Thirty people who contacted the centre said they were interested in finding out more about how they could get involved in improving the neighbourhood. They included equal numbers of men and women; just over half were Asian and the remainder were white; two thirds were working and five had not undertaken any civic activity in the last year. By varying the contact centre routines and providing neighbourhood support, the local authority altered its institutional rules and practices and this relatively minor change over a short period of weeks attracted people to become involved in community activities. They wished to be better informed and wanted more influence over agencies that delivered services.

However, in the first round of the project, people's interest was not sustained. When interviewed eight weeks later, only ten of the 30 were actively planning action to improve their neighbourhood. These ten were more likely to be, older, already involved in civic activity and did not include the eight Asian women who had initially come forward. For the others, their initial interest was not sustained; why this might be is an interesting question. One perspective is that the success of this initiative depends on local government changing institutional factors in two ways: first, at the recruitment stage; second, by adapting the structure of opportunities in a way that makes citizens feel that their involvement would be worthwhile and not too burdensome. Council staff were keen to encourage people to join or set up community groups, rather than listening to individual voices. One parent was initially interested but later said:

'I just want to put my opinions forward, not go to meetings and things. I will be more proactive when my children are in education. I am happy to put my views forward and be consulted.' (Cotterill and Richardson, 2009)

Family support

The third project was an attempt to deter and prevent anti-social behaviour. Low-level but pervasive disorder often causes as much public concern as the more serious crimes that the formal criminal justice system is designed to deal with (Halpern et al, 2004). A number of policies have attempted to address such behaviour, most notably anti-social behaviour orders.

This project aimed to pre-empt the need for legalistic intervention by providing support to families who were already known to the police or children's services, and whose children were judged to be at risk of engaging in anti-social behaviour. The judgement was based on various indicators relating to social deprivation, history of problem behaviours in the family, low school attainment (Hobcroft, 1998; Beinart et al, 2002) and substance misuse by parents (Barnard and McKeganey, 2004). The project aimed to provide low-level support for families who were in need but not at crisis point. The interventions were short-term and focused on ensuring that the various public agencies that families had contact with were responsive and co-ordinated. The underlying assumption was that, if services were able to work with families on low-level concerns, the risk of anti-social behaviour among children would decline.

The project was led by the local authority but delivery was through a third-sector organisation – a children's charity. The organisation was selected for its expertise in dealing with families and anti-social behaviour, and to distance the project from statutory services – associated with crisis-level intervention – to encourage families to be involved. The project had some initial difficulty recruiting families to participate. However, those who did become engaged remained so over the duration of the project. In-depth interviews at three-monthly intervals tracked the families receiving the intervention with a comparison group of families not receiving support. The two groups were similar in terms of their risk factors and levels of family disorganisation. Overall, the families in the intervention group made progress on: increased engagement of children and parents with appropriate services; improved family relationships; improved children's behaviour; reduced episodes of crisis; and additional practical support for issues relating to housing, finances and respite. In general, the families in the comparison group experienced higher levels of disruption, such as, frequently moving house faced more frequent crisis episodes and had no new service contact unless in crisis. One family (out of six in the comparison group) made progress independently. The early, pre-emptive nature of the support was valued by interviewees. Subsequently, after short periods of project intervention, families felt able to coordinate their own support and deal with problems within the family, as illustrated by the following quotes from parents:

> 'It's knowing someone is out there that can help us if we need to be helped … we don't need to get into trouble to be helped.'

> '[The project worker] helped me get through the bad parts and put a lot of things in place. And I don't feel like I need as much contact. I have his phone number, I know if there is anything bothering me then I can ring him.'

The ability of the project workers to coordinate agency action was a result of the support received from the local authority and other agencies. The strand leader was influential and kept the momentum going with the project, especially in early stages when recruitment was difficult. A multi-agency steering group was crucial as it maintained awareness and gave a chance for services to feed back and respond to the project as it developed (see Askew and Richardson, 2008 for full findings). Although the long-term effects of the project have not yet been established, the experience of the project suggests that relatively light-touch family support for short periods of time can prevent an escalation of problematic behaviour. It also illustrates that this group of families are capable of defining their own needs in relation to public services and resolving issues within the family.

Community drug support

The drug support design experiment was conducted in a housing estate of a northern town. It provided support in the community to 'problem substance-users' – who exhibited particularly entrenched behaviours based on dependence and addiction (heroin, alcohol and amphetamines were the dominant drugs) and various issues relating to unstable lifestyles, such as problems with health, accommodation and relationships with others. The intervention was based on a rounded rather than merely 'treatment' approach to the addiction, focusing on changing the lifestyles of users as well as reducing drug use, as suggested by Parker (2004). As such it went beyond the prescription of substitutes – such as methadone – to provide an intensive and flexible community approach to reduce the barriers associated with coming off drugs. It represented a fundamental shift in the way this local authority offered drug services.

Each project worker had a small caseload of five clients and offered each individual a combination of diversionary activities, one-to-one support and advocacy work on areas such as housing, relationships, finances, health as well as advice and support on harm reduction and treatment options. It operated on the premise that there is no 'one size fits all'. Drug workers need to respond to personal circumstances, such as the particular form of drug dependence and the associated psychosocial problems (Gossop, 2006). This project was focused on changing behaviour at an individual level and there was a strong focus on personal responsibility. It was designed to focus on supporting individuals to deal with the range of problems associated with the misuse of drugs, break down barriers to engaging with treatment and help clients 'gain control over their own lives' on the basis that a reduction in drug use would follow. For the majority of clients this involved restructuring their lives and changing their daily routines.

As with the family support project, successfully engaging with the client group was an important part of the support. There are statutory means available to ensure compliance in drug treatment such as, the Drug Rehabilitation Requirement (DRR) but, in an effort to avoid coercive treatment strategies, involvement was voluntary for this project. Recruitment and implementation was a long process but, of the 20 original participants, 16 remained in contact over the two years of the research project.

The outcomes of the project were broadly positive as assessed over seven waves of measurement (Askew et al, 2008). Overall the health of clients had improved; the number of clients reporting health problems decreased by 9% from Wave 1 to Wave 7 (from 24.5% to 15.4%). A senior nurse practitioner at the Community Drug Team said she felt that the project had encouraged clients to attend health screenings and that the close client–worker relationships had helped address health problems. By Wave 7, 87.9% of the clients had stable accommodation; this was an increase from a low of 55.6% (in Wave 2). Clients also reported better relationships with others and an increase in self-confidence; 6.3 % of people had problems getting along with others in Wave 7 compared with 39.9% in Wave 1. Clients reported that the project had helped build relationships with friends and family. One client re-established contact with their children who were in care; another felt support from the project worker had helped his parents understand his issues in relation to drug use. In terms of overall illicit drug use, the data showed fluctuations over time but with an overall decrease from 30.6%

of the client group using illicit substances in Wave 1 to 15.8% in Wave 7. The project was successful in encouraging vulnerable and chaotic individuals to accept treatment, as one participant stated:

> 'It was them [project workers] that got me into treatment.
> I wouldn't have bothered otherwise. I needed help to make
> the first move.'

It also increased the skills and knowledge of individuals and assisted in positive social engagement through diversionary activities. A participant at a cooking session run by the project commented:

> 'I learn something new every time ... It has helped me to
> meet people, become more social and open up more socially.
> I realised I had the ability to talk to people and make friends.
> It has helped me in a different way than I thought.'

 The project did empower the clients but did so in different ways, to different levels and by different means. This reflects the heterogeneity of substance misuse and those who misuse substances. Each individual had different levels of dependence, circumstances, reasons for using substances and issues to resolve. In this sense the flexibility of the service was useful to address the variety of need.

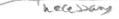

Governance change and behaviour change

The policies outlined above range from fairly straightforward canvassing to complex intervention in the lives of individuals and families. The target groups vary from all residents to a small group of people with chaotic and unstructured lives. The results show that such policies can be successful in changing behaviours. One factor that was critical to success or failure in all four projects was the level of sophistication of their implementation. The projects have in common the aim of changing citizens' behaviour in some way and using soft persuasive strategies to achieve this change, but the scale of the challenge to local governance varies considerably. In this section we discuss a number of themes related to the implementation of projects and citizens' experience of them, examining a second doubt about behaviour change programmes: whether local institutions have the capacity to deliver these policies effectively.

Flexibility and tailoring

Behaviour change policies can range from fairly standardised and general (for example, food labelling) to intensive programmes that are flexible and tailored to a diverse client base. The experience of these four behaviour change experiments suggests that projects that were flexible and tailored to need were received well by citizens and encouraged them to take personal responsibility. Conversely, where local institutions were not able to tailor and be flexible, citizens did not respond as well. There is a broader recognition in policy of the need for, and difficulty of, personalising public services (Cabinet Office, 2006). With the community engagement project, the initial message was a standardised script read to callers to the council and it was fairly successful in getting an initial 'lead'. However, when faced with the actual routes for participation, the enthusiasm of some residents tailed off. People said they wanted to make a difference on crime, litter and community facilities, and the local authority response was to put them in touch with relevant community groups. But groups are not what everyone wants, and some people, particularly those busy bringing up families and working, did not want to join organisations. They wanted different opportunities to make their point and have their voice heard.

Among the families involved in the family support project, some primarily needed support on practical things; others were looking for emotional support as well as practical help. The aim was to be flexible, responding to these specific needs; this can be resource intensive and requires a particular way of working from the project workers and service professionals. Even where new projects succeed in being flexible they have to work with existing services that may not have the capacity to work in this way. For example, the drug support project experienced difficulties in working with the local authority's housing department because of differing institutional practices and priorities.

All four programmes involved some additional costs, including things like employing and training the recycling canvassers, and extra resources for intensive targeted work with families and substance users. There were concerns about costs from local politicians and other practitioners in three of the projects, with perceptions that these tailored approaches were more expensive and difficult to adopt beyond a small pilot area. However, others involved in the projects pointed to the potential long-term savings that could be made by the upfront investment in preventative work. But, while tailoring of services can have long-term benefits, it may put short term-pressure on public services that have to meet the needs of a wide range of citizens.

Those who advocated in favour of resourcing these intensive projects argued that the programmes (particularly the drug and family support projects) were based on a complicated understanding of the drivers of particular types of behaviour. Rather than exclusively tackling the anti-social behaviour or substance misuse, they tried to influence the context in which individuals found themselves in the hope that improving services would help prevent anti-social behaviour or that stabilising lifestyles might give those who misuse substances greater opportunity to regain control over their habits. If the projects are successful in engendering personal responsibility in clients, and preventing further costly behaviour, they offer potentially significant long-term savings to a range of public services and benefits to society. Until further experimentation is conducted it is hard to judge what savings and benefits may be achieved.

It can be useful to segment the population and tailor behaviour change policies differently depending on the known behavioural characteristics of a particular group. In attempting to influence behaviour change, government can use marketing techniques more commonly associated with the commercial world, identifying and segmenting different target groups and tailoring interventions according to what might be most effective for each section of the population (Knott et al, 2008). The recycling project first identified whether households were recyclers or not and then targeted the canvassing accordingly, treating people differently. Existing recyclers were thanked for using the recycling box; reminded of the variety of recyclable materials and – if they seemed enthusiastic – asked if they would like to become recycling champions. Non-recyclers were encouraged to recycle, informed of the day and date of collection and materials collected, and asked if they could be counted on to recycle regularly. *what about barriers to recycling?*

Engagement and participation

The initial process of engaging with participants presented similar challenges for the projects but to different degrees. The recycling project required minimal time with people who were contacted at home on a relatively uncontroversial issue. The process of locating and engaging citizens was much more problematic for the other projects. In the community engagement project, while the initial recruitment was successful, the involvement in general did not last. Exactly why this was is hard to say, but it seems likely that policy makers and citizens had different expectations about what it was feasible to ask of people, especially where they had little spare time. While a broad selection of people showed initial interest in the community engagement project, young people, Asian women and those without previous experience of participation did not sustain their involvement. One possibility, to be tested in future research, is that they needed activities tailored to their interests if they were to stay involved. Nor was the project able to overcome the well-known barriers of engaging minority ethnic groups. For example, one woman said:

> 'I wear a hijab and I don't want to go into an environment where they don't know about normal Muslims, only the terrorist extreme. If there were other people of my origin I might go. If I go the first time and it is accepting then it is fine.'

The family support and the drug support projects were at the most extreme end of the continuum. They were asking people to behave differently on sensitive issues, requiring change around private behaviours. Both the recycling and community engagement projects used voluntary participation, as did the family support and drug projects. All four projects were non-coercive and relied on people agreeing to take part. However, the barriers to the families and substance users getting engaged were greater, and the stakes for those citizens personally were more immediately obvious and arguably higher than for individuals going to a community meeting or doing recycling. Therefore, the initial process of engaging with clients was critical for the family and drug projects, which required building and maintaining good client–worker relationships to sustain involvement. Subsequently, both projects were delayed by long lead-in times of several months for the recruitment and engagement of clients. However, once clients were engaged, there were very few dropouts and those engaged had positive outcomes. In this sense, the process of successful recruitment and engagement of individuals should be recognised in the evaluation process and highlighted as a positive outcome. The professionals who delivered these projects needed to have strong relationships with citizens in order to broach delicate subjects, such as drug misuse and issues within the family home, to persuade people to engage in lifestyle changes and parenting support. Research found that few of the public sector agencies had this kind of relationship with people as they only intervened at crisis level. For example, families felt they had personalised support from health visitors at children's centres but identified a support gap for low-level problems beyond this. The clients in the drug support project and the parents in the family support project appreciated a trusted professional who they felt understood the strains on their lives and could offer support and guidance.

A two-way process

Citizens involved in these experiments often regarded their own behaviour change as part of a contract with expectations on both sides. If citizens are to consider changing their behaviour, they will have high expectations about the behaviour of public agencies. Canvassers went door to door to promote the use of a recycling service. While the majority of householders seemed happy with the service, those who were dissatisfied with its standard – missed collections, rude staff, dirty boxes returned, pedantic over contamination – had given up on recycling altogether and had to be persuaded to restart. Canvassers felt they had to win round people who were fed up with the service, as one canvasser commented:

> '[If] collections weren't right or something went wrong or they got disenchanted because they don't get their bin back or they are confused about how things should be sorted ... we have tried to persuade them to give it another go.'

The canvassers were negotiating a contract with the householder – persuading people to recycle in expectation that the service would be better than before.

Similarly, in the community participation experiment, people who considered action to improve their neighbourhoods expected that the local authority would play its part in maintaining the neighbourhood. If the citizen made an effort but then found that the council was failing to deliver its services effectively they got disheartened. A bin strike during the experiment meant rubbish was left uncollected and people got angry and disheartened. As one resident commented:

> 'The original phone call was about the back alley and it is still in the same state. I have cleared it and then it has deteriorated again. I was promised that flyers would be put through every door explaining the system and nothing has happened. And the bin strike has made it worse.'

Empowering citizens

3. A third doubt about behaviour change is whether citizens are willing to accept government interference. Behaviour change policies have attracted some critical attention for expanding into areas of life that many would consider private or nagging citizens unnecessarily. Yet, in these local experiments, there was little evidence that citizens resented the interventions to change behaviour. Fears of being too heavy handed were raised by local authority staff rather than citizens. For example, at the outset of the community engagement project, contact centre staff were worried that citizens with other concerns would respond angrily to being asked about civic activity, but their worries were alleviated during the trial. Similarly, local services were initially apprehensive about the willingness of families to be part of the family support project for fear that they would regard it as an intrusive intervention. The one public service that did have good enough relationships with families to broach parenting issues was reluctant to talk to families about getting the additional help because the provider felt this could damage their relationship with families. This was one of the reasons why the programme was delivered by a third-sector organisation. There were some difficulties recruiting for the family support project, although it is not possible to analyse the reasons for non-participation. However, once participants had been recruited, they tended to 'last the course' and our interviews with them show no indication that they felt the interventions to be intrusive.

In these instances the worries about an overbearing or intrusive state were unwarranted. But can the more positive claim that the interventions were empowering be supported? This is a complicated question because, as discussed earlier, 'empowerment' can be understood in two different ways. On the one hand, people and groups can be empowered to solve problems for themselves with the provision of the required resources, skills and capacities. On the other hand, people and groups can be empowered in their relationship to public service providers by giving them greater opportunity to influence and shape how they receive services.

The interaction between these two understandings of empowerment is most apparent in the family support and drug support projects. In both projects, the assumption was that making public services more flexible and responsive for clients would allow the clients to take greater personal responsibility for their own behaviour – that 'empowering' clients in relation to public services would also 'empower' them in a more general sense. The projects produced generally positive, though limited, findings on that issue.

In the community engagement project the policy makers were hoping to empower residents in the first sense of the term, to encourage them to 'take action on community issues in the area'. However, at least some of the residents were more interested in the second meaning of empowerment, wanting to increase their ability to influence the services provided to them rather than take a very active role in dealing with community issues.

Conclusion

The chapter examines the experiences of citizens in four projects relying on persuasive policy tools to change citizen behaviours. In each, citizens and public institutions were engaged in implicit negotiations about their respective roles and expectations. Far from being pliant and malleable, the citizens we spoke to often had clear ideas about how that balance should be struck while demonstrating willingness to adapt their behaviour where they felt public governance was meeting its part of the bargain. The chapter has shown that policies, when sensitively done, can be effective and deliver results.

However, the successful implementation of all but the simplest behaviour change policy posed challenges to the existing structures of governance. As with all government intervention, behaviour change policies operate in a context of resource constraints, competing demands, dispersed authority and differing views. Flexibility and tailoring can be challenging and costly. It is therefore commendable that the local authorities in these four examples have made efforts to develop innovative strategies to allow services to adapt better to citizens' needs. The outcomes of these projects have been so far encouraging and provide the opportunity for further development.

References
APSC (Australian Public Service Commission) (2007) *Changing behaviour: A public policy perspective*, Barton, Australia: APSC.
Askew, R. and Richardson, L. (2008) 'Preventing and deterring anti-social behaviour and crime in young people: research based design project', IPEG Working Paper.
Askew, R., John, P. and Liu H. (2008) 'Intensive support for problematic substance users: outcomes of a design experiment', IPEG Working Paper.

Barnard, M. and McKeganey, N. (2004) 'The impact of parental problem drug use on children: what is the problem and what can be done to help?', *Addiction,* vol 99, no 5, pp 552-59.

Beinart, S., Anderson, B., Lee, S. and Utting, D. (2002) *Youth at risk? A national survey of risk factors, protective factors and problem behaviour among young people in England, Scotland and Wales,* London: Joseph Rowntree Foundation/Communities that Care.

Brannan, T., John, P. and Stoker, G. (2006) *Re-energizing citizenship: Strategies for civil renewal,* Basingstoke: Palgrave MacMillan.

Cabinet Office (2006) *Reaching out: An action plan on social exclusion,* London: Cabinet Office.

CLG (Communities and Local Government) (2008) *Communities in control: Real people, real power,* London: CLG.

Cotterill, S., John, P., Liu, H. and Nomura, H. (2008) 'Mobilizing citizen effort to enhance environmental outcomes: a randomised controlled trial of a door to door recycling campaign', IPEG Working Paper.

Cotterill, S. and Richardson, L. (2009) 'Changing the nature of transactions between local state and citizens: an experiment to encourage civic behaviour', presentation at the Political Studies Association conference, Manchester, 7-9 April 2009.

Gossop, M. (2006) *Treating drug misuse: Evidence of effectiveness,* London: National Treatment Agency.

Halpern, D., Bates, C., Mulgan, G., Aldridge, S., Beales, G. and Heathfield, A. (2004) *Personal responsibility and changing behaviour: The state of knowledge and its implications for public policy,* London: Cabinet Office: Prime Minister's Strategy Unit.

Hobcroft, J. (1998) *Intergenerational and life-course transmission of social exclusion: Influences in childhood poverty, family disruption and contact with the police,* Case paper 15, London: London School of Economics and Political Science, STICERD, November.

Knott, D., Muers, S. and Aldridge, S. (2008) *Achieving culture change: A policy framework.* London: Prime Minister's Strategy Unit.

Lewis, M. (2007) *States of reason: Freedom, responsibility and the governing of behaviour change,* London: IPPR.

Lowndes, V., Pratchett, L. and Stoker, G. (2006a) 'Diagnosing and remedying the failings of official participation schemes: the CLEAR framework', *Social Policy and Society,* vol 5, no 2, pp 281-91.

Lowndes, V., Pratchett, L. and Stoker, G. (2006b) 'Local political participation: the impact of rules-in-use', *Public Administration,* vol 84, no 3, pp 539-62.

O'Leary, D. (ed) (2008) *The politics of public behaviour,* London: Demos (www.demos.co.uk/publications/politicsofpublicbehaviour).

Ostrom, E. (1998) 'A behavioural approach to the rational choice theory of collective action', *The American Political Science Review*, vol 92, no 1, pp 1-22.

Parker, H. (2004) 'The new drugs intervention industry: what outcomes can drugs/criminal justice treatment programmes realistically deliver', *Probation Journal*, vol 4, pp 379-86.

Shaw, P.J., Lyas, J.K., Maynard, S.J. and van Vugt, M. (2007) 'On the relationship between set-out rates and participation ratios as a tool for enhancement of kerbside household waste recycling', *Journal of Environmental Management*, vol 83, no 1, pp 34-43.

Timlett, R. and Williams, I. (2008) 'Public participation and recycling performance in England: a comparison of tools for behaviour change', *Resources, Conservation and Recycling* vol 52, no 4, pp 622-34.

Verba, S., Schlozman, K. and Brady, H. (1995) *Voice and equality: Civic voluntarism in American Politics*, London: Harvard Press.

Acknowledgements

We thank all those local government officers and citizens who generously gave their time to participate in our research. Our colleagues in the Institute for Political and Economic Governance (IPEG) – Peter John, Hanhua Liu and Liz Richardson – made a substantial contribution to these research projects. The projects were funded by the Economic and Social Research Council, Communities and Local Government, the North West Improvement Network and local councils. The views expressed are the authors alone.

Note

[1] Information gathered from the Office for National Statistics Neighbourhood Statistics, 11 August 2008 (www.neighbourhood.statistics.gov.uk/).

TEN

Every child's voice matters?

Harriet Churchill

Introduction

The publication of *Every child matters* (DfES, 2003) began a radical reform of children's services in England and Wales. The reforms were driven by concerns to improve child protection systems and children's outcomes, particularly among the poorest children. As a result children's services have undergone major institutional reform. Local education and social care authorities have been reorganised into 'children's authorities' and new structures seeking to improve accountability and interagency working have been introduced. Within these governance arrangements, authorities have been expected to involve children and young people (DfES, 2003), initially in terms of consulting service users and more recently in the 'planning, commissioning and delivery of public services' (DCSF, 2007).

This chapter examines children's participation in this service context. The terms 'children and young people' will be used interchangeably to refer to the age range targeted by the reforms (young people aged between 0-19 years old or up to 21-24 years in the case of looked after or disabled young people). The first part of the chapter reviews the drivers of change and national policy framework for reform and participation. The chapter will then examine the conceptualisation of children's participation and the implementation framework for reform drawing on theoretical and empirical work in this area. With several tensions between child welfare and children's participation agendas highlighted and a number of critical issues for local practice identified, the final section of the chapter examines change within a case study local authority. I argue that in this case there was evidence that children's involvement in local governance has not merely been tokenistic and has stretched beyond managerialist consultation. This was because children's participation was viewed as citizenship education and related to social inclusion and cohesion objectives in New Labour's communitarian approach. However, participation was not as yet 'embedded in organisational cultures' (Kirby et al, 2005) or leading to 'shared child–adult agenda setting' (Hart, 1992). The analysis seeks to demonstrate that, in the case of children's services reform, this is because of weaknesses in both the conception and implementation of children's participation. In thinking about the way forward there are tensions between current child welfare/children's participation agendas that need to be addressed as well as a number of factors curtailing local implementation.

Children's services reform and children's participation

In this section the drivers and framework for reform will be set out, illustrating the shift from an emphasis on consulting children and young people to more extensive participation in service review.

The reforms and policy agendas

Every child matters (DfES, 2003) set out a programme of reform aimed at improving five key outcomes for children and young people: their health, safety, enjoyment and educational achievement, making a positive contribution to society and economic well-being (DfES, 2003: 14). With a focus on these outcomes, *Every child matters* made the case for reform to encompass all children's services (DfES, 2003: 2).

Improving accountability, coordination and performance monitoring across children's services were key aspects of reform. Between 2005 and 2008 local children's social services and education departments were to form children's authorities, under the leadership of a 'children's director'. Children's directors were to establish local strategic partnerships, 'children's trusts', made up of senior officers from health, social services and education, working in partnership with the voluntary and private sectors. Children's authorities were required to initially conduct a systematic review of services and local needs, in order to produce a Children and Young People Plan (CYPP). Against this framework for local reform, children's authorities would then be subject to performance monitoring in respect of the five key outcomes for children. Ofsted, the standards and inspection agency for education, had its remit expanded to monitor standards across all children's services in line with the new outcomes-focused approach. At the local level of service delivery, services were to be devolved and more integrated, so that health, social services, education, youth services and other professionals delivered services through local partnerships, 'children's centres' or 'extended schools'.

With concerns about child protection failures, children's authorities were also to establish local safeguarding boards (LSBs), to review and reform child protection procedures and services. The reforms stressed the need to improve intervention powers and information sharing in response to child welfare concerns. A controversial 'children's database' was proposed and legislation was developed so that public service professionals had a duty and power to report child welfare/protection issues at the point of 'concern' rather than at the point of evidence of harm (Parton, 2006). These institutional changes were in line with New Labour's approach to modernising public services, whereby factors such as improving partnership working were thought to be the most cost-effective way of improving children's services (Churchill, 2008). For example, partnership working was viewed as important in reducing the duplication of services, improving information sharing, facilitating the pooling of budgets and raising awareness of needs (DfES, 2003).

In assessing the drivers of change, Parton (2006) argued that New Labour's reform of children's services represented the coming together of New Labour's programme to reduce child poverty and social exclusion alongside the need to respond to child protection concerns raised by the case of the death of Victoria Climbié (when concerns about her welfare had come to the attention of a range of public services on several occasions). Within this synopsis of the drivers of change, there is also a need to emphasise the significance of policy and public concerns about youth anti-social behaviour and offending. Ultimately, then, there were three dominant agendas driving reform. The first agenda has involved an emphasis on more preventative measures for safeguarding children with a strategic review of child protection policies, the establishment of LSBs with strategic responsibilities to oversee that review, new powers for professionals to raise child welfare concerns and the more controversial extension of information gathering, surveillance and monitoring of children's welfare (Parton, 2006). The second agenda, concerned with taking forward New Labour's anti-poverty initiatives aimed at children, has led to an emphasis on reducing health, income and educational inequalities between poorer and better off children. Several commentators have highlighted the importance that New Labour placed on educational attainment as a route out of poverty and this has been further indicated within children's services reform where the former Department of Education and Skills took the lead role, Ofsted became the inspection agency and children's authorities have often been headed up by children's directors with backgrounds in education. There has been criticism, though, that New Labour's approach to tackling child poverty is based on a narrow view of child well-being in terms of hard and fast indicators of physical health or educational attendance and attainment (Williams, 2004).

The third dominant policy agenda has been that of addressing youth anti-social behaviour and offending. New Labour has been concerned to present an image of being 'tough on crime' and has governed during an era of grave public concern about levels of youth violence and crime. There are concerns about a crisis in childhood where Britain has been cast as the 'worst place in Europe to grow-up' (UNICEF, 2007), with a 'yob culture' (Duncan-Smith, 2006). One of the critical outcomes for children therefore sought within the reforms was to promote young people's 'positive contribution' to their neighbourhoods and society. Under this agenda the reforms refer to involving and consulting with children, and investing in citizenship education and creative/leisure opportunities for disadvantaged young people as preventative measures.

The reforms and children's participation

From the outset the reforms conceptualised and related to children and young people as more than mere recipients of welfare services. Consultation events with young people were undertaken during the development of the Green Paper and it was stated that children's authorities and agencies were to 'seek out the views of children and young people', which should be evidenced in their CYPPs (DfES, 2003). This built on service-specific consultation requirements that were established within the 1989 Children's Act, 2001 Health and Social Care Act and 2002 Education Act. *Every child matters* also represented recognition of the importance of 'child-friendly language'. The consultation events, for example, had illustrated how children prefer the term 'keeping safe' and promoted an active role for themselves and adults in helping to 'keep safe' over the more passive notion of adult-led 'child protection' (DfES, 2003). While the requirement for consultation was welcomed by many, several criticised the reforms as only marginally concerned with a children's participation agenda. The work of initiatives such as the Children's and Young People's Unit (CYPU) and Children's Fund projects (aimed at improving the coordination and provision of services for disadvantaged youth) were viewed as more radical, promoting an ethos of youth participation in 'the design, provision and evaluation of policies and services' (CYPU, 2002: 3). While the language of inclusion and participation was present in the Green Paper, many felt that children were conceptualised in homogeneous and developmental terms that express political and economic interests in securing a future workforce that is disciplined and skilled (Williams, 2004). Williams states the reforms 'set out the structures of accountability to protect children ... and created educational opportunities to enable them to become productive future citizens' but were less about 'fostering the active enjoyment of, and negotiation of, childhood' (Williams, 2004: 80).

More recently, though, authorities have been encouraged to 'build a culture of participation' with children and young people, actively involving them in the 'commissioning, development, running and performance monitoring of local services'–performance in this area to be monitored as part of 'joint service reviews' (DCSF, 2007). This shift could be due to effective campaigning. It also represented mobilisation across political parties to set out reforms of the conduct of politics itself and the political system. New Labour has focused on local government reform and sought to establish devolved governance structures, to 'forge more influence, control and ownership by local people of local services' as 'place shapers' (CLG, 2008: 1). Informed by the 'crisis in childhood' narrative, this agenda has also involved political pressure to review citizenship for young people. A Youth Citizenship Commission was established in 2007 to review youth political engagement, the civic values of young people and support for reducing the age at which the right to vote is gained.

Analysing the framework for reform

This section analyses the reform objectives set out above with reference to theoretical and empirical work on children's citizenship and participation in local governance.

Conceptualising participation

It appears children's involvement in New Labour's reform of children's services concurs more with liberal and communitarian conceptions of children's citizenship than radical or feminist perspectives. Liberal notions of citizenship are concerned with individual legal status whereby citizenship is conveyed by political, civil and social rights and duties laid out in law (Hart, 1992). Children are not granted the same rights and duties as adults because of their immaturity and because they are seen as 'welfare dependants' – that is, as dependent on, and primarily the responsibility of, families. Citizenship is granted when young people are deemed able to exercise citizenship rights and duties effectively. However, within this framework, the age at which children are considered mature and competent citizens varies between countries, cultures and different areas of law. Currently, young people in England can undertake paid work from the age of 13 and yet cannot vote until the age of 18. In criminal law the age for criminal responsibility in England and Wales has been lowered to ten years old, challenging the welfare paradigm and causing controversy over whether young people and adults should be treated in such similar ways. Overall, the current legal framework is criticised for inconsistency, where children are treated either as welfare dependants (emphasising their vulnerabilities and incompetence rather than their strengths and capabilities) or the same as adults (which fails to recognise their dependencies and vulnerabilities) (Neale, 2004). Further, citizen rights and duties are granted on an age basis so that 'young people are suddenly expected to become responsible, participating adult citizens at the age of 16, 18 or 21 without prior exposure to the skills and responsibilities involved' (Hart, 1992: 5). Childhood, therefore, is accompanied by citizenship education and young people are viewed as 'citizens in the making'.

Communitarian perspectives are particularly interested in citizenship as social practice and citizenship education. Etzioni (1993), for example, argued that citizenship is about how we live on a day-to-day basis, our social values and how we relate to one another, which in turn fosters communities, shared responsibility and solidarity. In this sense, children as 'citizens in the making' are an important concern as civic values are seen as primarily learnt during childhood, mainly within families (Etzioni, 1993). Communitarianism then emphasises micro-level community, family and self-governance. Further, thinkers such as Etzioni put forward a particular view of what our shared values and duties should be as citizens, which include being productive paid workers, responsible parents and law-abiding citizens. Although communitarian theory differs, what has been significant about the communitarian contribution to New Labour's social policies is a pessimistic narrative that social solidarity is under threat and citizens have become more individualised or individualistic (Etzioni, 1993; Blair, 2006). These general narratives, though, tend to downplay continued intergenerational social solidarity within the context of family and socioeconomic changes (Williams, 2004). Communitarianism is thought to blame deficient citizens for social problems rather than acknowledge the effects of inequalities and discrimination (Williams, 2004).

More radical conceptions of children's citizenship seek to integrate notions of children as agents, dependants, citizens in the present and citizens in the making. A strong line of argument for children's participation is that of democratic principles:

> ... children's citizenship is about participation in the process of sharing decisions which affect one's life and the life of the community in which one lives. It is the means by which a democracy is built and it is the standard by which democracies should be measured. Participation is a fundamental right of citizenship. (Hart, 1992: 5)

The right for children to express their views in decisions and services that affect their lives (in ways that foster their evolving capacities to do so) was established by Article 12 in the UN Convention on the Rights of the Child (UNCRC), which was ratified in the UK in 1991 (United Nations, 1990). Feminist sociological conceptualisations of children's citizenship tend to expand on democratic principles and look at everyday adult–child relations. Neale (2004) formulates children's citizenship as entitlements to recognition, respect, protection and participation. Neale argues that young people should be:

- recognised as being individuals with identities, concerns, views and interests that are respected and valued;
- viewed as agents with strengths, competences and influence in their own childhoods and in society;
- entitled to protection from harm, care and welfare, and to participate in decisions that affect their lives;
- provided with opportunities to learn about and develop the skills, competences and dispositions of active citizens (Neale, 2004: 8–10).

I would argue that the *Every child matters* reforms in England are more concerned with the third, and increasingly the fourth, set of issues identified by Neale but are weak on the first two. Interestingly, children's services reform objectives in Wales and Scotland refer more explicitly to respect for cultural diversity and multicultural belonging (Leverett, 2008).

Realising participation in practice

This section considers theoretical and empirical work on effective youth participation in local governance. For Kirby et al (2005) effective children's participation is participation that is 'meaningful for children and young people', 'effective in bringing about change' and 'embedded within the organisational ethos' (Kirby et al, 2005: 3). There is no doubt in their minds that effective children's participation demands radical organisational change rather than merely empowerment of young people to participate:

not just children .—

> This change is about the whole ethos and culture of the organisation and needs to happen within senior management, as well as within frontline staff, and across policy and practice. It is about developing new ways of working with children and young people. Developing the infrastructure and building organisational capacity needs dedicated commitment, sufficient staff support and an undertaking to adopt an organisational learning approach. (Kirby et al, 2005: 7)

In their research on children's participation in 29 local authorities and agencies they distinguished between three ideal types of 'cultures of participation' (Kirby et al, 2005).

* *Consultation-focused organisations*, which consult children and young people on a one-off or regular basis to inform managerial decisions about services, policy and product development.
* *Participation-focused organisations*, which consult and involve young people in making decisions, although in relation to time-limited initiatives or specific service contexts (for example, youth forum, school council).
* *Child/youth-focused organisations* where 'participation is central to all practice with children and young people within the organisation'. The organisation 'establishes a culture in which it is assumed that all children and young people will be listened to about all decisions – both personal and public – that affect their lives' (Kirby et al, 2005: 16).

Kirby et al (2005) suggest that the level/type of participation would differ according to organisational objectives. Where organisations work regularly and directly with children and 'services impact a lot on children' they should be child/youth focused. However, 'strategic planning organisations and bodies should be participation focused so that young people have a specific scrutiny role'; and organisations that sell goods and services to young people should be 'consultationary' (Kirby et al, 2005: 18). Their research has reviewed evidence for the range of managerial, service, societal and child/youth development benefits that can be secured from working in these ways (Kirby et al, 2005). However, research has also highlighted constraints and contradictions that local authorities face as organisations (and collectives of organisations). These include the constraints of national policy; lack of support from senior management; limitations of local/institutional funding and partnership frameworks; and the challenges of realising change across all levels and sectors of public services (Hart 1992; Kirby et al, 2005). In the context of children's services reform under New Labour, the national policy framework places emphasis on the managerial and social welfare outcomes of participation (rather than democratic) – namely with targets to safeguard children, reduce health and educational inequalities and reduce youth offending. The requirement to involve young people is rarely associated with considerations of the complexities of implementation raised by empirical work in this area.

Children's participation: local policy and practice

This section examines local reform in one local authority, fictitiously called Gatsborough City Council, between 2004 and mid-2008. The Council serves a post-industrial northern city with relatively high levels of educational underachievement (compared to national educational attainment targets), social services caseloads and youth offending rates. The analysis draws on data that was collected as part of a larger investigation of children's services reform implementation in five local authorities. The study examined local priorities for reform and the development of service user/children's involvement. Semi-structured interviews with youth participation workers and children's services professionals, documentary analysis of strategic documents (such as the local CYPP), interviews with parents and family carers, and focus group discussions with young people informed the larger study. The analysis below is informed by this data and aims to illuminate the directions of local policy and practice in this case (rather than provide conclusive findings on the specific outcomes of all the main participation activities, which would require more extensive research).

The aims and development of children's participation

Children's participation in Gatsborough City Council since the early 2000s can be characterised by four overlapping phases. The first phase, from the mid-1990s to 2004, was orientated towards two key focuses – political representation for young people and service-specific consultation. There was a focus on promoting young people's political literacy and representation across the city via the Youth Council (YC). The YC was established in 1996 and was made up of elected representatives from secondary schools with, at its most active, around 100 members aged 11-18. It operated as a formal structure, with termly meetings held at the Council's Town Hall, meeting agendas set by council officers and members making decisions via member discussion and voting. From 2001, the YC received resources and support from a council officer whose role within the chief executive's department included some time to organise, chair and develop the YC. At this time, the council officer reported in an interview for the study on children's services reform that her role with the YC work was "well supported" as an "innovative youth participation initiative". Between 2001 and 2004, the officer extended the consultation and political literacy aims of the YC by developing more representative and effective school councils, such as by providing training for teachers on engaging students in school councils and developing meaningful consultation activities with them, and providing training for students in formal political representation methods (the use of election methods to aid school council selection and decision making). Her efforts were focused particularly on secondary schools. The second element of children's participation during this phase involved service-specific consultation – for example, in relation to social care services as required by the 1989 Children's Act.

A change in focus, though, emerged from the development of Children's Fund projects in the authority, which orientated consultation towards disadvantaged young people as a group and as recipients of Children's Fund initiatives. Gatsborough received Children's Fund investment for many local projects. The local Children's Participation Partnership (CPP), made up of agencies delivering Children's Fund projects, promoted a strong ethos of participation within these projects, consulted widely with disadvantaged young people and established a significant youth advocacy role for third-sector agencies. This development heralded a change of emphasis where participation initiatives moved away from political objectives and the citywide involvement of young people to improving services for disadvantaged young people and empowering those most in need. This work was informed by the growing body of good practice in engaging with young people. Informed by this, by 2004, the council officer reported in an interview for the implementation study that she felt the YC's approach to youth engagement was "too formal and adult-led", primarily concerned with meeting Gatsborough Council's "feedback needs". She also felt her remit in working with the YC was quite limited (to conduct formal meetings with the YC three times a year) and that she was afforded little time or funding to "dedicate to development work with schools and young people" outside these meetings. Related to this, the officer felt that the YC was initially "blessed with a really engaged group of young people" but by 2003/04 their engagement had dwindled and the amount/skills of new members had declined.

The reorganisation of children's services, from 2004, then led to the second phase of participation activity. In line with national policy and building on the significance of the CPP in local reforms, this phase can be characterised as concerned with the empowerment of disadvantaged youth and the expansion of service-specific consultation (which moved into the realm of young people contributing to the establishment of issues for review). In 2004, the council officer working with the YC became the lead youth participation worker and relocated to Children's Services. During the development of the CYPP, Children's Services ran several consultation events/activities seeking to gain young people's views on services and hear about their concerns. The voluntary sector agencies involved in the CPP continued to have a strong role in organising these events, which used traditional consultation methods such as surveys and focus groups with service users and more creative methods. For example, young people attending youth groups in neighbourhood regeneration areas have been supported to make films about their experiences and views, which were then shown to decision-making committees within Children's Services. In Kirby et al's (2005) terms, the strategic review of children's services provided a window of opportunity for a more participatory role for young people in 'establishing issues for service review'. The youth participation team also recognised other differences beyond the focus on economically disadvantaged youth, with effort to represent the views of boys and girls, disabled young people and people from minority ethnic communities. However, the views of younger children have not been so widely accessed. These developments were further prompted by criticism in a 'joint area review' that Gatsborough Council needed to develop a more long-term participation strategy. One development has been children's involvement in the work of the Scrutiny and Overview Committee in Children's Services, instigated by the former youth participation worker and members of the CPP, who sat on the Committee. A decision was taken within the Scrutiny and Overview Committee to seek the views of young people on every appropriate agenda item. This took many creative forms so that a committee discussion about looked after children was stimulated by a DVD made with children in social care about their experiences and views.

The third phase of participation, emerging from 2006, involved the reorganisation of youth participation into district youth forums. This development again reflected national and local policy developments, with concern within the Council to develop a more long-term participation strategy and the 2006 Local Government Reform Act coming into force. The Children's and Young People's Engagement Strategy was devised and finalised in mid-2008. This strategy has been informed by an emphasis on district-level community involvement. The strategy formulated a vision of district youth forums, with four forums covering the city and expected to feed into the six new district-level committees. These district decision-making structures have service review roles, but by mid-2008 did not have extensive devolved budgets or commissioning roles. In two districts the youth forums developed out of the youth engagement work of Children's Fund and local regeneration projects. The other two youth forums were established following some developmental work establishing networks between statutory and third-sector agencies, and in particular recruiting members from local secondary schools. It was envisaged that, as the new district-level decision-making structures (which are concerned with district/ neighbourhood issues) were established, the youth forums would be consulted by the district forums on issues concerned with provision for young people in neighbourhoods. The aims of participation were now cast strongly in terms of neighbourhood regeneration and social cohesion as well as the individual empowerment of youth forum members. The former youth participation worker stated that young people could "make a positive contribution" to their communities and were being "empowered to improve their neighbourhoods". This development had meant the return of more citywide structures for youth engagement (akin to the YC) but the remit was towards improving localities and it is unclear how the forums may work together. Another aspect of this development was the relocation of youth engagement into the work of Youth Services, with local youth workers organising youth forums. The full-time youth participation post in Children's Services ended and there was a fear this work could become compartmentalised as the responsibility of the Youth Services (which does not work with younger children). However, the role for young people in the Scrutiny and Overview Committee may prevent compartmentalisation.

A further, more recent development in Gatsborough Council is also worth noting. A fourth phase of participation, which involves moves to reinvigorate the YC seems to be emerging. The interest for this has developed out of concern about political apathy and citizenship education among young people, as well as interest within the local authority Children's Services to consult young people more to get a clearer picture of their needs 'across the board' (across the age ranges, localities and services). However, much will depend on the extent to which lessons are learnt from the past when the YC relied on the active engagement of skilled young political actors and limited resources were available for developmental work.

Evidence of 'listening to children' and strategic impact

The discussion now turns to examine the issues raised by young people and evidence that young people have influenced strategic decisions in Gatsborough Council. I will argue that youth participation activities did lead to some 'organisational learning' but this occurred mainly at the level of individual committee members and participation workers rather than informing service-level reform. Where the issues raised by young people did not support council priorities, they did not influence agenda setting.

To demonstrate aspects of organisational learning, it is possible to track some decisions to youth participation work. On remarking about the impact of the films made by young people and their involvement in the Scrutiny and Overview Committee, the youth participation worker and committee minutes reported how young people had "influenced decisions", "changed members' attitudes" and engendered a commitment among members to "spread this work out to other committees in the council". The films about being in care, being a disabled young person and living in different localities in the city had been received as "real eye openers" highlighting daily concerns about safety, poverty and peer pressure. Children's Services had reported a renewed commitment to invest more resources into localities and groups that were not classed as in the highest need but where young people nevertheless had expressed the need for improved facilities and services.

As part of the larger study, 11 members of the most newly formed youth forum were interviewed in two focus groups in early 2008. The group met weekly and involved young people aged between 11 and 16, with a fairly even gender balance and students from several schools in the neighbourhood. On attending one of the group sessions it had the feel of a youth group, with the young people involved provided with leisure and social opportunities, IT and entertainment facilities, creative opportunities (such as music courses) and a place to meet up. Many members of the group were siblings or cousins, or knew each other through school. These benefits of group involvement, such as social, leisure and educational opportunities, were seen as important aspects of improving the lives of the young people and the young people themselves referred to how much they valued the facilities and opportunities provided. The group had also engaged in consultation activities but these were in their early stages – the young people had undertaken training on 'expressing their views'. When asked for their views about services in the focus groups, members talked at length. The issues raised related to homework, school councils, anxiety about school exams, health concerns (such as the effects of smoking or alcohol use), bullies at school, the health of family members, the quality of family relationships (particularly contact with non-resident fathers), getting into trouble with the police and restrictions in using public spaces. For example, there were several issues raised about schools, such as around homework and student feedback:

Sam: 'You're at school for about six hours. Then you come home and you have homework.'

Louise: 'And you can't play out with your friends. All your life is just work. When school's over you're supposed to chill out, not work more.'

Sam: 'Homework is important, but you should have another hour at school to do it.'

James: 'We have a school council. When we were in it we would give them ideas. They didn't listen to them though.'

Sam: 'They would look at them and then choose the opposite! We don't have our dinnertime until 1.30 and I am starving by then. We complained, we had a box for complaints. They got loads of

complaints but they didn't do anything about
them.'

James: 'We were going to have a fun day and we got
funding for it. But then they pulled it. I did
complain about that but they didn't do anything
about it.'

The young people also talked about feeling judged and disrespected
by adults because of the way they dressed, their age or perceptions of
their families; and linked these to negative stereotypes of poor, male
or minority ethnic young people. There was particular concern about
the police stopping them using the local park, although there was also
recognition of their families' concerns about their safety when using
this park. The issues raised were about these young people's everyday
experiences of family relationships and relationships with services.
They remarked on a lack of practical advice from agencies, such as
from schools about future employment options, and their concerns
being dismissed by authority figures, such as teachers.

Is there evidence of these concerns being acted on and becoming
strategic priorities within Children's Services? Although more extensive
research is needed to address this question, overall council strategic
priorities continue to be firmly set by national targets and priorities,
with a focus on improving health, social care and educational attainment
outcomes among the most disadvantaged children. Gatsborough's
CYPP described its main priority as 'ensuring children and young
people have the skills, abilities, self-esteem and positive outlook to
get good jobs and be successful in adult life'. These priorities, while
important, can contribute to the kinds of pressures within schools
that the young people are reporting concerns over. Strategic priorities
have not articulated the need to review student engagement practices
in schools or developed extensive reforms/training for more effective
service user participation in the everyday work of mainstream services.
This would suggest the Children's Services and partner agencies in
this case would not be classed as 'child and youth focused' using Kirby
et al's (2005) schema. Perhaps the work of youth forums and the
renewed commitment emerging around reinvigorating the YC will
lead to a more collective youth voice. However, the views of younger
children remain neglected in this framework. The visit to the most
recently developed youth forum described above suggested this group
was initially focused on benefiting those involved with social and

educational activities and opportunities, with some additional training for consultation activities.

Conclusion

Children's services reform in England has been concerned with reducing health and educational inequalities among children and preventing youth offending. There has also been an increasing commitment towards children's involvement in governance, primarily conceptualised as consultation to aid the identification of need as well as recognition of the positive individual benefits/skills and social cohesion outcomes to be realised through youth engagement. The case study example demonstrated that, at the local level, much consultation and participation activity had developed, particularly in relation to secondary schools, social care services and youth district forums. These agendas and contexts are important. However, children and childhood are constructed in relation to child development, skills deficits and social threats rather than children's rights. A more child/youth-focused approach would seek not only to improve children's outcomes and neighbourhood provision but also to change adults' thinking, services and structures. On a positive note, young people were involved in the new district governance structures and in scrutiny work, with their involvement leading to some 'organisation learning' among senior council officers and professionals. However, such participation work was also vulnerable in terms of resources and compartmentalisation as the work of youth services.

References

Blair, T. (2006) Speech on social exclusion (www.epolitix.com/EN/news).

Churchill, H. (2008) 'Communities in control? The challenges of neighbourhood governance with reference to local government reform in England', *Commonwealth Journal of Local Governance*, no 1, pp 1-21 (http://epress.lib.uts.edu.au/ojs/index.php/cjlg).

CLG (Communities and Local Government) (2008) *Unlocking the talent of our communities*, Leeds: Communities and Local Government Publications.

CYPU (Child and Young People's Unit) (2002) *Learning to listen: Core principles for the involvement of children and young people*, London: CYPU.

DCSF (Department for Children, Schools and Families) (2007) *The Children's Plan: Building brighter futures* (Cm 7280), London: HMSO.

DfES (Department for Education and Skills) (2003) *Every child matters* (Cm 5863), London: The Stationery Office.

Duncan-Smith, I. (2006) *Breakdown Britain*, London: Centre for Social Justice.

→ Etzioni, A. (1993) *The parenting deficit*, London: Demos. *Summary?*

Hart, R.A. (1992) *Children's participation: From tokenism to citizenship* (Innocenti Essay no 4, pp. 19-22), Florence: UNICEF.

→ Kirkby, P., Lanyon, C., Cronin, K. and Sinclair, R. (2005) *Building a culture of participation*, London: DfES.

Leverett, S. (2008) 'Children's participation', in P. Foley and S. Leverlett (eds) *Connecting with children: Developing working relationships*, Bristol: The Policy Press/Milton Keynes: Open University.

→ Neale, B. (ed) (2004) *Young children's citizenship*, York: Joseph Rowntree Foundation.

Parton, N. (2006) *Safeguarding children: Early intervention and surveillance in late modern society*, Basingstoke: Palgrave.

UNICEF (2007) *Child poverty in perspective: An overview of child well-being in rich countries* (Report Card 7), Florence: UNICEF Innocenti Research Centre.

United Nations (1990) *Convention on the Rights of the Child*, New York: United Nations.

Williams, F. (2004) *Re-thinking families*, London: Gulbenkian Foundation.

e-citizenship: reconstructing the public online

Rabia Karakaya Polat and Lawrence Pratchett

Introduction

The internet and other new information and communication technologies (ICTs) are not intuitively associated with promoting concepts of localism. Indeed, it is a defining feature of these technologies that they are global in their potential and generally uncoupled from localities in their application. It is as easy to access a web page, send an email or meet someone in *second life* from another continent, as it is to correspond online with a neighbour. In this respect, the internet and its related technologies are a major threat to notions of the local, and particularly to any idea of local citizenship. New technologies threaten to create virtual communities on a global scale – communities that are linked less by geography and more by the shared interests, values or prejudices of individuals, regardless of where they may live. Citizenship in this global context, in so far as it might exist at all, is unlikely to make much reference to place but will be premised on ways in which individuals have needs or interests in common. In the online world, locality is arguably an irrelevance.

At the same time, however, these supposedly global technologies are being enacted in ways that are explicitly local in their focus, with the potential to enhance rather than undermine localities. From the e-government developments of local authorities that enable residents to access services online, through to local applications of global social networking sites such as Facebook, it seems that people are as likely to use the technologies for local purposes as they are to go global. Despite the global reach of these technologies, there is plenty of evidence that both individuals and organisations are not only willing, but also want, to use ICTs to strengthen interactions at the local level. The potential of the internet might be global but its enactment is decidedly local.

This global–local paradox lies at the heart of this chapter. We are interested in the way new ICTs, and especially the internet in all of its various forms (from 'traditional' websites through to more recent adaptations of Web 2.0 and social networking), affects notions of citizenship, especially in relation to existing and emerging institutions of local governance. Our concern is with whether online practices of citizenship through different applications are compatible with traditional notions of local belonging. Will the internet eventually lead to the death of local notions of citizenship or can it be an instrument for building community engagement and developing new understandings of citizenship at the local level?

To explore this paradox the chapter focuses on the UK local e-government programme that ran between 2000 and 2006, and analyses its limitations in terms of supporting or building any sense of local community. The chapter starts by looking at three different dimensions of citizenship and reflects on their significance in the online world. We then examine how each of these is being enacted in the online world, by both governments and citizens, focusing especially on the nationally promoted local e-government programme. A final section examines the consequences of the current enactment for the development of citizenship.

Three dimensions of citizenship

The debate around citizenship is primarily one of change. Kivisto and Faist (2007), for example, analyse change around four competing trends that they observe in relation to citizenship. First, they see issues of *inclusion* as being fundamental to citizenship and reflect on the changing way in which states are more or less inclusive of social groups. Second, they concentrate on *erosion* and the extent to which citizen rights have been eroded in the context of the limitations of the welfare state. Third, they examine *withdrawal* as a concept and the extent to which citizens are disengaging or withdrawing from conventional political institutions. Finally, they look to *expansion* as a way of understanding current concepts of citizenship, reflecting on the multiple or 'nested' citizenships that come about in a globalised polity (Kivisto and Faist, 2007). Equally, Lord Goldsmith's review of citizenship for the Ministry of Justice is premised on the assertion that 'we are experiencing changes in our society which may have an impact on the bond that we feel we share as citizens' (Goldsmith, 2007: 7). From academic analysis to policy makers, the assumption is that change is fundamental to understanding citizenship.

The problem with the contemporary debate on citizenship, however, is that it tends to ignore two aspects of change, which, we argue, are central to any understanding of modern citizenship. First, the role of locality is understated in each of these analyses; they remain locked in an assumption that citizenship is primarily the preserve of the nation state. In contrast to this assumption we see locality as being the foundation on which other forms of identity, community membership and citizenship are built. Individuals see their membership of other communities in the context of the locality in which they live and the forms of citizenship that it promotes. In some instances they may take positive experiences from their locality as the basis of engagement with other communities, whether they are nested multiple and overlapping geographic communities or more general communities of shared interest. In other instances the experience may be a more negative one, in which individuals seek alternatives to their experience of local citizenship. Either way, their sense of citizenship elsewhere is shaped by their personal experience of the locality in which they live.

Second, the role of technology in shaping the experience of citizenship is downplayed or even totally ignored in many debates. Contemporary ICTs, and especially the internet, create new and different opportunities for political engagement (Chadwick, 2006). At the very minimum, a significant proportion of citizens access public services on line. For some the political experience is greater; whether engaging through online discussion forums, using an online petitioning system to lobby for a particular policy, or simply forwarding on political videos on YouTube, new opportunities for engaging with both the state and the community are emerging all the time. Furthermore, as more and more people use these technologies in their everyday life, so their expectation of using them for their routine engagements with government, politics and their communities will grow. The internet and its various enacted technologies (Fountain, 2001) are no longer new; they are now mainstream.

We see the relationship between online forms of citizenship and other citizen identities, not as being in competition with one another, but rather as an overlapping and nested process of engagement in which individuals learn what it means to be a citizen through their exposure to different geographic and virtual communities. Being active in an online community is not necessarily an alternative to having a sense of belonging to a particular geographic community or, for that matter, to a community of interest. Indeed, those who engage online are also more likely to be (or become) politically active in the offline world. However, it is also clear that different communities, whether online or offline, will have different expectations of their members, work through different rules and will lead to potentially very different understanding of what it means to be a citizen.

The challenge, therefore, is to understand how new forms of identity correspond to or compete with conventional approaches to citizenship. In particular, we are interested in the way in which the different enactment of ICTs by governments, politicians, citizens and so on leads to different forms of citizenship and identity. There are at least three dimensions of citizenship that can be considered in this context: citizenship as status, citizenship as rights and responsibilities, and citizenship as identity. In this section we consider each of these in turn.

Citizenship as status concerns formal membership of a community and who has access to it. Conventionally such status is associated with membership of a nation state. Thus, nation states determine who can be citizens, what immigration and naturalisation policies should consist of, and so on. Broader definitions of citizenship go even further and include all the political, economic and social structures that constitute membership of a nation state. As Turner (1993: 2) puts it, 'citizenship may be defined as that set of practices (juridical, political, economic and cultural) which define a person as a competent member of society, and which as a consequence shape the flow of resources to persons and social groups'. In effect, this dimension of citizenship is concerned with who is included within a community and the rules that determine such membership. At the level of the nation state such membership is normally clearly defined in law. At the sub-national or local level the position is often more confused. The political constituency at the local level might include residents of a community (not all of whom might be citizens of the nation state) and people who work in that locality but live elsewhere, as well as other local interests. The Maastricht Treaty and the expansion of the European Union has further complicated the position, bestowing denizen status on migrant workers, giving them political and economic status at the local level while not recognising them as full citizens at the level of the nation state (Schmitter et al, 2004). The key point here is that, both below and above the nation state, people belong to multiple communities and have varying status as a citizen in many of them. Unlike at the nation state level, the rules governing the membership and conferring the status of citizen are often ambiguous and variable.

Citizenship as rights and responsibilities concerns the relationship of individuals to the state, and focuses on the formal capacities and immunities associated with the membership of particular communities. It is the combination of both rights and responsibilities that is significant here. Citizens of a community lend legitimacy to its institutions by giving their consent to governance and, in return, they expect certain protection and benefits from their membership. Membership of that community requires individuals to perform certain duties in return for the benefits of that community. As David Held (1996: 81) puts it, 'membership of a political community, ie citizenship, bestows upon the individual both responsibilities and rights, duties and powers, constraints and liberties'. Such duality is evident at the local level. Indeed, it is at the local level where the rights and responsibilities of citizens are most evident. Citizens in their everyday activities both sustain the communities in which they live and are bound by the social norms and formal rules that make the community effective. Where this duality does not exist, communities often fail. However, this duality becomes more challenging in the multiple, nested communities to which most people belong. Different norms and rules apply to the membership of these communities, and each brings different benefits. While the rights and responsibilities associated with living in a specific locality are relatively immediate and clear, the converse is true of membership of the European Union or other higher-level political communities. Locality, therefore, suggests particular interpretations of nested rights and responsibilities, which may vary subtly from place to place.

Citizenship as identity concerns the behavioural aspects of individuals acting and conceiving of themselves as members of a particular cultural, ethnic or political community. Individuals identify themselves as being associated with particular collectivities and as being distinct from others. Such distinctions and identities are as much a feature of locality as they are of distinctions between nation states. The broadcaster Stuart Maconie (2006) offers an amusing but nonetheless typical illustration of local rivalry in his contrast of the personalities of Lancastrians and Yorkshire people:

> We each nurture deeply held prejudices against one another. They [people from Yorkshire] think that we are soft and a bit silly. Easily led and somehow lightweight. We [Lancastrians] think they are humourless and mean-spirited, arrogant and dull. Compared to us Lancastrian bon vivants, we say, waving our pints around for emphasis, they are suspicious and cold. (Maconie, 2006: 178-9)

While the rivalry between Lancashire and Yorkshire might be one of the more celebrated local enmities, there is no doubt that such distinctions are maintained between cities and communities across Great Britain; as, indeed, they are elsewhere.

Community as identity is not only about distinction from neighbouring communities, however; it is also about celebrating shared interests or common bonds within communities. People want to be seen to be citizens of particular communities because of the legitimacy it appears to give them and because of the values that they share. Communities reinforce identity in this way. Indeed, the development of online communities is primarily about this type of citizenship, in which members belong to these communities because of the identity that they are able to share with others.

These three dimensions of citizenship provide a basis for understanding the different trends that are emerging in the world of electronic citizenship and its relationship with changes in citizenship at the local level. As a response to the decoupling of citizenship and nationality, partly due to increasing levels of migration (see Leila Thorp's chapter in this book), states have tried to load citizenship with new meanings. Such new meanings are the object of contemporary campaigns for unity and integration, which aim predominantly at the incorporation of immigrants and people from minority ethnic communities (Joppke, 2007: 44). Other parts of this book have dealt with issues around community cohesion, the role of faith and the underlying values that are supposedly associated with Britishness and British values. However, new ICTs also affect these three dimensions of citizenship. On the one hand, they have the potential to bring easier access to citizenship, introduce ways to enjoy civil rights in a more convenient way (such as political participation, e-voting and so on) and transform citizenship identities by promoting certain values such as multiculturalism. On the other hand, they also have the potential to add greater levels of complexity to these dimensions, by increasing the multiplicity of identities that citizens might have, alienating individuals from their geographic communities and encouraging individualistic modes of engagement with political institutions.

None of these outcomes is given properties of the technologies. How ICTs will affect citizenship depends on how they are used or enacted. How governments, politicians, pressure groups and individuals use the technologies for political engagement matters to the development of citizenship. It is to this enactment of the technologies that we now turn.

Enacting citizenship online

The growth of the internet and its related technologies has not been a linear process. While the take-up of first the internet and then later broadband internet has generally been one of consolidated growth, the applications that have emerged over the period since the mid-1990s when the internet first gained popular use have varied widely: from the e-commerce developments that characterised the dot.com revolution and bubble of the early 2000s, to the highly specialised *usenet* facilities promoted by certain communities in the late 1990s. The internet has grown across a number of different trajectories at one and the same time. It has multiple uses and meanings, which vary in different social, political and economic contexts as well as across time. Its diversity is part of its mainstreaming into everyday culture. For many sections of society it is a fundamental feature of daily life.

Of course, for a significant minority of people (mainly the older and economically disadvantaged sections of society) access to the internet is still limited or even non-existent (Dutton and Helsper, 2007). For those caught on the wrong side of the digital divide the concept of e-citizenship is still meaningless. However, as this chapter is primarily about e-citizenship, we will concentrate on those individuals for whom the internet is a part of their daily routine and for whom, therefore, there is the potential for changing forms of citizenship online.

Because it has been enacted in different ways at various periods of history and encompasses a range of different meanings for those who use it, the internet also holds a number of dichotomous ambiguities in terms of its implications for citizenship. One of these we have already alluded to – that of the possibility of it being a wholly global technology that exists beyond any geographic community but that, in reality, is often used at a very local level to promote those very same communities. However, there are a number of other ambiguities that are inherent in the different ways in which the internet is being enacted. Three of these are particularly relevant to understanding the changing nature of local citizenship.

First, there is a tension between the individual and the collective. One of the features of the internet is that it tends to promote highly individualised relationships, especially between citizens and political institutions. Proposals for e-voting, for example, have been heavily criticised by some because voting from home by computer supposedly breaks the link between the voter and the collective institutions of democracy that are symbolised by all voters attending a polling station (Pratchett and Wingfield, 2004; Gibson, 2005). The concern among these critics is that voting from home online becomes a random and non-reflective act, whereas traditional voting in person at a polling station involves a small but significant investment in the political process, giving space for reflection and encouraging a person's identity as citizen of that political community. At the same time, however, the internet has a long history of promoting collective engagement. One of its strengths is that it enables communities that are geographically dispersed to be in continuous and sustained contact. Furthermore, the advent of social networking sites has exploited this capacity to the full. The internet is now home to many communities of interest, many of which are explicitly geographic and local in their focus. This first ambiguity, therefore, concerns the extent to which contemporary enactments of ICTs in governance foster a sense of collectivity and community as opposed to individualism and alienation from political institutions.

Second, there is tension between the identity of those engaging electronically and the anonymity that the technology can also afford them. This dichotomy is not so much about the privacy, or lack of it, that the individual has from the state in the online world, although that debate is in itself an important one for notions of citizenship because it addresses the extent to which citizens can trust those who govern (Raab, 1999; 6 et al, 2002). Rather, it is about the way in which individuals choose to reveal or protect their identity in online engagements. Whether it is sending anonymous emails to a politician, 'flaming' a rival discussant in an online forum using a pseudonym, or operating an avatar in Second Life with invented characteristics, new ICTs provide the user with many opportunities to hide, disguise or even distort their identities to fit different images of themselves. As a consequence, there is the possibility for behaviour, much of it rude or abusive, which would not take place in face-to-face meetings. This potential for anonymity poses significant problems for citizenship, especially where it is premised on concepts of status and belonging. Anonymity can at the same time be vital for freedom of expression through the internet. In authoritarian regimes, internet is the last refuge where anonymity provides some freedom of expression, although these governments increasingly use new methods of filtering, censorship and restrictive legislation on its use.

Potential of the ICTs to provide anonymity is not always taken up by the people. On the contrary, many individuals do not seek to protect their anonymity, but, rather, use the technology to promote their self-identity. Indeed, enacted technologies such as Facebook seem to encourage individuals to reveal far more about themselves than they would in their offline communities. Again, therefore, the internet is ambiguous in terms of its implications for citizenship. In many contexts, anonymity militates against responsible citizenship, not least because individuals who seek to hide or disguise their identity are working against the status dimension of citizenship. However, in other less democratic contexts, anonymity enables citizens to express critical and/or opposition views that they would hesitate to express in their face-to-face relations. In these cases, people chose to stay anonymous, not to insult others more easily but to protect themselves against any government persecution.

Third, there is a longstanding debate within the study of ICTs as to whether they are the triggers for change and transformation or whether, in reality, they tend to reinforce existing biases and institutions. For those who see technologies as being revolutionary and transformational in their impact, the assumption is that ICTs provide a unique opportunity to radically change organisational, political and democratic behaviour (Hazlett and Hill, 2003; Jaeger and Thompson, 2003; Heeks, 2005). It is not much of a stretch from such optimism to assume also that technologies will have a significant effect on the nature and practice of citizenship. Others, however, are sceptical about the so-called revolutionary effects of new technologies in the political domain, arguing that the technologies become 'normalised' by their social and political context over time (Margolis and Resnick, 2000) or, even, that new technological applications and their effects reflect the interests of dominant actors, thereby reinforcing or even aggravating existing socio-political cleavages and patterns of interest (Danziger et al, 1982; Dutton, 1999; Kraemer and King, 2005). Rather than being inherently revolutionary, therefore, the implementation of ICTs is often seen to reinforce and advance the interests of dominant powers in the polity. From this perspective, ICTs are unlikely to enact new forms of citizenship but, instead, will support dominant modes of citizenship that already exist in the offline world.

It is not sufficient, however, simply to observe the ambiguities that lie at the heart of the internet and its development. To understand how the internet is being enacted in relation to local citizenship it is also necessary to examine how different actors are shaping this enactment, either through explicit attempts to develop particular modes of citizenship or more implicitly through the way in which they use them in their everyday activities. To this end, we focus on the government's enactment of ICTs at the local level through the local e-government programme that the Department for Communities and Local Government (DCLG) ran between 2000 and 2006. This programme was targeted at getting all local government services available electronically. It has led policy at the local level in terms of developing online access to local government and politics, and defined the way in which UK localities operate in the online world.

The local e-government programme had its roots in the 1999 *Modernising Government* White Paper (Cabinet Office, 1999). At the heart of this strategy was the belief that government services should be available continuously and not just during conventional working hours. Consequently, the White Paper established targets that '50% of dealings [with the public sector] should be capable of electronic delivery by 2005 and 100% by 2008' (p 52). These targets were revised by a subsequent strategy statement from the newly created Office of the e-Envoy to involve 50% by 2002 and 100% by 2005 (e-Envoy, 2000). The targets were not restricted to central government departments or agencies but covered the entire public sector, including local authorities. Indeed, as the primary location of most day -to-day services, local government is seen as being central to the delivery of the information age strategy. As the e-Envoy's second annual report acknowledged, 'the number of transactions involved [in local government] vastly exceeds those of the rest of central government put together' (e-Envoy, 2001: 57). For local as well as central government, therefore, these were tough targets on e-government that needed to be met by 2005 (Pratchett, 2004).

To support the implementation of e-government, the strategy involved a number of different initiatives, some of which were more coercive than others. At the coercive end of the scale, a performance indicator (BVPI157) was used to measure and compare the quantity of council services that were available electronically. This indicator measured the performance of local authorities in relation to 22 different functions where electronic services were expected to be introduced, ranging from the payment of council tax and other bills, through to applying for planning permission and even voter registration. Local authorities were also required to produce an annual strategic statement on how they were progressing towards the 2005 targets and were awarded a sum of money for successful submissions, to support their strategies for the forthcoming year. At the less coercive but more supportive end of the scale, a series of 22 local government led 'national projects' that developed generic tools and instruments for councils to use in their bid to achieve the 2005 targets were commissioned. These 'national projects' provided a range of resources that councils could use in relation to particular e-government challenges, from best-practice guidelines through to actual software.

The local e-government programme was a major policy aimed at changing both the internal operation and external relationships of local authorities online. It was arguably one of the biggest initiatives of its kind in the world. It sought to be both comprehensive in its approach and detailed in its implementation. Little scope was given for individual local authorities to ignore or reject the targets. Although many countries have implemented e-government solutions, no other country sought to do so in such a comprehensive and unbending way. As a result, most local authorities met the 2005 targets either before the deadline or shortly after.

The implications of the local e-government programme for local citizenship, however, were not really part of the programme, despite the same government's ongoing commitment elsewhere to support enhanced political participation and the building of sustainable communities (Pratchett, 2000; Stoker, 2004) The programme was driven by the dual themes of 'modernisation' and 'efficiency'. The modernisation theme was captured by the slogan '21st century services' and was aimed at encouraging the public sector to mirror the supposedly best practice of the private sector in terms of making all services available 24 hours a day. It was supposed to enhance consumer choice both in the types of services available and the channels through which they are accessed. The efficiency theme was linked to the Gershon review of public spending and the idea that effective implementation of ICTs could reduce the transaction costs of particular services, especially those that had a high volume of use (Pratchett and Leach, 2005). The emphasis, therefore, was on efficiency savings and passing on the costs of services to the public wherever possible.

The implications for citizens of this modernisation and efficiency process are not necessarily all positive. While there are generally high levels of satisfaction among those who use e-government services, the experience has been one of a largely consumerist nature. People have individual contacts with organisations at the local level. Moreover, these contacts are of a more impersonal and distant nature, with little if any opportunity for personal contact. In effect, the e-government programme has largely depoliticised many of the contacts that individuals might have with local public services, reducing them to the level of customer-style transactions. It is notable, for example, that only one of the 22 national projects within the local e-government strategy had anything to do with enabling local politicians to operate more effectively (the £4.6 million local e-democracy national project) and even that project had only a small part of its budget devoted to that particular goal. To the extent that the programme has anything to say about citizenship, therefore, it is largely what Clarke et al (2006) have described as developing 'citizen consumers'.

This argument is backed up by the existence of a whole project within the local e-government programme entitled 'e-citizens'. Somewhat surprisingly, this £2.5 million project did not seek to understand or encourage new forms of citizenship online. Indeed, it did not even seek to promote traditional forms of citizenship in the new environment. Instead, it focused on encouraging take-up of the new channels being developed elsewhere in the interests of modernisation and efficiency. Its resources were invested, therefore, in surveying the e-activities of the public and marketing e-services to them. The 'e-citizens' strand of the programme, therefore, captured perfectly the overarching message of the local e-government programme in relation to citizenship. Creating citizen customers was the primary goal of the programme.

The local e-government programme sits in stark contrast to the way in which the public understand the technologies for community engagement and citizenship. In the United States, the use by Barack Obama of social networking sites and viral video campaigning to raise both money and votes in his successful campaign to be US President is well documented. In the UK, there is an equally pervasive use of such sites for political campaigning, even if it is not on the same scale as in the US. However, much of this activity is not linked directly to political parties but is generated by active individuals acting independently or semi-autonomously of traditional party politics. A key feature of the way ICTs are being enacted by the public is in relation to small groups who spread information online among small communities of interest. Such communities may or may not be geographically linked.

There is a significant disjuncture, therefore, between the way in which local governments are seeking to enact citizenship and the way in which citizens themselves are realising their own political efficacy online. It is evident that, in most local authorities, the e-government initiative ended when the 2005 targets were met. The technology and the way it has been enacted is clearly based in the Web 1.0 understanding of the internet. Local authorities provide information and services to the public through different channels. In all but a few cases they have not really started to embrace the Web 2.0 technologies. While citizens are using Facebook, YouTube and MySpace to reassert their political interests and develop campaigns on behalf of their communities, most local authorities are largely ignorant of their existence.

Conclusions: the prospects for local citizenship in the online world

The local e-government programme says little about citizenship directly, even in those areas in which it is supposedly seeking to. The way in which it is being enacted, nevertheless, has a significant impact on the development of citizenship. In this concluding section we match the three dimensions of citizenship set out earlier to the processes of enactment created by the local e-government programme, to develop some conclusions on how e-citizenship is emerging in the UK.

Citizenship as status has been a significant issue in the development of e-government more generally in the UK. The need to be able to identify individuals and confirm their identity has been at the heart of many of the developments. This need emerged both as a result of the requirements of modern life and the post-9/11 political atmosphere that brought security to the agendas of many governments. The push to develop smart ID cards based on biometrical information to confirm identity, and which contain 'a biographical footprint' of the individual linked to the ID card and summarised on its chip, is probably the highest-profile example. ID cards lie at the heart of the state's desire to be able to confirm the status of all residents and to distinguish citizens from non-citizens. By linking smart chip technology to a national database containing more detailed biographical information, the state will have the basis of a unique identification system for all citizens. The fact that the roll-out of the cards began with them being issued to foreign nationals living in the UK highlights their role in conferring full or partial status on individuals as citizens.

The ID card scheme is not the only e-government application associated with citizenship as status. Indeed, the authentication of individuals is a key feature of many e-government systems. This authentication is particularly relevant at the local level in relation to payment and benefit systems but it also extends further. For example, local authorities are responsible for maintaining an electronic register of voters – something that defines citizenship more than anything else. The move towards online registers has made this process more flexible, allowing citizens to register at any point during the year rather than just at one fixed time. As local authorities and other agencies have moved on line, so the identification and authentication of local residents has become more critical, not less. Indeed, such authentication is justified, in part, by the fact that, in the online environment, people can claim to be resident in a particular city from anywhere in the world. Local governments, therefore, have become increasingly concerned with authenticating status and identity in relation to services (whether online or offline). In terms of the tensions identified in the previous section, therefore, the emphasis of the local e-government programme has very much been on removing all types of anonymity from the use of their systems. Interestingly, however, local e-participation schemes aimed at getting citizens to influence policy through such systems as e-petitioning or online forums have been far less concerned with any such authentication.

Citizenship as rights and responsibilities is largely shaped by the need for authentication in ICT systems. Indeed, the drive for authentication is less about the general status of citizenship and more about the specific rights of individuals to particular services. One criticism of the way in which local e-government has been enacted, however, is that it is primarily concerned with supporting citizens' rights to particular services (especially in relation to welfare) and has done very little to promote the responsibilities side of citizenship. A notable exception would be online tax paying. Citizens' rights to particular benefits are exercised more easily through the use of technology. However, citizens are also invited to fulfil their responsibilities, such as tax payments, electronically. Therefore, ICTs are used to enhance both rights and responsibilities of citizenship.

Most of the systems and applications that have been developed have been targeted at individuals and encourage a particularly individualistic approach to relationships with public organisations. Whether it is paying a bill or examining a planning application, the online systems have added another layer of alienation from local government and other public organisations. Even where interactive engagement is encouraged through, for example, emailing a complaint, the response is often generated automatically, thereby creating further distance between citizens and governments. Few, if any, of the major e-government applications developed at the local level highlight the collective responsibilities that citizens have to their community. In the tension between individualism and collectivism, therefore, citizenship as rights and responsibilities tends to emphasise the individual rights aspects and ignores almost entirely the collective responsibilities side of the dimension. We tend to talk about *individual* rights and *collective* responsibilities. However, rights are not always enjoyed individually – that is, right to organise a pressure group, right to group protest, right of an ethnic group to access public information in its own language. These are rights that are enjoyed as a group. Although the e-government applications have a bias towards promoting individual rights, there are examples where these applications advance collective rights.

For example, Leicester City Council's website offering information in languages of different ethnic groups demonstrates the council's recognition of the collective right of these people to the use of their own language.

Citizenship as identity is largely ignored in the local e-government enactment process. Some local authorities and other public agencies at the local level do seek to 'badge' local identity in their online presence. Few, however, go beyond such marketing approaches. From an e-government point of view, therefore, citizenship as identity is an irrelevance. A notable exception would be web content in government websites in different languages. For example direct.gov.uk offers content in Welsh, which contributes to recognition of Welsh identity. Likewise local authorities provide content in different languages used by ethnic groups; Leicester offers limited information in languages like Gujurati and Punjabi. Except these few cases, identity remains largely an irrelevance. This perspective sits in stark contrast to the way that citizens themselves are using ICTs, and especially Web 2.0. Much of their activity, especially on social networking sites, is about reasserting identity with particular pre-existing communities and establishing new identities (whether existing or invented) with others. Although some of these communities are truly global, or at least non-place specific in their nature, many of them have their roots in geographic communities that have then become more dispersed as individuals have moved localities. While the local e-government programme, therefore, has been primarily about reinforcing conventional understandings of citizenship, citizens are using the technologies in a much more innovative way to transform their relationships with various communities.

This chapter started by questioning whether concepts of citizenship at the local level are compatible with the global capacity for engagement that ICTs offer. It is certainly clear that this global capacity affects localities. The political experiences of citizens and their ability to interpret events are no longer limited, or even necessarily shaped significantly, by where they live. Instead, they increasingly take cues and influence from nested networks in which they exist to make sense of social, political and economic factors. These cues and influence in turn shape how they understand citizenship. Of course, locality remains an important factor in understanding citizenship but, increasingly, this factor needs to be set in the context of the wider online experiences to which citizens are exposed.

References

6, P., Leat, D., Seltzer, K. and Stoker, G. (2002) *Towards holistic governance: The new reform agenda*, Basingstoke: Palgrave.

Cabinet Office (1999) *Modernising Government*, White Paper, London: Cabinet Office.

Chadwick, A. (2006) *Internet politics: States, citizens and new communication technologies*, Oxford: Oxford University Press.

Clarke, J., Newman, J., Smith, N., Vidler, E. and Westmorland, L. (2006) *Creating citizen-consumers: Changing public and changing public services*, London: Sage.

Danziger, J., Dutton, W.H., Kling, R. and Kraemer, K.L. (1982) *Computers and politics: High technology in American local governments*, New York: Columbia University Press.

Dutton, W. (ed) (1999) *Society on the line: Information politics in the digital age*, Oxford: Oxford University Press.

Dutton, W. and Helsper, E. (2007) *The internet in Britain 2007*, Oxford: Oxford Internet Institute.

e-Envoy (2000) *e-Government: A strategic framework for public services in the information age*, London: The Stationery Office.

e-Envoy (2001) *UKonline 2001*, London: The Stationery Office.

Fountain, J. (2001) *Building the virtual state: Information technology and institutional change*, New York: The Brookings Institute.

Gibson, R. (2005) 'Internet voting and the European Parliament: Problems and prospects', in F. Mendez and A. Trechsel (eds) *The European Union and e-voting*, London: Routledge, pp 29-59.

Goldsmith, P. (2007) *Citizenship: Our common bond*, London: Ministry of Justice.

Hazlett, S.A. and Hill, F. (2003) 'e-Government: the realities of using IT to transform the public sector', *Managing Service Quality*, vol 13, no 6, pp 445-52.

Heeks, R. (2005) *Implementing and managing e-Government: An international text*, London: Sage.

Held, D. (1996) *Models of democracy: Second edition*, Cambridge: Polity Press.

Jaeger, P. and Thompson, K. (2003) 'e-government around the world: lessons, challenges and future directions', *Government Information Quarterly*, vol 20, no 4, pp 389-94.

Joppke, C. (2007) *Controlling a new migration world*, London: Routledge.

Kivisto, P. and Faist, T. (2007) *Citizenship: Discourse, theory and transnational prospects*, Oxford: Blackwell.

Kraemer, K. and King, J. (2005) 'Information technology and administrative reform: will e-government be different?', *International Journal of Electronic Government Research*, vol 2, no 1, pp 1-20.

Maconie, S. (2006) *Pies and prejudice: In search of the North*, London: Ebury Press.

Margolis, M. and Resnick, D. (2000) *Politics as usual: The cyberspace revolution*, London: Sage.

Pratchett, L. (ed) (2000) *Renewing local democracy? The modernisation agenda in British local government*, London: Frank Cass and Co.

Pratchett, L. (2004) 'Local e-government in Britain', in M. Eiffert and J. Puschel (eds) *National electronic government*, London: Routledge, pp 13-45.

Pratchett, L. and Leach, S. (2005) 'A new vision for local government: rhetoric or reality? ', *Parliamentary Affairs*, vol 58, no 2, pp 318-34.

Pratchett, L. and Wingfield, M. (2004) 'Piloting e-voting: lessons and limitations from the UK experience', in N. Kersting and H. Baldersheim (eds) *Electronic voting and democracy: A comparative analysis*, Basingstoke: Palgrave Macmillan, pp 172-92.

Raab, C. (1999) 'Protecting privacy', in W. Dutton (ed) *Society on the line: Information politics in the information age*, Oxford: Oxford University Press, pp 199-250.

Schmitter, P., Trechsel, A. et al (2004) *The future of democracy in Europe: Trends, analyses and reforms*, Strasbourg: Council of Europe Publishing.

Stoker, G. (2004) *Transforming local governance: From Thatcherism to New Labour*, Basingstoke: Palgrave Macmillan.

Turner, B. (1993) 'Contemporary problems in the theory of citizenship', in B. Turner (ed.) *Citizenship and social theory*, London: Sage, pp 1-18.

TWELVE

Conclusion

Catherine Durose, Stephen Greasley and Liz Richardson

The picture this collection paints is of a series of genuine attempts by different sorts of decision makers to fundamentally change the way that local areas are governed. The changes are designed to draw citizens in more closely towards the local state. The chapters illustrate that there are high stakes for decision makers in changing local governance in these ways. The public sector believes that it will not be able to govern effectively without the cooperation and active involvement of citizens. Reform is difficult, however, and governance stakeholders, particularly at the local level, do not have the capacity or resources to redress many of the biases in the system. The book shows how many gaps remain between citizens and governance structures.

This volume has sought to move beyond the often highly abstract debates around citizens and governance and examine the 'practice' of citizenship (Prior et al, 1995). Rather than looking at citizenship as a status that people possess, this text has focused on citizenship as a 'practice' that people engage in. By looking at the actual interactions between governance and citizens, we can better explore the implicit understanding of the nature and limits of citizenship.

This book has also attempted to unravel the language of citizenship. In the last two decades, a whole new language has emerged to try and describe and define the citizen–governance relationship. Terms such as 'civicness' and 'co-production' attempt to both describe change and influence the ways in which citizens act. By exploring contemporary interactions between citizens and governance we can begin to understand whether what is going on is simply rhetorical or something more substantive. The turn to governance has been much discussed but what is clear is that the 'turn' is an ongoing process and the rhetoric of citizen governance is not always matched by substance. While participation and empowerment are now concepts with significant currency there is clearly an ongoing tendency towards centralisation and standardisation. This raises the question of where is the citizen in this debate? In academic work, there has been a clear focus on the organisational impact of governance, but less on the demands now made of, and by, citizens and how citizens themselves reflect and respond to these changing demands.

What's at stake?

We argue that attempts to change local governance appear to be genuine endeavours to make governance more citizen-centred. Part of our conviction that our examples are not simply more of the same, or a lacklustre effort to tick boxes, comes from the sheer effort being expended by governance actors on getting closer to people and changing how decisions about localities are made. Another reason for believing that the role of citizens is being taken seriously by local governance is that there is a lot at stake for the public sector.

The chapters offer many different examples of both this effort and the high stakes. Catherine Durose and Liz Richardson (Chapter Three) consider developments in neighbourhood-based working. The neighbourhood has been a site of local government activity over the last decade and before, as evidenced in an almost bewildering array of different forms of neighbourhood-based working. It is now difficult to find a local authority without some form of sub-local working. This is not just a rhetorical commitment but a financial one, with a commitment to neighbourhood working now mainstreamed in local authority spending. Neighbourhood-based working is also seen as an opportunity to improve the efficiency and effectiveness of service provision, notably the joining up of services and the creation of more citizen-centred services, and to improve accessibility to and accountability of local decision making.

James Rees (Chapter Four) focuses on citizens' experiences of Housing Market Renewal (HMR). HMR is a vastly ambitious policy aiming not only to improve the economic vitality of the city, but also to reshape the city demographically and the aspirations of citizens. Its aims were no less than a re-envisioning of the fundamental rationale for neighbourhoods and places, and considerable central funding has been committed. Dedicated local governance structures have been created to steer these transitions.

Matthew Goodwin (Chapter Six) comments on attempts to develop cohesive local communities by promoting contact between different groups – particularly different ethnic groups – in order to prevent tension and even discrimination and violence between communities. Similar issues can arise between established communities and new migrant communities (see also Leila Thorp, Chapter Seven).

Rebecca Askew, Sarah Cotterill and Stephen Greasley (Chapter Nine) discuss varied examples of attempts to change the behaviour of citizens and communities. The aims of these policies ranged from fairly minor adjustments – for example, recycling behaviour – to fundamental changes designed to transform the lives of, often vulnerable, citizens. These attempts have often taken the form of cost- and resource-intensive pilots using new and sometimes controversial approaches.

Harriet Churchill (Chapter Ten) comments on the major restructuring of Children's Services in response to the Every Child Matters (ECM) agenda. The ECM agenda attempts to refocus on children and young people as citizens with the hope of turning around life chances and aspirations, along with tackling anti-social behaviour and child poverty.

What are perhaps both heartening and alarming are the hugely high hopes that public sector professionals have for the governance changes they want to make. These changes are going to make public services more efficient and effective, make citizens better parents and environmentalists, lever in extra resources to meet societal goals, bring communities closer together, tackle child poverty, prevent civil disturbances and improve the parlous state of local democracy. Failures to adapt governance structures appropriately and/or engage citizens therefore present serious risks. If changing governance to include people does not produce contented, active and empowered citizens, or better ways of managing services, or a vibrant democracy, then why go to all the effort?

Where are the gaps? How are citizens 'missing'?

Local governance is putting considerable effort into engaging with citizens and it is often assumed that, compared to national institutions, local governance can be 'nearer' to citizens. However, the chapters in this book raise questions about how citizens are grouped and defined by governance and the extent of meaningful engagement with citizens' needs, demands and priorities. In many cases highlighted by this volume, there are gaps in understanding and mismatches between citizens' own aspirations and what they are assumed to be by governance. The citizen is clearly often still 'missing' in the renegotiation of the relationship between citizens and local governance.

The first area of mismatch between local governance and citizens is the different ways in which citizens are grouped, defined and self-defined. Does governance engage with citizens 'in the round'? How does governance cope with new communities and new citizens?

Contributions to this volume have evidenced how citizens are often understood by governance in terms of identities that they have not chosen for themselves. Chapman (Chapter Eight) argues that a largely 'top-down' construction of faith identities that centres on collectives and tends to mask diversity within and between religious traditions and groups has emerged. Harries and Richardson (Chapter Five) discussed the housing aspirations of minority ethnic citizens, specifically second-generation south Asian women, and how the perspectives and preferences of these citizens are reflected in local authority housing strategies. Housing strategies have tended to emphasise the importance of citizens' ethnic identity in influencing people's housing aspirations. However important people's culture or ethnic background might be, this was not the most relevant aspect they referred to when they were asked about where and how they wanted to live. South Asian women were more likely to make choices about where to buy a home based on the fact they were mothers first and foremost and wanted good places to bring up children. More so than this, the Asian women did not live the sorts of lives or have the sorts of views that many housing providers assumed they did. The chapter provides an insightful example of how citizens might define and group themselves differently from the categories used by local governance actors. The disparity in these definitions and groupings can lead to a misunderstanding of the demands, needs and priorities of citizens.

Governance perspectives can often reveal narrow, limiting understanding of citizens. As Thorp argues (Chapter Seven) globalisation, and in particular the recent increase in economic migrants, has challenged the boundaries of citizenship. Groups who do not enjoy full formal citizenship rights are nonetheless being involved in governance processes. The character of this involvement is not fixed, however. Sometimes new migrants are seen to be participating in place shaping; sometimes they are seen primarily as a policing challenge. In this sense, citizenship can be seen to exclude or neglect particular groups; Churchill (Chapter Ten) reiterates this point in reference to children and young people.

Polat and Pratchett (Chapter Eleven) argue that, while e-government processes provide citizenship as a 'status' and allow citizens to assert their 'rights' in terms of accessing services, the notion of citizenship as 'identity' is largely ignored or considered irrelevant. This presents a clear disjunction with how citizens themselves are using new media and technology, which is in part about reasserting identity within particular communities. Thus far, e-government has not been able to capture the innovative ways that citizens themselves are using such technology to transform citizenship and relations with wider communities.

Governance can also see citizens as the 'wrong type' of citizens. Rees (Chapter Four) shows how the existing communities in HMR areas can be perceived as not economically active, lacking in aspiration and inhibiting the creation of neighbourhoods that new or potential citizens would like to visit, move to or invest in. Rebecca Askew, Sarah Cotterill and Stephen Greasley (Chapter Nine) look at the concept of behaviour change and its impact on citizens in a variety of policy settings. The chapter argues that strategies of behaviour change can sometimes lead to more responsive, effective service provision and encourage more 'civic' behaviour from citizens. This chapter offers a clear example of how governance asks citizens to become something they currently are not.

Local governance is clearly attempting to be inclusive in its engagement with citizens. However, a lack of knowledge and understanding of how citizens define and group themselves together impedes these efforts, and there are challenges in responding to the new preferences and interests brought as the practice of citizenship is expanded to include, for example, children or new migrants.

2. The second area of mismatch between citizens and governance is in the type and form of relationships developed and the underpinning reasons for seeking to engage with citizens.

Chapman (Chapter Eight) indicates that, while there have been significant efforts to include faith groups in governance, particularly at the local level, certain groups – notably from the larger faiths – have been able to dominate. Moreover, the underlying reasons for faith groups' involvement in local governance are not shared. Public sector actors tend to refer to resources-based reasoning, seeing faith organisations as repositories of social capital and community capacity. This chapter shows how one instrumental reason why faith communities have been approached has been to take advantage of their sizeable congregations and organising capacity, as well as to access easy routes into specific minority ethnic groups. However, some faith organisations have become involved in governance on the basis of their spiritual values. For governance structures more interested in faith organisations' resources, the expression of faith values, especially where they clash with equalities agendas, has been a source of tension. The potential for misunderstanding has been compounded by difficulties in translating faith-based concepts and values into the language of bureaucracy. Thorp (Chapter Seven) tells a story about how attempts by governance structures to engage new migrants appear at times to be too clunky. Structures predicated on British cultural values put off people with experiences of Eastern European political systems, and formal engagement opportunities were ill-suited to transient populations and those working in '3D' jobs (dirty, dangerous and difficult).

The extent to which the commitment to changing relationships with citizens is sustained and substantive is also questioned. Harriet Churchill (Chapter Ten) considers how children and young people are consulted and engaged around service provision, and the meaning this has for our understanding of their roles as citizens. Churchill argues that, while the government has made a commitment to engage with children and young people as citizens, the style of participation can take different forms depending on local context. Her case study of children's services in one local authority reveals a genuine consultation effort on the part of governance actors, but the efforts do not amount to a child/youth-focused service with a change in adults' thinking, services and structures in relation to children.

James Rees (Chapter Four) examines citizens' experiences of Housing Market Renewal. The chapter asserts that citizens are often co-opted into the process of change while simultaneously being sidelined. The priorities, demands and needs of existing communities in deprived areas undergoing regeneration are often neglected for a focus on potential communities, which are seen to be able to make a bigger economic contribution to the area and to fit better with strategic corporate aims of local government.

Local governance might struggle to build relationships with the community that are empowering for citizens. Durose and Richardson (Chapter Three) comment on the potential and inherent difficulties of the 'neighbourhood' as a site for empowerment. There are many different motivations for working at the neighbourhood level. However, it is difficult for local authorities to let go and see the neighbourhood as a site for citizen empowerment; local authorities also often lack the skills to empower effectively.

The third area of mismatch between citizen and governance is in terms of outcomes. If more is being demanded of citizens, then the process of engaging with them has to be meaningful and underpinned with results — and results that both governance and citizens think are positive. This is illustrated by examples in Chapter Nine where citizens trying to behave in a more environmental way became frustrated and demotivated by unresponsive governance.

The material in Chapter Ten is a poignant illustration of where children and young people have made substantive comments about changes that would add to their ability to perform educationally and otherwise, but they do not feel listened to or that their ideas are acted upon. Churchill's examples show that young people had offered positive suggestions, such as better advice on future employment options, but it was not clear how their input had produced different service outcomes.

Rees (Chapter Four) has indicated that policies such as HMR often explicitly go against the current preferences of existing citizens in a neighbourhood. The argument from those in charge is that wider social and economic outcomes for the city and for other sorts of people need to take precedence. Often the strategies of local governance in engaging with citizens gloss over some of the structural difficulties that citizens face. When seeking to engage with citizens, it is important to address underlying inequalities and the importance of socioeconomic factors (see Goodwin, Chapter Six, for example). Goodwin also discusses the level of sophistication needed to effectively implement interventions to bring people together from different backgrounds. If contact between groups is done in too superficial a way, then the outcomes can be no effect on prejudice or, worse, that prejudice is reinforced.

What demands were being made of and by governance and citizens?

The extent to which any gaps and failures in new governance modes are endemic or inherent is a crucial factor in the effectiveness of ongoing reforms. If simply too much is being asked of people, then the impact of co-production and active citizen governance will be limited.

What comes across in nearly all of the chapters is how big an 'ask' is being made of citizens. We have described the high hopes that governance actors have of changing governance. Running in parallel to these hopes are significant demands being made of citizens: to get out of their homes and attend meetings in draughty community venues; to come forward and offer their views about complex and sometimes tedious technical issues; to understand the wider needs of places and constraints on decision makers; to make new friends and be more tolerant of different groups; to deal with major change; to change their own habits and behaviours. It is easy for practitioners to become disheartened by the considerable scale of these challenges. The reality can be overwhelming. Public sector professionals doing engagement find it an uphill struggle to generate widespread involvement. Agencies working to change behaviour wrestle with deeply entrenched habits. The backdrop to the work discussed in Chapters Six, Seven and Eight around ethnic mixing, community cohesion and the integration of new migrants into communities is that some areas have a history of activity by the far right and that news reports in the local press offer a stream of negative stories about the reactions of existing citizens to new arrivals.

Despite these challenges, the evidence from the chapters overall is that citizens have not dismissed requests made of them. For example, in Askew et al's chapter on behaviour change (Chapter Nine), there were doubts raised by practitioners about whether citizens would be willing to accept government interference. Yet, in these local experiments, there was little evidence that citizens resented the interventions to change behaviour. Similarly, the ask being made of citizens to get on better with people from different backgrounds needs to be set against evidence that four fifths of the population already do feel people get on well and the same proportion already have some social contact (albeit limited) with people from different ethnic backgrounds.

What constraints exist for governance?

This volume has identified gaps in the citizen–governance relationship and places where the citizen seems to be missing. In doing so it presents some critical reflections. However, our understandings of these gaps are tempered by an acknowledgment that governing is an incredibly difficult job. Local governance is faced with a complex and changing social world with demanding and highly differentiated citizens. Policy development under such circumstances presents serious challenges in terms both of understanding what is required and of delivering it effectively. Governance institutions are characterised by limited cognitive capacity and the complexity 'out there' is partly mirrored by a complex institutional and power structure within the public sector. Taken as a whole, the public services are a complex tangle of bargains and picking at one thread is prone to cause unexpected unravelling elsewhere.

This complexity is compounded by the particular difficulty of some of the policy challenges faced. They require citizens to change behaviour, take greater responsibility for their own actions and see past their own prejudices. The boundaries of citizenship are being blurred while the ways in which the public groups, or is grouped, together are also changing, with a new emphasis on neighbourhood or faith, for example. Faced by such challenges, public sector institutions have to reduce complexity to proportions that allow concerted action over periods of time.

Some argue that, given the context in which it operates, governance failure is inevitable (Jessop, 2000). Others have argued that, despite the rhetoric of empowerment, 'managerialism has eroded the prospects for democratic partnership' (Davies, 2007: 780). Observers of the policy process would agree that there is more than an element of truth in these conclusions. However, such conclusions do seem to rely on applying exacting and abstract standards to governance. In our view this can lead to an overly fatalist understanding of the capacity of public governance to respond to social change in a way that is broadly beneficial. A more pragmatic approach involves asking whether the capacity of governance to respond to citizens' demands can be reformed in desired ways even if never perfected.

The inevitability of bias

Faced with a complex and uncertain world, governance relies to some extent on biases to simplify the problems and allow action. Here, 'bias' is not necessarily used in a pejorative sense. A bias might exist in favour of a particular solution, a particular scale for action, a way of understanding a group. Researchers have argued that bias is an inevitable part of institutions and public life more broadly. One writer, referring to interest group politics in the US, famously observed that 'organisation is itself a mobilisation of bias in preparation for action'(Shattschneider, 1960: 30). Similarly, institutional theorists have explored the link between, on the one hand, how institutions are organised and, on the other, biases in how they 'think' about the world and the solutions they offer to problems (Douglas, 1987).

In many contexts some governance bias is essential for timely and coherent action. Biases enter governance in the way that citizens and their demands are constructed by policy makers and by administrative processes; biases are introduced with the organisational structures that are designed to deliver programmes. It is impossible for complex organisations to structure themselves to do things without adopting some biases in favour of certain strategies and world views.

The consequences of bias

Social scientists have their own biases, and the chapters in this book have inevitably focused on areas where problems exist and improvements might be possible. In their chapter Durose and Richardson explicitly discuss how biases are associated, intentionally or otherwise, with institutional design. Across local government, what seems to be a substantial and sustained experiment with neighbourhood and area governance has been under way in recent years. The authors argue that different scales of institution can favour different priorities, styles of governance and styles of citizenship. While welcoming the experimentation, they note that the way that neighbourhood governance is often being designed makes it less likely to contribute to 'civic' engagement from the public and more appropriate for efficient service delivery, or as an annex of established institutions of representative democracy. Similarly, Askew et al discuss how institutional structures designed to provide generic services to client groups can struggle to deliver services that are more tailored.

Other chapters demonstrate the biases in the way that local governance thinks about the public. Chapters by Rees, Harries and Richardson, Chapman, Churchill and Askew et al provide examples of how the representations of citizens and citizen groups in the policy process are partial, limited by the interests, assumptions and usual practices of governance.

While the existence of some bias may be inevitable in governance, particular biases can be challenged. Having said that, the reform of governance in desired ways faces numerous barriers and reformers have to practise the art of the possible. Our chapters reveal a number of governance barriers to the reform of citizen–governance relations. In some instances financial and resource pressures limit the ability of local governance to innovate or adapt to citizens' interests and needs (Rees; Askew et al; Thorp). In other cases different goals appear to irreconcilable (Durose and Richardson; Rees). There are challenges that are specific to particular contexts – for example, Manchester City Council faces a particular fiscal challenge resulting from tight administrative boundaries around the city centre and the financial pressure to make Housing Market Renewal appealing to affluent professionals was therefore quite strong. Balancing this financial imperative and the view that mixed neighbourhoods were good with the desires of existing residents proved to be difficult (Rees, this volume).

Neighbourhood governance is being implemented with multiple goals that are proving difficult to reconcile. In particular there is a question about whether neighbourhood structures are to be new arenas for representative party democracy, or whether they are to be citizen-led organisations for community empowerment. Conflicting pressures are evident in Churchill's discussion of whether national structures and targets leave space for children's voices to be acted on as well as heard. Two of the projects discussed by Askew et al required a level of flexibility in service provision that was both administratively challenging and costly. More subtle barriers also exist in terms of the language of bureaucracy (Chapman) and the assumptions that are held about citizens and groups (Harries and Richardson; Thorp; Churchill; Askew et al).

Mobilising bias

The reality of change lies somewhere between the 'local government transformed' and the 'local government unmoved' narratives (Lowndes, 2004). Shifting the biases in governance towards an understanding of citizens as active, towards a more differentiated categorisation of groups and towards inclusion of a wider array of interests involves more than ad hoc or isolated victories: 'lasting change is a matter of establishing durable relationships of a kind that are a part of the system of governance' (Stone, 2009: 259). The reform attempts discussed in this book have involved trying to include citizens in the formulation and delivery of policy.

If governance cannot be completely 'debiased', then perhaps the biases that exist in governance might be tilted in particular ways. One clear example from Durose and Richardson's chapter is the involvement in one local authority of residents in drawing boundaries of neighbourhoods for the purposes of setting up governance structures. This involvement led to more and smaller neighbourhoods being defined than would have been the case if the local authority had been left to its own devices. The process did not eradicate bias because, as we know from a vast number of studies, the people who become involved in consultations are a self-selecting bunch whose view of what is the 'neighbourhood' is unlikely to be universally shared. It did however provide a challenge to the existing assumptions in the public sector and might nudge citizen–governance relations towards empowerment in the sense of recent policy documents (CLG, 2008). Selecting the appropriate organisation to deliver policy is another means for changing biases. Two of the projects described by Askew et al were delivered by third-sector organisations, either because of particular skills and greater flexibility or because it was believed that client groups might not trust local government staff. One strategy for reform, then, relates to institutional design and redesign.

A second strategy involves trying to understand citizens in new ways. Askew et al report on a project that attempted to shift the understanding of drug users from being seen as helpless dependants to being seen as citizens who are at least potentially responsible for their own well-being and actions. Another example is provided by Harries and Richardson who argue that the needs of second-generation members of minority ethnic communities can be very different from those revealed by surveys from the first generation, which often underpin policy initiatives.

A third strategy is to deliberately mobilise particular groups or citizens in relation to public institutions. Faith-based groups now have a largely assured position on strategic partnerships. Churchill describes how the success of the Every Child Matters reforms relies on children being seen as citizens as well as dependants.

Where next for policy?

There are examples going back to the 1960s and 1970s of attempts to activate and empower citizens (John, Chapter Two). The remaking of the citizen–governance relationship is a longstanding and ongoing process of change. This process is by no means complete. At times, citizens' views have been excluded, with their demands and priorities neglected and ignored, there have been repeated failures to differentiate between the needs and perspectives of different groups of citizens, with an emphasis on standardised ways of dealing with citizens rather than tailored or flexible understandings.

There are alternative governance models. It seems unlikely that policy, in the medium term, will move away from the governance model and return to the classical hierarchical model of government and public administration. However, as also described (see Introduction and John, Chapter Two), there are alternatives to facilitative styles of governance; there is a chance the pendulum will swing back again to a more market-driven approach based on individual choice. A reading of this book would suggest that this type of approach to governance is insufficient to meet the needs of many different groups of citizens, or to broker the sorts of discussions and compromises needed.

The effect of reform efforts to tweak governance bias remains to be seen. No doubt there will be some failures and the outcomes will fall short of democratic and governance ideals. On the other hand, there is evidence that local governance in some cases is starting to adopt processes, procedures and attitudes that are biased towards active citizens, differentiated services users and empowered communities. In any case our evidence strongly indicates that it is worth the attempt, however hard it is to do.

References

CLG (Communities and Local Government) (2008) *Communities in control: Real power, real people*, London: HMSO.

Davies, J. (2007) 'The limits of partnership: an exit-action strategy for local democratic inclusion', *Political Studies*, vol 55, no 4, pp 779–800.

Douglas, M. (1987) *How institutions think*, London: Routledge & Kegan Paul.

Jessop, B. (2000) 'Governance failure', in G. Stoker (ed) *The new politics of British local governance*, Basingstoke: Macmillan, pp 11–32.

Lowndes, V. (2004) 'Reformers or recidivists? Has local government really changed?', in G. Stoker and D. Wilson (eds) *British local government into the 21st century*, Basingstoke: Palgrave Macmillan, pp 230–46.

Prior, D., Stewart, J. and Walsh, K. (1995) *Citizenship: Rights, community and participation*, London: Pitman.

Shattschneider, E. (1960) *The semi-sovereign people: A realist's view of democracy in America*, Hinsdale, IL: Dryden.

Stone, C. (2009) 'Who is governed? Local citizens and the political order of cities', in J.S. Davies and D.L. Imbroscio (eds) *Theories of urban politics* (2nd edn), London: Sage.

Index